THE HEIST

ERNEST VOLKMAN
JOHN CUMMINGS
THE HEIST

HOW A GANG STOLE $8,000,000 AT KENNEDY AIRPORT AND LIVED TO REGRET IT

Franklin Watts 1986 *New York / Toronto*

Library of Congress Cataloging-in-Publication Data

Volkman, Ernest.
The heist: how a gang stole $8,000,000 at
Kennedy Airport and lived to regret it

Includes index.
1. Robbery—New York (N.Y.) 2. Brigands and
robbers—New York (N.Y.) I. Cummings, John, 1931-
II. Title.
HV6661.N72.1978.V65 1986 364.1'552'097471 86-13186
ISBN 0-531-15024-0

FOR
LILLE AND LOUISE

J.C.

FOR
ERIC AND MICHELLE

E.V.

Acknowledgments

The writing of this book would have been impossible without the cooperation of a long list of people on both sides of the law who shared their reminiscences and insights. Their vast reserves of patience, in the face of what must have seemed to be endless questions, were critical to this effort; we are grateful for their willingness to light up many dark corners.

It would be equally impossible to cite here all those people who rendered us invaluable aid—many would prefer not to be mentioned publicly—but we would like to express our thanks to the men and women of several organizations whose assistance was crucial. These include the Federal Bureau of Investigation, the United States Justice Department's Eastern District (New York) Organized Crime Strike Force, the New York City Police Department, the New York City Department of Corrections, the Police Department of the Port Authority of New York and New Jersey, and the Brooklyn District Attorney's Office, along with its Queens counterpart.

Naturally, none of the personnel in these organizations are in any way responsible for the opinions, conclusions, and assertions in this book; these remain our own responsibility, along with any errors of fact.

We would also like to express our thanks to several people not directly involved in the Lufthansa case who nevertheless were vitally important in the making of this book. Among them are Bob Guccione, editor and publisher of *Omni* and *Penthouse* magazines, for his encouragement and support; Peter Bloch, executive editor of *Penthouse* magazine, for equally valuable encouragement; and Eric Volkman, for important research assistance.

Above all, special thanks are due to our agent, Victoria Pryor of Arcadia Ltd., whose advice and direction were crucial; and Elizabeth Hock, our gifted editor, whose devoted work made it a much better book.

Ernest Volkman
John Cummings
New York, July 1986

Contents

THE HEIST

heist (hīst) *Slang.*— *tr.v.* **heist-ed, heist-ing, heists.** To rob; steal.—*n.* A robbery; burglary. [Alteration of HOIST.]

The American Heritage Dictionary
Second College Edition

Introduction

"The crime
of the century"

Even to this day, there are people in Ozone Park, New York, who insist they know exactly how it started.

Right there, in that place, they will say, pointing to a small, dingy bar on a street just outside the airport; that's where the ten men met one afternoon, plotting how they would steal more money than had ever been stolen before. It was millions of dollars they were talking about that day, more money than they had ever dared dream could be in one place, more money than they had ever seen in their lives. Like ripe fruit waiting to be plucked, the money lay, almost undefended, in an airport cargo terminal, and here was this little guy, telling them how to get it out. Easy, he said; like taking candy from a baby.

No, say others, it didn't happen that way. Actually, there were these seven guys in this other bar, and one night, they figured it all out. And when they were all finished, they suddenly realized that the years of hustling after dimes were over; they were going to be rich men. "Jesus, we're gonna make millions!" one of them shouted, and it was the first time anyone could remember that the bartender broke out the champagne, announcing all drinks were on the house.

None of that effete stuff like champagne glasses; these guys drank it straight from the bottle. They took long swigs and toasted this big Irishman, the guy with blue eyes and hands like hams. Laughing, they bragged about the new cars, the women, and the little businesses they would buy with their shares. They drank to the Irishman, the mastermind of it all, the man who had told them how to steal all those millions. He joined happily in the drinking and the toasts, never letting on that he planned to kill all of them, one by one.

———

Or there is the other story, the one about what happened to all those millions that nobody ever found. One of the robbers kept poisonous snakes as pets, so when it came time to hide the loot, the cash was stored in piles in the glass cages where the snakes slithered. But the sister of one of the crooks saw them; when she threatened to tell police what she had seen, her brother slowly pushed her head into the cage of a poisonous viper. She died, screaming and writhing on the floor after the viper bit her face, while her brother held her down on the floor, laughing.

———

It is the stuff of local legend in that community cowering in the shadow of Kennedy Airport. There seems no end to these accounts; at least half the population of Queens, apparently, has the "inside story" of what really happened in the event newspapers for a long time referred to as "the crime of the century."

The established facts are that in the hours just before dawn on December 11, 1978, a gang of seven men carried out a robbery at the Lufthansa Air Cargo terminal at Kennedy Airport and escaped with around $8 million in cash, unmounted jewels, foreign currency, and pure gold. Nearly eight years after that robbery, despite a strong effort by police and the FBI, not one cent of the money, or the gold and jewels, has ever been recovered. None of the actual participants in the robbery was ever charged with the crime. At least thirteen people connected with the crime have been murdered or are missing and presumed dead.

This bare-bones, police-blotter description, of course, is only part of the story and does not even begin to explain why

2

the Lufthansa robbery has exerted such a strong pull on the popular imagination. Or why, as the legends still floating around Queens attest, it continues to spawn such stories as the one about the unknown participant now living on a yacht in Florida, or the one about the millions buried under somebody's basement floor, waiting to be spent after the heat is off.

The Lufthansa robbery is the ultimate American true crime story. It has everything: sex, murder, huge amounts of money, the Mafia, a criminal mastermind. Moreover, it is surrounded by an aura of sinister mystery—how could they possibly have gotten away with it? Then, too, there is the American fascination with major robberies: Everyman's fantasy of the perfect score, the well-planned heist that takes millions from an impersonal target, preferably a little-loved one, such as a bank. For a series of complex reasons, Americans tend to regard such crimes with a mixture of awe, covert admiration and thrill, an outlook reserved for no other type of crime.

Statistically, the Lufthansa robbery's haul far exceeded that taken in what before 1978 was regarded as the greatest cash robbery in American history: the armed holdup of the Brink's Armored Car Company in Boston on January 17, 1950. In that case, seven men stole $2,775,395 in cash and securities in a daring operation that authorities first suspected was the work of master criminals. In fact, however, the robbery was carried out by a collection of local low-scale thieves who had discovered that the much-vaunted "impregnable" Brink's operation had all the security of a chicken coop in a hurricane.

In the end, the Brink's robbers did not get to enjoy the proceeds. Much of the money disappeared during "laundering" (a series of transactions to exchange money for new bills), and all those involved were later caught and sent to prison. The FBI took nearly six years and spent nearly $29 million of the taxpayers' money to crack the case. Some of the loot was recovered.

Judged strictly by size of haul, the Lufthansa heist remained the largest American cash robbery until December 1982, when a private armored car company in New York City was robbed of nearly $11 million in cash. However, that robbery was technically an embezzlement, since it was carried out by one of the company's employees, operating in conjunction with a number of friends and family members, none of them professional criminals. In any event, their triumph was short-lived; all were later arrested and convicted. A considerable portion of the money was recovered.

In 1983, a gang of robbers took $7 million from the Wells Fargo company in broad daylight. The FBI later solved the case, arresting all twenty participants. They turned out to be Puerto Rican revolutionaries, a connection suspected from the beginning, since they all disdained wearing masks during the robbery, as if they were proud of being identified. It was not, FBI agents noted, anything like Lufthansa, which involved professional criminals.

In all likelihood, the Lufthansa robbery probably will not be duplicated or superseded. For one thing, huge intercontinental shipments of cash are now increasingly rare. Today, such vast amounts are represented by computer commands; in milliseconds, millions of dollars can be moved thousands of miles between banks. That development is beginning to render obsolete those classic figures of the criminal world, the professional stickup crew led by a mastermind. Their replacement is the somewhat more mundane modern criminal, the computer thief who manipulates unquestioning machines into writing him a check.

Thus, the Lufthansa heist remains the most extraordinary such event in the annals of American crime. It is not merely that the crime was the only successful major cash robbery in American history—although, as we shall see, the word "success" in connection with that particular robbery has a terrible irony. More to the point, the basic facts of the robbery are almost incidental to its irresistible lure, for it has all the elements of a timeless drama: greed, betrayal, the dazzling appeal of the perfect score, the curious dynamics of the struggle between cops and robbers, the power of money over those who have never had much of it, and the gray world of the professional criminal.

And, most important, it is about life and death.

PART
ONE
THE ROBERT'S LOUNGE GANG

Chapter

1

"They ain't been doing right by Jimmy"

The morning of October 25, 1978, was bright and clear in New York City, with a strong hint of autumnal chill, among the first warnings of the inevitable cold and damp winter to come. It was an otherwise unremarkable day; much of the chatter around the crowded streets centered on the early-season chances of the Giants and Jets, along with complaints about rapidly rising prices in that year of double-digit inflation.

A black sedan exited the Lincoln Tunnel from New Jersey and moved up Manhattan's West Side into the noisy stream of traffic. It pulled up before the shabby facade of an old hotel at Broadway and West Fifty-fifth Street, and two federal marshals escorted their handcuffed passenger inside.

James Burke, Federal Bureau of Prisons No. 96380-131, was home.

He had returned to New York, his home, the place he called "New Yawk." After serving six years of a ten-year sentence for extortion, he had been released conditionally into an institution the prison authorities quaintly call a halfway house, by

7

which they mean a work-release program designed to phase convicts back into society. It is a laudable idea, although there has always been cause to wonder how convicts who have spent their entire lives in criminal activities are suddenly supposed to acquire the habits of good citizenship, including gainful employment, through a program that puts them back on the streets.

Burke was now part of what the federal government, with its love of euphemisms, referred to as the Community Treatment Center. It occupied two floors of the hotel, an old place that time had passed by; by 1978, it catered, sullenly, to the transient trade. Overhadowed by the glittering palaces in midtown Manhattan, the hotel gratefully accepted the federal government's rent checks for its halfway house.

In the language of the federal prison bureaucrats, the CTC was a means of easing convicted felons back into society. The prisoners were held there for at least ninety days prior to release from custody into parole. The condition of entry into the CTC was that prisoners must have a regular job on the outside. Each morning, they would be released to go to their jobs—or to seek new ones—and they would check back in by 11:00 P.M. On weekends, they did not have to stay in the CTC and were free to spend their time as they chose.

So much for the concept as it existed in theory. In practice, the halfway house was a joke. Professional criminals used their contacts on the outside to arrange some sort of phony no-show job. They spent their days in the very same criminal activities that had gotten them into prison in the first place. The sign-in requirement each night at eleven was also a standing joke. As every prisoner knew, a ten dollar bill would make the elderly federal guards look the other way.

As a professional criminal, Burke understood the system very well—and knew precisely how to take advantage of it. He was in the hotel only a few hours before he was back on the street. Officially, he had a job running a dress factory, but in fact Burke had no intention of spending a minute there. He also had no intention of seeking better employment.

Burke had more important objectives in mind. They centered on the urgent necessity to refurbish a minor criminal empire that had gone seriously to pot. And that task would set in motion a series of events he could never have anticipated.

8

In the vast, sprawling underworld of New York City, there were few who did not know about James Burke, known as "Jimmy the Gent." The nickname stemmed from Burke's habitual politeness and his reputation for paternalistic care of his confederates, a broad range of services that included providing bail money when needed, caring for the families of imprisoned men, and constant tutoring in the more intricate aspects of criminal enterprise.

But the nickname failed to reflect another side of Burke's personality—the strong-arm expert and vicious killer who was reputed to have killed over thirty men. It was whispered around the underworld that Burke once murdered a man with his bare hands during a temper tantrum. Burke's temper formed the cutting edge of his fearsome reputation as a criminal; those who have seen it erupt proclaim it a frightening experience.

Burke *looked* menacing. Born in the tough East New York section of Brooklyn of Irish immigrants from a class known as "shanty Irish" (as distinguished from the so-called "lace curtain Irish," the immigrant class that came to dominate the police and political establishments in New York), Burke spent the early part of his life working as a bricklayer. Those years of hauling brick and mortar up and down ladders in hods known contemptuously to some non-Irish as "Irish tea service" created Burke's huge arms and torso. Stocky, with curly gray hair and piercing blue eyes, he looked, ironically enough, like a tough Irish cop.

But Burke had never considered a career in law enforcement. Just after the Second World War, tired of eking out a living in the backbreaking world of the bricklayer, he began to dabble in criminal enterprise. It was small at first: a little bookmaking here, a little loan-sharking there. Entrée to the underworld was provided, not unnaturally, by some childhood friends with whom he had grown up in East New York who had become professional crooks. Among them was Paul Vario, Sr., in his youth a florist, a job he used as a cover to run a whole series of illegal gambling, bookmaking, and loan-sharking operations. (We shall hear much more of Paul Vario, Sr., later, for he was to occupy a critical fulcrum in Burke's later criminal career.)

The first dabblings in crime revealed that Burke had a natural talent for such enterprise. He was extremely active in soliciting new accounts and organizing an efficient system to serve bettors and borrowers, and he was noted for his ability to collect from recalcitrant debtors. And no wonder: Burke, who could be smiling and gracious one minute, lathering his considerable charm, would revert in a second when he discovered he had been cheated or that a debtor had no intention of paying. Then the other side of Burke's personality would emerge: his face would become bright red, the eyes would widen, the raspy voice would become a snarl. In such a mood, Burke was known to have broken every bone in the face of one debtor and to have beaten another into a bloody pulp.

Burke's reputation spread. By 1955, he was known as one of the most efficient—and frightening—bookmakers and loan sharks in New York. The word was that The Gent was not to be messed with. It was a reputation that came to the attention of two important organizations.

One was the New York City Police Department, which first arrested Burke in 1948 on bookmaking charges—Burke was seventeen at the time—opening a criminal dossier that by 1978 included thirty arrests, ten convictions, and five prison terms. The other was the Mafia, whose attention was drawn to Burke by Paul Vario, himself a rising star in the mob. And as Vario rose in the La Cosa Nostra hierarchy, he brought his childhood friend Burke with him, devolving upon him growing responsibilities: larger territories, bigger loan-shark accounts, and important assignments. These assignments involved, for the most part, Burke's specialty: collecting, by strong-arm methods, from debtors considered nearly beyond reach, even to the normally efficient Mafia collection methods.

By the 1960s, Burke had become one of the most notorious professional criminals in New York. In and out of police stations and jails with regularity, he was known to be deeply involved with illegal gambling operations, which also happened to be Vario's specialty. Burke was also acquiring a reputation for innovation: at one point, when barred from Aqueduct Race Track in Queens for illegal bookmaking, Burke simply moved his operation into the racetrack's parking lot, where, with a clear view of the tote board, he continued to book bets.

Burke inevitably found himself before several grand juries, the kind district attorneys used to convene regularly to get newspaper headlines. They would drag assorted criminals before these panels under grants of immunity, ask some self-incriminating questions, then indict them for contempt when they refused to answer. It led to a charade, the steady parade of criminals into jail for thirty days, where they would languish during the term of the grand jury. It was not a very efficient way of fighting the Mafia, and it later fell into disrepute. Before then, however, Burke found himself housed occasionally in the jail of Nassau County, a large suburban county just east of Queens. There an ambitious district attorney, vowing a fight unto the death against the mob, was forever running Vario—who had a home in Nassau County—and his associates before the grand jury.

It made for a lot of headlines (which was the real purpose of the whole exercise) and hardly bothered Vario, Burke, or anybody else in that crowd. They showed up at the grand jury on a Friday, fully aware they would probably go to jail after they testified that they had no intention of discussing anything having to do with the subject of crimes, especially any in which they were involved. They arrived with toothbrushes in their jacket pockets, regarding their imminent jailing as a necessary cost of doing business. Their deportment before the grand jury thus tended to be casual. One time Burke was asked if he knew the brothers Joe and Larry Gallo, infamous Mafia hoods in Brooklyn. "Are them the guys what make the wine?" Burke responded in wide-eyed innocence.

————

Even the cops had to laugh at that one, but they found less amusing the intelligence that Burke had begun to branch out into somewhat loftier enterprises, notably hijacking.

Actually, the hijacking was an offshoot of Burke's illegal gambling operations. In a moment of the kind of inspiration that fuels great criminal enterprises, Burke realized that an increasing number of his customers had jobs at Kennedy Airport. And not just any jobs; one of them held an important post as traffic operations supervisor for a major trucking company; one was a shipping clerk for another, a third was a loading dock foreman for still another trucking outfit. In other words, they possessed something far more valuable than their ability to pay.

Ability to pay was not always a consideration for the kind of people who gambled regularly. Like all bookmakers, Burke realized that working men who gamble are among the most foolish human beings on earth. Frequently, convinced that they can beat any odds, they bet far above their means. Rapidly in over their heads, they tend to "double down," or follow a losing series of bets by doubling the stake on the next series, in hope of recouping the loss and having a profit left over when the doubled bets win. In most cases, they do not, which usually leads to a debt that cannot be repaid. Enter now the loan shark, who, in the case of Mafia-connected bookies, tends to be the same person.

Burke was such an operator. To those who were swimming in gambling debts they had no hope of repaying on modest salaries, he offered a solution: a loan that would wipe out the debt and leave the debtor some extra money with which to keep betting. Such loans, the lifeblood of all organized crime, are made at usurious rates, with the interest—known as "vigorish" or "vig" in New York underworld slang—set at anywhere from 100 to 300 percent a week.

Normally, failure to repay such an unsecured debt is penalized by the standard Mafia treatment: a severe beating or, in especially difficult cases, kneecaps smashed by baseball bats. But Burke, with Vario's connivance, introduced a new twist: debtors were told their debts would be completely forgiven, provided they performed what was often described as "a small service to us." By which they meant that the debtor was to give them information—schedules of important shipments, details of highly valuable cargo, timetables of trucks moving expensive goods.

Soon the information began flowing. And the "Robert's Lounge Gang" was born.

———

Robert's Lounge—the genesis of its name remains obscure—was one of the workingmen's bars that dotted the streets just outside Kennedy Airport. It had been enjoying only modest success when its owners in 1969 gratefully unloaded

———

it on a local bookmaker and "connected" (Mafia) businessman named James Burke. Like many criminals, Burke used part of his considerable profits to buy a legitimate business. Such men often chose a bar or restaurant, which afforded a base of operations and a cash-basis business through which illegally obtained money could be laundered in the form of profits.

Burke's choice not only had the advantage of being near Kennedy Airport, increasingly his focus of operations, but also was fairly small and off the beaten path, the better to avoid certain undesirable customers, such as curious police detectives. The place may once have had some attraction for the airport workers, but in Burke's hands it was rapidly transformed into a Dodge City–style saloon. Into this plain-fronted bar with the neon "Bud" sign in the window came the underworld baddies who operated at Kennedy Airport just down the street: loan sharks, bookmakers, hijackers, hoods, strong-arm artists. The sinister looks of this scum of the underworld soon drove the working-class customers away; what remained was a steady clientele of crooks who regarded Robert's Lounge as their private social club and place of business.

Inside, there were five telephones near the front door, all of them busy around the clock with bookmakers getting the latest betting lines or booking their bets. Around the Naugahyde-padded bar gathered small knots of men, making assorted plans over their drinks. Other groups seated at some battered tables made their own plans, occasionally grinding out a cigarette on the old terra-cotta floor. (Cleanliness was not a strong suit at Robert's Lounge.) Downstairs, in the basement, which had been outfitted as a private lounge, a sort of club-within-a-club, dice and poker games ran almost constantly. The basement was also known to local hoods as "the gym," the place where obstinate debtors or hoodlums who had committed minor transgressions were beaten by groups of thugs. After they had finished beating a man into unconsciousness, the thugs would go upstairs to the bar and order cold drinks, grousing about how tiring their "workouts" were.

Burke presided over all this activity with the air of a grand patrician. Thanks to his chilling reputation and known connection to the Mafia through Paul Vario, he was treated with deference and respect, a man to whom other criminals began to turn for advice and support. Certainly by this point

Burke possessed an excellent grasp of the arts of criminal enterprise; as a man considered brighter and more shrewd than most criminals, he was clearly somebody good to know.

From the coterie of criminals who began to gravitate toward him, Burke recruited his own private gang. Depending on their usefulness to him, they ranged in the pecking order from close confidants to fringe members, to whom Burke would occasionally throw a few crumbs. Those closest to him were selected to commit the crimes that began to occupy most of Burke's time: hijacking goods out of Kennedy Airport. Others were given pieces of his bookmaking business, still others were assigned strong-arm tasks, and a few were let in on a racket that Burke was just beginning to experiment with: narcotics.

––––

In sum, Burke was becoming a crime boss in his own right. While he was technically affiliated with Vario's Mafia family, he had been granted a form of independent operator's status that was a tribute to his criminal acumen. As an independent affiliate—with the strict understanding that Vario was to receive proper tribute in the form of a cut of Burke's profits— Burke had the right to recruit his own people. Those he recruited represented a disparate collection of human beings who shared a regard for Jimmy Burke's abilities, believed he would help make them a lot of money, and assumed he would never betray them. Burke made it clear to them that they would always be taken care of if arrested and would always receive a fair share of the profits—in return for which they were expected to maintain eternal silence, no matter how strong the pressure. Burke did not need to add, as a man who had already killed a fair number of miscreants, that he would exact the ultimate penalty from any squealer.

––––

Still, compared to the rigid organizational structure of the Mafia, Burke's gang was a somewhat loose confederation whose members flitted in and out, depending on the availability of targets. On any given night, they could be seen in Robert's Lounge, sometimes playing the ancient-looking pinball machine near the bar, or watching the large-screen television set

––––

that never seemed to be off, or having drinks with their patriarch, discussing the latest scores, large and small.

Among the more interesting gang members was a man who did not look like a crook at all. But in fact Robert (Frenchie) McMahon, whose boyhood was spent as a numbers runner in the infamous Hell's Kitchen in Manhattan, had devoted his life to crime. A slight man who wore glasses, McMahon looked like an accountant or a stockbroker and liked to consider himself a gentleman. He cultivated that image by wearing expensive, hand-tailored suits.

His only real job in the thirty-seven years of his life had been a seventeen-year career at the Air France cargo terminal at the airport. Although most people assumed his nickname stemmed from that fact, actually the name "Frenchie" arose from an incident in 1972, when he helped rob an Air France truck of over $2 million. The robbery capped an interesting career during which he had helped the Mafia steal just about anything that was not tied down at Air France's cargo operations.

McMahon had also been involved in a long list of hijacking operations, a record that made him a natural for Burke's hijack gang. McMahon proved his worth almost immediately, carrying out a string of hijackings for his new boss. He was eager for as much work as Burke could find for him, to support his fondness for fine restaurants and beautiful women. Those interests swallowed up the bulk of what McMahon made from the hijackings; the rest went to two ex-wives whose lawyers seemed to be constantly hounding him for money.

McMahon was joined in the Burke crew by his close friend, Joseph Manri, whose real name was Manriquez. The change of name by the unmistakably Hispanic-looking Manri reflected his hope that he could pass for Italian and be inducted someday into the Mafia. Meanwhile, he was busy matching his friend's record for air cargo theft, bookmaking, and auto theft. In the process, he developed an intimate knowledge of the various loading docks at Kennedy Airport, priceless knowledge and experience that moved McMahon to recommend him to Burke. In addition to similar police records, Manri and McMahon shared a taste for beautiful women, who seemed to take the lion's share of what Manri earned. (Manri and McMahon sought to pare expenses by sharing the same small Ozone Park apartment.)

Although McMahon and Manri were considered the most trusted of the Burke gang, Burke's closest associate was a hood named Thomas DeSimone, whom he had known for years. Among other quirks, DeSimone had a thing about freshly shined shoes and would never appear in public for even the most casual encounters without a nice shine. This was a heritage of a childhood partly spent as a shoeshine boy. However, few dared to refer to the quirk openly, for DeSimone was known to be extremely sensitive on the issue; reputedly, he had murdered a local hood who made the mistake of twitting him about it.

DeSimone took pride in being "sharp" (a phrase implying attention to dress and appearance), for he had an abiding passion for female flesh—*any* female flesh. A tall man with the kind of dark good looks that reminded many of Errol Flynn, DeSimone had an all-consuming appetite for the opposite sex. Despite being married, he pursued *anything* that looked even vaguely female.

Sometimes called—albeit derisively—"Two-Gun Tommy" because of his habit of carrying a matched set of pearl-handled pistols, DeSimone's life was dominated by a passion even greater than the lust for female flesh: the desire to be "made" (formally inducted) into the Mafia family of which Paul Vario was a leading light. To that end, he had spent the last twelve of his thirty-two years dutifully carrying out a long list of crimes large and small for the mob and had maintained silence in the face of several prison sentences. In Mafia terms, he was a "stand-up guy," but alas for DeSimone's ambitions, Vario's family was in no rush to welcome him into the fold. The problem was that however stand-up, DeSimone was hopelessly stupid, demonstrating no ability to generate profit.

It was a fatal defect, for above all, the Mafia is a profit-making enterprise and prefers to choose its members on the basis of how much money they will be able to earn for the family. Aware of Burke's own mob connections, DeSimone had joined his hijack gang, hoping that a stellar performance there might enhance his chances with Vario's group. Meanwhile, he spent his free time with an assortment of women to whom he bragged of his Mafia connections.

However deficient DeSimone's brain, he was a positive genius compared to the mental acuity of another close associate of Burke's, Angelo Sepe. For students of the unfathomable, the relationship between Sepe and Jimmy Burke provided a rich field. Thin, just over five feet tall, Sepe was an unkempt, low-life hood who had a record of fourteen arrests that had begun when he was fourteen years old. The charges ranged from petty larceny to burglary. Despite the fact that Sepe was a singularly untalented crook, Burke enrolled him in the gang and had what amounted to a father-son relationship with Sepe, patiently instructing him in the finer points of crime and trying to correct Sepe's biggest problem—the tendency to get caught.

Burke's patience persisted, even though Sepe was a near-cretin whose consuming passion was a menagerie of small animals. Virtually every stray animal he encountered—rabbits, birds, turtles—became part of the menagerie, to which Sepe spent hours cooing in what he apparently thought was some kind of animal language they understood. Perhaps so; the animals seemed devoted to him.

———

Every criminal gang has its gofer, and Parnell (Stax) Edwards served that function in the Burke crew. A convicted credit card thief who had become a friend of DeSimone while in prison, Edwards performed a wide variety of low-scale functions for the gang, including occasionally acting as chauffeur.

Edwards was black, although his skin was so light many people took him for white. For many years his ambition was to be a successful blues singer, and to that end, he often performed in Robert's Lounge. It was, of course, a tough place for musical performances; no one went there for the entertainment. And when the crowd was in no mood for music, it was not unusual for a hood in the audience to suddenly yell at Edwards (who in any event had little talent), "Shut the fuck up, motherfucker!" before hurling a bottle.

Despite these setbacks, Edwards persisted in what he regarded as the beginning of a great musical career. Meanwhile, he continued running errands for Burke's crew and was rewarded with an occasional shipment of clothes or other goods that had been stolen from trucks. Edwards peddled these on the street. He used the profits to score some cocaine, which he snorted with some friends, to whom he boasted of his "important" criminal connections.

———

While Stax Edwards looked the part of the prototypical street hustler, Martin Krugman, another close Burke associate, looked like the prototypical bookie. Sometimes called "Bug Eyes" for his protruding eyeballs that stared nervously out at the world, Krugman was a thin man of fifty-two who appeared much older. Born in Poland of Orthdox Jews, he had long ago turned his back on what he considered their suffocating piety and ritual; in return, they discussed him as though he were dead.

Krugman was determined to be a "wiseguy" (New York slang for a Mafia crook), and to that end had hooked up with Burke years before in bookmaking operations. At first an eager errand boy who liked to hang around with hoods, Krugman demonstrated talent for bookmaking, and Burke had given him a large slice of the business at Kennedy Airport.

But that was only one part of Krugman's life, a secret to all but a handful of people. To everyone else, he appeared to be a hairdresser who operated a men's hairpiece operation out in Nassau County. From the salon Krugman also dealt some cocaine to a selected few. The rest of the time, he made book out of an upstairs room at Robert's Lounge, overseeing a growing business. He had a number of interesting customers, among them, Burke knew, several operations supervisors in air cargo terminals at Kennedy Airport.

———

No greater physical contrast existed than the one between Krugman and one of his colleagues in the Burke gang, Louis Cafora. If nothing else, Cafora stood out: of medium height, he weighed over 300 pounds (he was called "the whale") and he moved his bulk around New York in a gaudy white Cadillac that barely seemed big enough to contain him. He was noted, additionally, for an appetite that defied belief. He always seemed to be eating, and Burke was not especially pleased that every conversation with Cafora seemed to be dominated by the subject of food. Nevertheless, Burke, aware of Cafora's involvement in loan-sharking and heroin trafficking, felt that the fat crook was a valuable addition to the gang because of his additional expertise in stickup jobs.

———

By far the most curious member of the Robert's Lounge Gang was Henry Hill, who enjoyed a close relationship with Jimmy Burke that puzzled most of the other gang members. They were unaware that the link between Hill and Burke extended back nearly twenty years. Hill, then a fourteen-year-old street punk, had begun running errands for the players in a Mafia-run poker game in Brooklyn. Among those players were Burke and Paul Vario, Sr. Impressed by the youngster's eagerness to please, his street smarts, and his apparent desire to become a real crook, the two men adopted him as a sort of mascot. Later, Hill became part of Burke's crew, participating mostly in gambling operations and disposal of hijacked goods.

Over the years, Burke and Hill developed a relationship that was nearly father-son, and under Burke's tutelage, Hill demonstrated something of a flair for crime. Quick to spot any angle that could be exploited, Hill became a personal favorite of Vario, Sr., who tended to take credit for Hill's development. Vario could not sponsor Hill for Mafia membership, however, much as he admired Hill's moneymaking abilities: Hill was only half Italian. He had an Irish father who despaired of his son's choice of a criminal career.

Burke in effect became Hill's surrogate father, much to the dismay of some other Burke associates, who thoroughly disliked the thin, fair-haired man with the pronounced paunch that made him look like a pregnant pencil. And they wondered why Burke continued to treat Hill like a son, even after his protégé developed a serious drinking and narcotics problem that by 1973 was beginning to make him act more like a junkie than the street-wise moneymaker he was reputed to be.

———

Possibly, part of the answer to the Burke-Hill riddle was in the difficult relationship Burke had with his own son, Frank James Burke.

Invariably called Frankie, to his intense annoyance, Frank

was the elder of Jimmy Burke's two sons. The younger was named Jesse James Burke. The names were Burke's tribute to the men he admired most, the leaders of the infamous Jesse James gang of the old West. Both sons had grown up in an atmosphere that can only be described as different; their father always cheered for the bad guys in television police dramas, and he never failed to be touched by movie scenes showing the death of Jesse James.

Although his father had schooled Frank in the arcana of crime, the boy did not seem suited for his chosen profession. Despite his precise imitation of his father—including the swagger and the nearly impenetrable Brooklyn accent—Frank failed at virtually every crime he attempted. He had acquired, by the age of nineteen, an undistinguished record of petty larceny, drug-related offenses, and possession of burglary tools.

Openly scornful of his son's lack of criminal abilities, Burke tried everything, including taking Frankie to his first "hit," during which he carefully instructed the boy in the proper method of disposing of inconvenient human beings. Frank seemed to have learned the lesson imperfectly, however, and he became the laughingstock of the New York underworld.

———

It would seem, at first glance, that this variegated collection of low-lifes was not the stuff of criminal greatness. Yet, by the early 1970s, the Robert's Lounge Gang was among the most successful criminal enterprises in New York, racking up vast profits in hijacking operations, mostly at Kennedy Airport. No one was quite sure how much stuff was being hijacked—air cargo operations had the bad habit of deliberately understating their losses—but it was clear there was a serious problem. That problem centered on the personnel Burke and Vario had carefully assembled: truck drivers in hock to the mob, key air cargo employees who were providing inside information, and a gang that thus knew exactly when to strike for maximum profit. As Queens police detective Robert Mackey observed at the time, in what was only a slight exaggeration: "It's a race between the airport and the crooks to see who gets the goods out of the airport first."

From the moment construction began on the airport in the 1950s, it was a prime target of the mob. Like the waterfront, with its profusion of riches, which had provided such tempting targets a generation before, the airport represented an irresistible lure to the mobsters who understood a basic economic fact of life: literally billions of dollars' worth of stuff poured into New York, the world's richest port, every year. All that was required was a system to make sure a certain portion of it did not reach its chosen destination.

In the case of Idlewild Airport—as it was known before being renamed in honor of the slain President in 1963—thievery was considerably eased by circumstances. One was the sheer size of the place: Kennedy Airport, among the world's largest, sprawled across more than 5,000 acres once occupied by marshland and a huge golf course. A city unto itself, it was a self-contained community where over fifty thousand people worked and through which millions of passengers moved. The airport's cargo operations were the biggest and most active in the world, with a volume of nearly $35 billion a year by 1975. The place was a beehive; just about everything produced by human hands was shipped through it at one point or another by fleets of trucks that shuttled in and out of the airport around the clock.

And it was precisely there that the mobsters discovered the airport's weak point. Air cargo operations had plenty of security to guard the Swiss watches, cash shipments, computer parts, designer clothes, and other expensive goods, but once the goods were loaded aboard delivery trucks, it was all in the hands of a truck driver. As Burke and the other mobsters discovered, a driver could be bribed to forgetfully leave his keys in the ignition when he stopped for a cup of coffee. Or he could be promised forgiveness of a large gambling debt if he failed to remember what those three guys who held him up on that side street looked like. Or his supervisor could be bribed to overload the truck, and the surplus could disappear somewhere between the terminal and its intended destination.

Police found a little playlet enacted with monotonous regularity. The truck driver would sit in a detective squad room, being questioned about details of the robbery he had just undergone. Three men, he said, had run up to him while he was stopped at a traffic light. They had ordered him from the cab at gunpoint and then had driven off in the truck. All this at a major intersection with thousands of people in the area.

"What did they look like?" a detective would ask.

"Uh, three niggers with ski masks."

"Yeah? You mean to tell us that three black guys, wearing ski masks, just pop up in *broad daylight* on a busy street waving guns around? Sure. Try another one on us."

"Uh, maybe they weren't niggers. Maybe they were white guys; I can't be sure."

———

Police did not find these encounters amusing, for while the alleged victims of such hijackings were demonstrating an astonishing vagueness of memory, the man detectives knew was behind most of them was raucously celebrating his success in uproarious celebrations at Robert's Lounge, and occasionally in other mob hangouts, where Jimmy the Gent was known to show off by casually flicking one hundred dollar bills as tips to bartenders and waiters.

The success made Burke a "man of respect," as the Mafia term has it—someone who makes a great deal of money. Although Burke, a non-Italian, could not be formally inducted into the Mafia, he won the status of associate member, a powerful position that afforded him protection against any possible maraudings from other Mafia families. It also gave him authority (known as "sanction") to mete out discipline to members of his own group when necessary. The methods of "discipline" included murder.

As a reflection of his growing status, Burke moved from Brooklyn to one of the more expensive Queens neighborhoods, Howard Beach, just west of Kennedy Airport. To the distress of its law-abiding residents, Howard Beach had become known as "the Mafia's bedroom" in New York, because of the significant number of successful hoodlums who had moved in. The upward mobility of Burke and other mobsters was for Howard Beach a mixed blessing: while the crime rate was remarkably low—even the stupidest burglar knew better than to rob the house of a Mafioso—the community suffered the indignity of recurring newspaper reports listing Howard Beach as the home of hoodlums. It also endured the presence of unmarked cars containing detectives checking up on interesting neighbors.

As befit his background, Burke chose a house of solid brick. In fact, the place looked like a bricklayer's fantasy. It had a certain flamboyance, very much the dominant characteristic of Burke's life as he reached the pinnacle of criminal success during the beginning of the 1970s. Indeed, he became increasingly flamboyant, as though he were some kind of 19th-century robber baron. There was the afternoon, for example, that he walked into a friend's restaurant and complained about the terrible odor in the place.

Informed that the smell came from a filthy pizzeria next door, Burke asked his friend why he hadn't taken the matter up with its owner.

"I did, Jimmy," the friend replied, "but I can't do nothing with that guy; he don't care."

Burke excused himself—to make a phone call, he said—and returned several minutes later. People in the restaurant began to smell smoke. Then flames shot out from the pizzeria. Burke paid hardly any attention to the tumult. Instead of making a phone call, he had gone into the pizzeria, ordered everybody out of the place, then set it afire. End of problem.

More ominously, there was the time a crook from Atlanta, hearing that Burke was getting into the narcotics business, made the mistake of walking into Robert's Lounge, flashing $50,000 in cash in front of Burke's face, and asking to buy some high-grade stuff. Burke, the very picture of easy charm, put the man in touch with three men who, Burke said, would take care of him. During that subsequent meeting, three of Burke's hoods put three bullets into the man's head, then took his money.

It was only a matter of time, of course, before Burke, despite his criminal cunning, would make a serious mistake. He simply was taking too many chances. Ironically, he made that mistake not in New York, but in Florida. There, in 1972, wandering somewhat afield, Burke was running a growing illegal gambling operation with Henry Hill. Two big gamblers refused to pay, and an infuriated Burke had one of them on his knees, a gun pressed to his head, sobbing and begging for mercy.

Federal law primly calls this "extortionate extension of credit," and it earned Burke and Hill ten-year sentences for extortion.

The incarceration of Burke in a federal penitentiary did not necessarily mean the end of his criminal enterprise in New York, for he was perfectly capable of issuing orders from his jail cell. But, as he came to realize, the nature of his gang members necessitated his personal presence to keep their heads straight. Without Burke on the spot to direct, cajole, and threaten, they tended to rely on their own brains—a serious mistake by people who did not have much brains to begin with.

Very soon, word reached Burke that his gang had fallen on hard times. Sepe, for instance, had tried to carry out stick-ups on his own. They had failed ignominiously, including one in which he had used, for some odd reason, a dog's winter sweater as a mask—the kind of detail that tends to stick in witnesses' minds.

And Frenchie McMahon had played a major role in the hijacking of an Air France truck the year Burke went to prison, but led police to himself by spending his cut wildly and bragging all over town about his role. Suspicious of what they perceived as a strange delay by the authorities in prosecuting this crime, the rest of the Robert's Lounge Gang became convinced that McMahon had become a police or FBI informant. To prove he wasn't, McMahon and another hood hijacked a truck in Queens. With the driver between them, a gun pressed to his ear, the two hijackers discovered they could not operate the truck's gears. McMahon, who was sitting on the passenger side, ordered the driver to take the wheel. With that, McMahon's fellow hijacker opened the door and got out. Impatient, McMahon pushed the driver toward the wheel. But he pushed too hard; the driver fell out of the truck.

Now panic-stricken at the thought that all this might be attracting attention, McMahon and his confederate drove off in the truck, gears grinding, the vehicle hiccupping forward. Police, who found the whole thing hysterically funny, arrested them both a short distance away. (For these lapses, which he believed had caused the organization to suffer a severe loss of face to the police, Vario had McMahon thoroughly beaten by two thugs as an object lesson.)

Meanwhile, Krugman was arrested in Nassau County on a gambling charge. When police found some cocaine in his possession, he stupidly tried to bribe a detective. The detective played along, then arrested him on a bribery charge.

As for others in the Robert's Lounge Gang: DeSimone, along with six other men, hijacked a truck with $1 million worth of merchandise, but fouled up the job so badly that police grabbed them all. Cafora was convicted on a loan-sharking charge, while Manri botched a gas station robbery in which a police officer was killed during a high-speed chase.

———

It was thus an extremely angry James Burke who returned to New York that October morning in 1978. His foul mood consisted of equal parts of fury directed at the members of his organization for their incompetence, and rage at the lack of money that he was now feeling acutely.

For months, the underworld grapevine had buzzed with news of Burke's fulminations against the "morons," "shit-heads," and "assholes" of his once prosperous gang. In Burke's view, the gang was directly responsible for the fact that money —the prime ingredient of all criminal enterprise—was in short supply. What money there was had been swallowed up in legal fees and other expenses, and since the gang members had been busy getting arrested instead of making money, the Robert's Lounge was experiencing what a different sort of business might describe delicately as a negative cash flow.

"Jimmy's real pissed off," an underworld informant close to the Robert's Lounge Gang whispered to a police detective at the time of Burke's return. "They [the gang] ain't been doing right by Jimmy. There ain't been a dime coming in while he's been in the joint [prison]. You watch: Jimmy will tell them to either shape up and get some money coming in, or the bodies are gonna fall."

That is precisely what Burke told his crew; to DeSimone, one of his earliest associates, he put it plainly: "We got a lot of catching up to do." It was, as DeSimone understood, a strong warning, signifying Burke's deep dissatisfaction with the course of events during his prison stay. It meant that the gang was expected to make up for past incomeless incompetence— and fast.

They needed no reminder of Burke's willingness to use violence to make his point. As they became aware, Burke's initial hours outside the halfway house were spent traveling around in a chauffeured car thoughtfully provided by Vario. The chauffeur, one of Vario's more loyal hoods, was the very model of discretion, never once looking in the rearview mirror as his passenger made stops all over the city, inviting various people to sit in the back seat with him and have a conversation as the car was driven around. Some of those so invited owed money to Burke. He beat them up, then dumped them out of the car a few miles away.

Through it all, the chauffeur never gave a sign that he had heard Burke's fists smashing into one man's flesh and bones, or heard another man weeping piteously, vowing that he would pay the debt—if only Burke would let go of his testicles.

And when a man had been dumped from the car, accompanied by Burke's threats, the chauffeur calmly asked, "Where to now, Jimmy?"

Such debt-collection methods were, of course, a mark of Burke's desperation at that point. With the treasury dry, he had to get money as quickly as possible. However, even if he collected on a number of debts outstanding, he would still not have the large amount of capital required to refuel the bookmaking and loan-sharking operations that in turn drove the hijack operations.

In short, Burke needed a big score. The members of his organization did not seem to be exactly fertile with ideas in this area. DeSimone came up with a few harebrained schemes, none of them even remotely feasible, and even more ill-conceived schemes were advanced by Manri and McMahon.

Burke was slightly more moved by some ideas advanced by Henry Hill, who had been released from prison just a short while before. Hill noted that he had made an important connection in prison: a major Pittsburgh drug dealer, who had proposed a big interstate narcotics scheme. Even better, Hill pointed out, the drug dealer happened to be friends with a player on a major college basketball team. The player might be willing to do business in a gambling scheme in which point spreads could be manipulated, promising vast profits for people who knew the right way to bet.

Burke's interest wavered in these proposals, for they involved an immediate capital investment of some size, money that Burke did not have. He needed something that required minimal or no investment and that guaranteed an immediate return. In other words, some sort of major heist.

"Ain't anybody got something real good?" Burke asked, a general question revealing his frustration at having failed to find what he was looking for.

Actually, Burke was under even more pressure to come up with a big score than his confederates realized. And that pressure was coming from Paul Vario, Sr., *caporegime* (captain) in the Mafia.

They were all to discover that it was a very deadly pressure.

Chapter

2

"Somebody dropped a dime on us"

Like a jungle telegraph, word of the return of Jimmy Burke flashed around the community most interested in that piece of intelligence—the array of forces that constituted the law-enforcement establishment in New York. In the detective bureaus of the Queens, Brooklyn, and Manhattan district attorney's offices, and in the squad rooms of the Federal Bureau of Investigation, the New York City Police Department, and the Police Department of the Port Authority of New York and New Jersey (the bi-state agency that controls the airports), the intelligence was noted and filed away in dozens of memories.

They knew all about the man they had come to call "the Irish Godfather." They knew he was not sufficiently chastened by six years in prison to become a model citizen. And they also understood that Burke's sole intention, from the moment of his release, would be to restore the tattered remnants of his criminal organization.

Among those most interested in Burke's return were members of the Safe, Loft and Truck Squad of the New York City Police Department. One of the oldest and most famous squads in the department, it had been established around the turn of the century to combat the elite of the criminal world at that time—cat burglars and safecrackers. Some seventy years later, its mandate was broadened to include truck hijackings, bringing the sixty detectives of Safe and Loft, as it was called, into intimate contact with the Robert's Lounge Gang.

That contact was most often made by a small unit of six detectives who specialized in hijackings, an elite task force that amounted to six walking encyclopedias on the subject. For years, these detectives had conducted a running war with Burke and his crew; while the cops had won most of the battles, there was the uneasy sense that they might be losing the war. Despite arrest after arrest—including one of Burke himself—the system that Burke and Vario had created at the airport survived virtually intact; arrested men were replaced, and the group went on as before. It was a huge free-floating organism that absorbed the latest setback, readjusted, then went back to work.

Actually, however, although the police did not realize it at the time, that organization was beginning to show serious cracks around the edges. The combination of Burke's imprisonment—removing on-the-spot leadership—and continued ineptitude by the directionless hijackers contrived to put things in some disarray. True, the basic organization remained, but there was a catastrophic drop in income, and since profit was the name of the game, a restiveness had begun, a vague sense of uneasiness around other important sectors of the Mafia that perhaps all was not well with the Burke-Vario airport operation.

———

Among the first to recognize this uneasiness was one of Safe and Loft's star detectives, Robert Hernandez. Usually called "Bobby," Hernandez had been a street cop whose amazing record of arrests had won him a detective's badge and, later, assignment to Safe and Loft. He eventually wound up in the hijacking section where, like the others, he spent most of his time on the streets, fighting the hand-to-hand encounters that marked the war against the hijackers.

One result of those skirmishes—in addition to a lengthy list of arrests—was what became the police bible, a group of thick black notebooks that contained constantly updated intelligence on the hijackings and the men who had committed them. It was all there in those books, which were full of organization charts, names, dossiers, cross-referenced arrest records, and informants' data: a depressing picture of the giant clockwork that made the hijackings one of the more highly organized crimes around. The intricate system was composed of corrupt union locals, truck drivers enslaved by Mafia loan sharks and bookies, a network of fences, and greedy businessmen who knew that the goods they were buying below wholesale price were stolen merchandise. And behind it all lurked the crime bosses, such as Vario and Burke, who were raking in their shares.

––––

The foot soldiers of that organization—the hijackers and assorted supporting cast—came to know Hernandez quite well, as a cop who not only had arrested them but had also demonstrated during interrogations an uncannily accurate knowledge of how the hijacking operations worked. Although they assumed Hernandez was Puerto Rican, he was in fact the son of Cuban parents who, he would occasionally point out with some irritation, had lived in this country for fifty-two years. His New York accent contained not a trace of Spanish inflection.

Hernandez often appeared to be upset. A man who took his job very seriously, he was hyperactive, a bundle of nervous energy who seemed to be everywhere at once. He possessed the combination of talents that made him an uncommonly gifted detective: strong intelligence, street smarts (Hernandez had grown up in a tough New York neighborhood), and that sixth sense most good detectives have.

Burke's crew greatly feared the anti-hijacking squad, in particular Hernandez, a man they came to regard as their nemesis. Occasionally they wondered how Hernandez and the other cops often seemed to know operations in advance (hence, the suspicion attached to McMahon at one point), not realizing that such knowledge was usually the result of educated hunches and simple deduction of criminal patterns of behavior. They wondered, for example, how Hernandez and several other detectives knew about the drop (a site where stolen goods were temporarily stored) they had set up on a farm in New Jersey, and how they knew it was to be the place where the goods would be divided up before being dispatched to fences.

The fact was that Hernandez and the other detectives had decided to use that most ancient of all police techniques, "sitting on" (surveillance of) known associates of Burke. Their chosen target one morning was a man named Howard Weiner, an associate of Burke known to be involved in the disposal of hijacked goods obtained by Burke's crew. A part-time bartender at Robert's Lounge, Weiner was what police call "cherry," meaning a suspect who is inexperienced in dodging police surveillance. Apparently warned by Burke always to check for unmarked police cars that might try to follow him, Weiner, to the amusement of Hernandez and the other detectives on the surveillance detail, constantly checked his rearview mirror as he drove in his car—not realizing that the detectives were watching from in *front* of him.

Such surveillances only rarely produce anything significant, but that morning, Weiner, who seldom left New York City, headed south into New Jersey. There he suddenly pulled into a barn on a small farm. The detectives looked at one another. Since Weiner was not known to be interested in agriculture, what was this city guy doing on a farm? They decided to wait and watch.

They spent nearly two and a half days watching, and were rewarded by the sight of a huge tractor-trailer bumping over the plowed fields and into the barn. The truck had been hijacked out of the airport only a short while before. Then a car showed up with four men, all of them known associates of Burke. When the detectives struck, they discovered not only that they had recovered a huge shipment of hijacked goods, but that the car's trunk contained carefully prepared samples of material stolen in six previous hijackings. The display was apparently intended as a selection from which prospective buyers could choose, much as they would from a traveling salesman's display of his wares.

Burke was furious at Weiner's ineptitude, which had led Hernandez and the other detectives straight to the drop. He became almost apoplectic when, in a later raid, the police discovered an interesting account book in which Weiner had listed in some detail the amount of hijacked goods he was handling, plus the profits received after they were fenced. The

Burke mood could not have improved some time later, when another police surveillance operation uncovered a second drop where Burke was stashing loads of cigarettes smuggled to New York from North Carolina. This time, Burke himself made the error of checking up on his stash just at the moment when Hernandez and and several other detectives were there. Spotting Hernandez standing beside the stash with a big grin on his face, Burke read the situation in a glance. Wordlessly, he held out his wrists to be handcuffed.

———

At first glance, these victories appeared to be significant, and yet, as Hernandez argued, the police had not yet attacked the great clockwork that made the hijackings work, the corrupt system that had transformed truck shipping operations in the City of New York into something of a roulette game. At any given time, the chances were only five in ten that a valuable shipment would reach its destination. There were more than enough arrests, to be sure, but they had failed to result in significant jail sentences (Burke only got six months on the cigarette smuggling charge), and they did not have any noticeable impact on the system underlying the crimes.

During Burke's imprisonment in the extortion case, Hernandez and his fellow detectives sensed that Jimmy the Gent's organization was becoming badly frayed. Now there existed a real opportunity to attack deep in the bowels of the organized system of corruption that made the hijackings work.

But the problem was that the people in the corrupt unions and other components of the clockwork represented an impenetrable personnel system that was tightly controlled by the mob. The system represented maximum security; unless a man had been carefully checked out and vouched for by others, he had no hope of getting in. Those already in could spot an undercover cop instantly. (It was the same story for cops who had tried to infiltrate Robert's Lounge: even the most experienced undercover cop knew he was identified the minute he walked through the front door.)

The answer was somehow to get one of the mobsters to vouch for an undercover cop, who would then infiltrate part of the airport operation, and build a case from there. One segment of the airport operation seemed to hold some promise—

———

a freight-forwarding outfit known as VGS Delivery Service Company.

Although most freight forwarders were honest, dutifully forwarding lost baggage and freight to customers, with the airlines footing the bill, the mob had taken over several of them, finding such operations almost ideal cover behind which to transport stolen goods. VGS was one of the more active outfits. It was supposed to operate under the same stringent personnel-control rules as similar operations, but police had noticed that VGS tended to be sloppier than most. It appeared to be most vulnerable to penetration.

The necessary instrument to effect this penetration came in the person of a man we'll call Tony. A fringe mobster who had dabbled in airport and hijacking operations, Tony had been jailed on a battery of serious charges that left him facing lengthy prison time. Considering his options, Tony put the word out early in 1977 that he wanted to cooperate with police. In return, he hoped for "consideration in reduction of sentence."

Hernandez was the detective assigned to discuss this subject with Tony. He was moderately interested in most of what the prisoner had to say, but came fully alert when Tony suddenly said, "I can get the cops into the airport." It turned out to be a simple proposition: using his mob connections, Tony would introduce an undercover cop into VGS, then vouch for him.

Some weeks later, Tony walked into VGS with a stranger. "He's good people," Tony informed the men working there. This was a Mafia imprimatur, signifying that the stranger was loyal and mob-connected, thus differentiating him from "bad people" such as cops, FBI agents, and prosecutors.

The stranger was introduced as Robert DiStefano, known, Tony noted, as "Bobby the Beard" because of his distinctive black beard. To further establish DiStefano's bona fides, Tony cited the names of several notorious mobsters for whom DiStefano had worked (all the mobsters cited were conveniently deceased). As additional certification, Tony mentioned that he had just gotten out of jail, where he served time with DiStefano—a man, Tony noted significantly, who was known to be very tough and violent.

Certainly the stranger looked the part. Swarthy and husky, he walked in a kind of loose swagger much favored by Mafia hoods from Brooklyn. His distinctive hand gestures and body English marked him as an Italian, an impression that was reinforced by the Italian phrases he dropped into his conversations. It took only a short time during that winter of 1977 for DiStefano to come to be regarded by the mobsters of VGS as one of their own. Soon he was working out deals, buying up some of the astonishing amount of hijacked goods of every description that poured into VGS—crates from deliberately overloaded trucks, boxes stolen from special shipments, and entire truckloads of merchandise. The airport was hemorrhaging.

It was something of a revelation to DiStefano—who was actually Detective Robert Hernandez—for his position inside VGS afforded an unparalleled view of how much stuff was being stolen. And it was also an unparalleled opportunity, for he was now able, as a fully trusted business associate of VGS, to work his way into larger and larger deals. And as he slowly moved up the ladder, he hoped to encounter more important underworld figures, perhaps among them the big mobsters—such as Paul Vario, Sr.—along with the major fences, crooked businessmen, and labor leaders.

But it was not to be. To Hernandez's fury, the Queens District Attorney's Office, which had prosecutorial jurisdiction in the case, decided to end the infiltration operation and prosecute whatever cases could be made on the evidence already at hand. To be sure, Hernandez had managed to accumulate an impressive pile of evidence. In addition to the VGS operatives themselves, he had snared a crooked company financial officer who tried to peddle $42 million in stolen stock certificates through mob auspices. To boot, police recovered $1 million in hijacked goods.

Hernandez, however, was not pleased. "You blew it," he insisted to the Queens authorities who were basking in the glow of media publicity. He argued that if they had let the operation run its full course, they would have had a good chance of dealing the organized hijacking operations a deadly blow—possibly a fatal one.

It seemed at best an arguable proposition to the Queens prosecutors, but there was one man who understood that Hernandez was quite right. On one hand, he was grateful that the police mugging of VGS had ended prematurely, before everything had fallen apart. On the other hand, as the man behind

VGS, he had lost quite a bundle, among other bundles he had lost recently.

Paul Vario, Sr.—*caporegime* of the Lucchese Mafia family, famed mob moneymaker, presiding godfather over the Kennedy Airport hijacking operations, master of one hundred killer hoods, lord of the richest gambling and loan-sharking operations in the United States, and one of the most feared and respected dons in all of organized crime—was in big trouble.

———

Squat, with large hanging jowls that made him look like a mean bulldog, Vario regarded the world from large, bulging eyes behind thick glasses. In his early sixties, he had achieved, by the mid-1970s, the rarefied status of "a man of respect."

Vario's mob family—as distinct from his own, which included a wife and three children—was the Thomas (Three Fingers Brown) Lucchese organization. By 1977, Lucchese himself was dead, but as was the custom, his family continued to bear the name of its founder as a gesture of respect. It was one of the five Mafia families that controlled organized crime in New York. Collectively, as one of the most powerful organized crime outfits in the country, they had major influence in that field throughout the rest of the nation.

Vario began his career in the 1930s, and over the next thirty years, accumulated a criminal record that ranged from burglary to murder. In middle age, however, Vario began to concentrate almost exclusively on illegal gambling, partly because he had a real talent for organizing such operations, but mostly because gambling promised the greatest financial return.

Although he had the intellectual capacity of a boulder—he spoke in a sort of Pidgin English that sounded like a combination of Chico Marx and a parody of Marlon Brando—Vario nevertheless was regarded as one of the Mafia's shrewdest operators. He had developed a network of bookmakers, loan sharks, and numbers (illegal lottery) operators into a large, smoothly functioning organization that was a veritable money machine. Respectful mobsters would watch as Vario held court at a table in his favorite restaurant, presiding over relays of runners who brought in the day's receipts, sometimes spreading $20,000 in cash out on the table. These deliveries occurred with clocklike regularity, for Vario had a fearsome reputation as a mob leader who would not hesitate to kill those who transgressed in any way As the rumor had it, Vario "don't like no loose ends." He was reported to have had people killed on the merest suspicion that they had tried to shortchange him or that they had considered talking to police.

"Oooh, nice, Paulie," one of the mobsters would say, watching as Vario stacked up his cash. Vario, who barely tolerated the nickname, would grunt in reply, his standard response to statements that he thought not worth the effort of a sentence. At such moments, those who knew Vario were reminded that he not only bore a vague resemblance to a pig but often acted like one as well. Vario was a thug who liked to hang out in various Mafia-owned restaurants, gorging on food and drinking vast quantities. On such occasions, he was customarily surrounded by a retinue of hangers-on and aspiring hoods. They would laugh at his jokes and butter up this man who by a nod of the head could start a man's mob career—by giving him a contract "hit" assignment, perhaps, or letting him perform some other deed that would put Vario's family in his debt. For a would-be gangster, that might mean eventual induction into the mob, "getting a button," a status that would be accompanied by a small piece of the action someplace.

As Vario's status rose in the Lucchese family, he was eventually promoted to *caporegime,* or *capo,* a rank just below that of the godfather of the family. The increased status led Vario to behave with even more excess than usual in his personal dining habits, and police surveillance reports were soon filled with tantalizing tidbits about his wilder escapades. There was the night, for example, when Vario ordered a huge shrimp cocktail, which he polished off by simply upending it and letting the contents slither into his open mouth. Or the night at a Manhattan nightclub when a female friend of Vario's, apparently of the same school of social etiquette, became annoyed at the attentions he was paying to two shapely showgirls. She went into the ladies' room, took off all her clothes, and then paraded through the nightclub.

Vario's status in the Lucchese family increased in direct proportion to his moneymaking ability, and as his gambling operations continued to grow, there was talk he was due to become the next leader of the family. The talk was enhanced by the brilliant success of Vario's Kennedy Airport operation, where the interlocked combination of gambling, loan-sharking, and hijacking had produced gargantuan profits. Then, too, Vario's reputation suffered no harm when he was able to recruit and develop such talent as Jimmy the Gent Burke.

In addition to his business acumen and ruthlessness, Vario required another talent to make his airport operation hum smoothly: diplomacy. The problem was that another of the five New York families—the extremely powerful one run by the country's most feared godfather, Carlo Gambino—also had its hooks into the airport. But the Gambino operation centered on corrupt union locals that extorted millions each year from frightened shippers eager to keep labor peace in a competitive market that fought for slices of the billions of dollars' worth of cargo that moved in and out of the airport. The Gambino crowd preferred such operations, believing that corruption and payoffs were preferable to such crimes as robbery, which tended to attract too much law-enforcement attention.

The Gambino operations at the airport created tension with the Vario-Burke operations, which concentrated on theft. The tension, in turn, spawned all sorts of intricate diplomatic arrangements—mostly in the form of money paid as "shares" to potentially competing Mafia operations at the airport. Both the Gambino and Lucchese families dreaded the possibility of a shooting war over the issue, so both sides bent over backwards to accommodate each other's needs. Often, the issue of contention was Jimmy Burke; the Gambino family considered him a maniac who was certain to get them all arrested. An especially delicate incident was touched off one day when Burke rushed into a Mafia-controlled restaurant and demanded to use the meat scale. When asked why, Burke casually showed a stack of gold bars just hijacked off an airport truck, then asked if the restaurant manager wanted one. Alarmed at the possibility that the police would suddenly arrive and arrest everybody in the place, the manager went to the Lucchese family's chief *capo* for overall airport operations, a sinister hood named John (Johnny Dio) Dioguardi.

"Those stupid motherfuckers!" Dioguardi exploded, smashing an ashtray into his desk as he heard the complaint. "That fucking Paulie Vario! I told him, I'm getting the fucking blame and we're not getting a fucking quarter out of it. That son of a bitch is gonna blow my business over there with labor. I told that bastard to cut that fucking shit out. My business is labor, not stealing fucking hijacked goods."

Later, when Dioguardi had calmed down, he met with Vario. Paulie explained the economic necessity of the Burke hijacking operations; there were promises of a cut of future profits from hijacking, and in the end Dioguardi was mollified —even to the extent of rescinding an order to fire a corrupt union official known to have given Burke inside information on important shipments.

"You gotta prestige for me," Vario had said during the negotiations, and it was a tribute to Paulie's mob standing at this point that Dioguardi grasped the point instantly: failure to get the firing rescinded would cause too much damage to the reputation of one of the godfathers of airport crime.

And so the great clockwork mechanism rolled on, and by 1975, Queens District Attorney John Santucci was complaining publicly that because hijackings were so common at the airport, air cargo companies and shipping outfits had been deliberately understating their losses for fear of driving insurance premiums to unreachable heights. According to Santucci, goods worth nearly $1 billion a year were being stolen, although the officially reported loss figures were about one-tenth that figure. Burke's Robert's Lounge Gang was responsible for a good portion of the thefts.

———

And yet, at the very moment the district attorney was complaining about a problem that seemingly was out of control, the very man who dominated the airport crime scene began to lose his touch.

No one could quite explain it. Perhaps, some suggested, it was the combination of ill health, age, and hubris. Whatever the cause, Vario's operations began to go sour; with Burke in jail and the hijackings beginning to fail, Vario turned to several other areas, including a huge loan-sharking scheme. But an increasing number of them failed, and like the rumors surrounding an aging athlete whose eyes and legs were going, the whispers began: Paulie was losing it.

———

Vario was out of earshot of most of these whispers, for he spent an enlarging portion of his time at a relative's home in Florida, from where he tried to direct operations by pay telephone (concerned over FBI wiretaps, he avoided regular phones like the plague). The distance only made things worse, and squabbling broke out among some of the lower-echelon hoods in the section of the family he controlled. Vario was beginning to lose prestige, and the decline in his status was confirmed when another *capo* was named godfather of the family.

To Vario, who had once been considered the odds-on favorite for godfather, the blow was devastating. He had read a newspaper report on the succession struggle in his family. According to the article, the FBI accurately predicted that Vario would be passed over on the grounds that he was no longer "astute enough."

"Hey, what means this 'not astute'?" an infuriated Vario complained to a mob friend, waving the newspaper at him.

"It means," said the friend, one of the few men who could talk with brutal honesty to Vario, "that you're a dumb fucking guinea."

———

Dumb or not, Vario had come under mounting financial pressure, and in his search for an operation that would restore his magic touch, he turned to the man who was known within the mob as someone who could convert a modest investment into vast profit—albeit at enormous risk, legally.

The man was Joseph (Joey Beck) DiPalermo, Vario's fellow *capo* in the Lucchese family. A gaunt, thin man who weighed less than 140 pounds, DiPalermo was the Mafia's leading narcotics kingpin. He was also known to be a vicious killer who had attempted, unsuccessfully, to poison informer Joseph Valachi in prison. By 1977, back on the street, DiPalermo had returned to the narcotics business with renewed vigor, despite his seventy years. He had also returned to the business of killing, for he was part of a nasty internecine struggle within the mob for control of lucrative narcotics distribution territories, a bloody war that had already taken twelve lives.

———

Vario's connection to DiPalermo was a mark of desperation, for Vario had always avoided dealing in drugs, an activity he considered too dangerous in terms of possible legal consequences. But he needed a lot of money quick, and in early 1977, a meeting in Florida with DiPalermo offered a solution.

DiPalermo had a plan that promised immense return on investment. Simply, he had arranged for purchase of a large shrimp boat, which, after being stripped of all identifying marks, would pick up a big shipment of assorted narcotics in Colombia. It would then return to the United States and dock secretly at an unused pier on the Queens shoreline. Its cargo would be offloaded quickly, then fed into DiPalermo's distribution networks. Total investment would be $1.5 million, and since the anticipated street sale value was around $40 million, the return would be spectacular. Vario agreed to chip in as his share a huge chunk of dwindling capital. That, added to DiPalermo's share and others collected from various mob figures, set the deal in motion.

DiPalermo rounded up the crew to handle the operation, and when he was finished, close to two dozen people knew what was to happen. From the standpoint of both DiPalermo and Vario—and, as things turned out later, a lot of other people—it would have been better if not so many had known.

Especially the young woman with the bewitching eyes.

———

It was the general consensus among the wretched low-lifes who constituted the Robert's Lounge Gang that Theresa (Terry) Ferrara was the most spectacularly built woman in the history of the world.

That may have been only a slight exaggeration, even for those to whom extreme voluptuousness in a woman meant only exaggerated curves. And those who had seen Terry naked had no doubt that she was spectacular.

Actually, a good number of men had seen Terry naked, for she moved in the fast lane and had shared her bed with many men. To them she seemed like a tigress, this sexual animal whose passions had become something of a local legend in Queens. Not that she confined herself to Queens; she always appeared to be going somewhere: a yacht cruise to the Caribbean, a quick jaunt to Las Vegas, a few weeks in Florida

For the most part, the trips were the result of her liaisons with a long string of Mafia hoods—she seemed to have an abiding attraction for them—and vaguely connected older men whose income derived from certain activities on the fringes of crime. They had also provided her with a new sports car and a $1,000-a-month penthouse apartment.

She had grown up in Queens with Tommy DeSimone, and that connection eventually brought her to the fringes of Burke's organization. She occupied something of a curious position in that group, for Burke discouraged the presence of women in the area of crime; a traditionalist on social questions, he believed that a woman's place was in the home. Nevertheless, because of her connection to DeSimone and a number of other hoods, Burke tolerated her presence and even allowed her to deal a little cocaine.

Ferrara dealt cocaine while pursuing her other career—running the small hairdressing salon in which Martin Krugman conducted his hairpiece (and bookmaking) operation. The salon, a gift from one of her older boyfriends, did not enjoy land-office business, but that was a matter of small concern to Ferrara. She much preferred to spend her time planning a night at an expensive disco in the Hamptons or preparing for her next trip.

Like many girls from the Italian neighborhoods in Queens, Ferrara always had ambition. Given the remarkable physical attributes nature had bestowed on her, it was no surprise that she wanted to be a model and actress. But Ferrara was lazy, and she became convinced that a shortcut existed that would allow her to bypass the years of study and struggle on the way to the top. Her chosen method was to cultivate—sexually, usually—men of power who she believed could help her by boosting her straight to the top. Most of the men had no such power, however, and by 1977, she was twenty-six (ancient by modeling standards) and no nearer to being a top model and actress than she had been ten years before. The stark fact was that she had become a pseudo-prostitute, a party girl who combined the fatal illusion of a career with an equally fatal attraction for Mafia hoods.

Still, thrilled as she was by her proximity to real-life criminals, Ferrara always had a dread of being arrested. Thus, on a summer day in 1977, when she sold some cocaine to an under-

cover narcotics agent, she was ripe for the standard blandishments in such situations. There would be no arrest and no jail
time she was informed, but she would have to pay for her
crime with the only thing of value she possessed: information.
She wouldn't have to probe for information; just call a certain number whenever she heard something "of interest." It
was unnecessary to spell out the consequences, should she
decide not to cooperate: jail or worse—the little whisper in
the right ears that Theresa Ferrara was that most despised of
all human beings, a snitch, a stoolie, a rat. And then, she was
reminded, it required little imagination to divine what hoods
would do to a woman stool pigeon.

She had been hooked, neatly and perfectly, and from that
moment, she was an informant, caught in a web from which
there was no escape. The men she knew saw the same startling
coal-black eyes and the incredible body, but they did not
realize that it was now a different Theresa Ferarra whose
gyrations on a disco dance floor never failed to rivet the attention of every man in the place. In addition to her life in the
fast lane, Ferrara now had another life, a secret life she spent
in hurried conversations on pay phones.

She delivered a number of interesting news items picked
up from pillows and other places, but the most interesting of
all came one early autumn night in 1978 when a hood who
was dancing with her in a Manhattan disco began to brag. He
was involved in a big drug deal, he confided, one in which he
stood to make a good pile. How would she like to go with him
to Florida and help him spend it? Perhaps, she hinted, parrying the question while learning more of this big deal. In an
effort to further impress her, he revealed more details, enough
to move her to excuse herself and go to the ladies' room.

There she dropped a dime into a pay phone, dialed a number she had committed to memory, and then half whispered the
details she had just heard.

———

A chilling fog had begun moving across the bay just after
dark, and by midnight, the darkened marina in the Queens
waterfront community of Far Rockaway was completely socked
in. The dozen men standing around the marina felt the damp

cold of that November 11, 1978, envelop them. With hands wrapped around Styrofoam cups of coffee, tap-dancing to keep their feet warm, they peered out anxiously into the bay, vainly trying to spot the boat.

But the fog and the darkness conspired to make any sighting impossible, so they listened for the distinctive sound of a boat engine. It came just after midnight, a *thwock-thwock* echoing in that remote area of the peninsula of Queens facing the Atlantic Ocean. It was the unmistakable sound of a large fishing boat. Several men clambered aboard as it docked; other men readied the half-dozen vans parked on the dock.

The men aboard the boat had just begun unloading large cloth bags when one of them heard the sound of a high-powered boat engine in the bay, closing on the docked boat's stern. "Coast Guard!" he yelled. As the alarm went up, the men fled in all directions, running through the tall marsh grass and reeds as the Coast Guard boat's searchlight swept the area.

The following day, the Coast Guard and the federal Drug Enforcement Administration basked in the glow of a major media extravaganza. Television camera crews and newspaper photographers lavished their attention on the piles of cloth bags containing 30 tons of seized narcotics—including 10 million Quaaludes—at the time the largest seizure ever made in the northeastern United States. DEA officials would say only that an anonymous phone call had led them to the site.

DEA agents regretted that they had not been able to grab any of the smugglers during the raid. They began the standard process of trying to determine whom they might be able to link to the boat, named the *Darlene C*. They suspected from the outset, however, that the paper trail of the boat would soon run cold.

And it did: the boat was officially registered to an Alabama trawler outfit, but it had been sold to a Florida fisherman. He claimed he had resold it only a short while before to some men he remembered only as Panamanians. He could not recall their names, try as he might. As for clues aboard the boat, there were precious few. The narcotics had been wrapped in Colombian chicken-feed sacks, so it was safe to assume that the boat had come from that country. A further clue was the expensive ocean navigation equipment on board, indicating that the boat had been outfitted for a very long journey. Obviously, the shrimp trawler had been picked up in Florida, sailed to Colombia to pick up the drugs, and made its way to New York.

Beyond that, nothing much could be learned about the boat, except for the curious matter of its name. DEA agents discovered that the *Darlene C* nameplate had been attached after a recent rechristening. It covered another, older nameplate that bore the boat's original name.

That name was *Terry's Dream*.

Paul Vario, Sr., was not happy. As he stared out the living room window of his Florida home, he looked like many of the other elderly people who had settled in that community near Fort Lauderdale—sitting in their little homes with nothing to do, staring out their living room windows, just waiting to die.

"Somebody dropped a dime on us," growled Joseph Di-Palermo as he paced the other side of Vario's living room.

Vario grunted, for it did not require a doctorate to deduce that someone with knowledge of the big drug deal had taken the dangerous step of "dropping a dime"—surreptitiously informing the authorities of an upcoming criminal operation.

"Whoever did it is gonna pay," said Vario, quickly reviewing the various horrible forms of revenge that could be inflicted on the body of the informant. He did not spend an undue amount of time on this matter, for as he was aware, there would be plenty of time later to track down the informant and exact a terrible vengeance. Vario at the moment had a more pressing concern, which was the matter of recovering the nearly $1 million he had sunk into the abortive drug operation. Already in serious trouble with the mob, he knew that this disaster represented another count in the gathering indictment against him, the lengthening list whose bottom line, unmistakably, would reveal that Paul Vario was finished.

The solution was clear. After DiPalermo left, Vario went to a nearby street corner and began feeding rolls of coins into a pay phone. One of the calls he made was to Jimmy Burke, and the message was unambiguous: "Jimmy, I need a big score, real big."

Burke was more than willing to help his old friend and godfather, but since Vario's urgent plea coincided with his own troubles, he was in no position to help. In fact, Burke at the moment was feeling somewhat depressed, for a review of the current situation revealed prospects that ranged from fair to bleak. Even visits to Robert's Lounge failed to lift his spirits. He had sold the place while in prison, and without his presence, it seemed to have sunk into a dingy sleaziness that lacked the spark which animated it during the heyday of his gang.

Familiar faces also failed to lift his spirits, for none seemed able to offer the brilliant idea that would mean a major score, the gusher that would restore the Burke gang's fortunes and at the same time help out Paulie.

"Who've we got at the airport?" Burke asked the bookie Martin Krugman, who then reviewed the list of debtors with possible access to important information. It was a list of only vague promise, and Krugman became aware of Burke's scowl, the certain sign that he was deep in thought.

"What are we looking for?" the bookie asked.

"Something big," Burke replied, smiling. "I'll tell you how big: we may have to steal the whole goddam airport."

Chapter

3

"I know where I can get millions"

In horseplayers' parlance, it was a "lock"—a horse so prohibitively favored to win that nothing short of nuclear attack would prevent the inevitable. Unless, of course, the horse fell just after leaving the starting gate.

Which, to Louis Werner's shocked disgust, is exactly what that guaranteed winner did early one June afternoon in 1978 at Aqueduct Race Track in Queens. The bell rang, the starting gates clanged open, and there, right in front of the horseplayers clustered along the rail, the horse suddenly dropped to its knees. Amazingly, however, the horse got up, galloped off into the dust kicked up by the six horses already on their way, and, in the characteristic burst of speed that had made the horse the can't-lose betting favorite in the weak field, managed to finish only a half-length behind the winner.

"Son of a bitch!" Werner cursed at the heavens, angrily decrying his fate. He ripped up his betting ticket, and the pieces floated to the ground, which was already littered with thousands of other losing tickets, more snowflakes in the drifts of shattered dreams.

Only the truly desperate can appreciate the depth of Werner's rage at the heavenly fates that day. He had bet $1,000 on that "lock" to win, and it was $1,000 he could scarcely afford to lose, for Louis Werner was just about at the end of his rope.

———

If, as Thoreau once said, "The mass of men lead lives of quiet desperation," then Louis Werner was among the most desperate of all. He had exhausted all his options and then some. He was a man for whom absolutely nothing seemed to go right. Not even his final wild throw of the dice had worked, the bet on a prohibitive favorite at short odds. Ordinarily, as Werner knew, such a bet, while it does not produce big earnings because of the constricted odds, nevertheless has the virtue of at least keeping a bettor's head temporarily above water. But it hadn't worked, and now Werner faced the daunting task of coming up with a miracle that would lift him out of his financial hole.

That hole was solely of Werner's own making. In financial terms—the only terms in life that he seemed to grasp—the situation was stark. Out of a $15,000 annual salary (minus taxes), he had to pay his own living expenses, support payments to the wife and daughter from whom he was separated, the modest but very real expenses of a girlfriend, car payments, and the cost of his low-scale drinking habit.

All of which a thrifty man might have been able to handle, but Werner's problem was compounded by an addiction that rendered all budgets meaningless: gambling. And not just ordinary gambling, the few-dollars-here-and-there kind indulged in by a good portion of American men, but a foolish and compulsive gambling that by 1978 was taking the bulk of what money he earned. Werner had by then amassed a debt of $18,000 to bookies who allowed him to play on credit.

It was a typically accommodating gesture bookies made to people like Werner, for gamblers of his type represented a steady source of income, much like blue-chip stock dividends. Come what might, there was no question that Werner, like the legion of other equally foolish gamblers of the working class, would bet on just about anything that was bettable. Equally inevitable was the anticipated result: usually Werner would lose.

Werner was representative of a type who had been en-

———

riching bookies for more than a century. He wagered year-round on every professional sport on which odds-makers would give "lines"—the anticipated margin of victory, the critical figure that bettors bet either for or against. Often, like other addicted gamblers, he would bet on several sports at once. He might have $200 riding on a day's racing card at Aqueduct, while another $500 assumed that the odds-makers had no idea what they were talking about when they deduced that a particular football team would beat another by at least three points.

Werner's central motivation, like that of other gamblers, was to get rich quick, an illusion the bookies did nothing to dispel. They had nothing to gain by telling their client that nobody ever got rich betting over his head on sports he knew little or nothing about—certainly not enough to bet on the margin of victory or loss. Instead, they encouraged Werner, the typical wiseacre, and listened to him as he spoke with a loud assurance on every sublety of the strategies of football, baseball, hockey, basketball, and thoroughbred racing. He insisted that all of his bets were the result of sophisticated analysis of such esoterica as the superiority of the Dallas Cowboys' pass rush. All the while, the bookies knew that people like Werner bet on vague hunches, half-inspired guesses, and sheer stupidity.

When, as was predominantly the case, the bettors lost, the bookies clucked sympathetically, commiserating with them about the fluke play or bizarre happenstance that had undercut a "smart bet." To Werner, the perpetual loser, they provided a sympathetic ear for his rages about how assorted incompetents on various teams had committed blunders and thus ruined his brilliantly conceived betting strategy. Then the bookies would determine how much he wanted to "get down" (bet) on upcoming events, followed by the grim task of reviewing Werner's credit rating and the size of his outstanding debt, which was growing at compound interest. Whenever he could—which was not often—Werner would pay a modest amount to reduce that debt, very much like the Siberian in the sled tossing out pieces of meat to keep the pack of wolves temporarily at bay. But time was running out: he had borrowed nearly $7,000 from a finance company and from the credit union where he worked. He was in hock up to his eyeballs.

To those who knew Werner, his desperate attempt to become rich seemed very much in keeping with the man, a dreamer with no special intellectual (or other) gifts, who was consumed by the desire to be important—which, to Werner, meant having a lot of money. He was always somewhat vague about what he intended to do with all that money, once he got it, for he had no special interests that would have consumed large amounts of capital. Sometimes he would talk about getting a new van, then heading west across the country, to live indefinitely as a well-heeled nomad with a large stake. Other times he talked in general terms about leaving New York and starting anew someplace else. These were, in fact, a small-timer's dreams; at root, Louis Werner was small potatoes.

A man of medium height with rimless eyeglasses, Werner reminded some people of a bloodless accountant. To others, he looked like a large weasel, a simile occasioned by Werner's habit of squinting, as though he couldn't quite make out the world around him. He was forty-five years old—he tried to hide signs of encroaching age by dyeing his thinning gray hair —yet he struck some people as the quintessential New York bigmouth: a brash, opinionated know-it-all who constantly bragged about the "big break" that always seemed to be lurking around the corner.

It had never come, of course, and the small circle of people who knew Werner became accustomed to his endless rhapsodizing about the golden dawn guaranteed to arrive the following morning. Certainly the others saw no evidence of it. Werner's estranged wife, Beverly, was certainly not impressed. While he talked on and on about how he was going to make it big some day, the support checks were either late or nonexistent. Equally unimpressed was Werner's girlfriend, a divorcée named Janet Barbieri. She would have preferred to hear Werner propose to marry her (he seemed to avoid that topic), and explain how he intended to support them, should that unlikely event occur.

About the only person who seemed to have any faith in Werner's ability to bring forth the golden dawn was his friend, Peter Gruenwald. It was a faith connected with two circumstances that were to change both of their lives forever: (1)

they both worked at Lufthansa Air Cargo at Kennedy Airport; and (2) they planned to rob their employer.

———

Gruenwald saw Werner's yellow Plymouth pull into the parking lot of Lufthansa Air Cargo that June morning, and from the ashen look on his friend's face when he emerged from the car, Gruenwald knew that Werner had suffered still another setback in his endless quest to beat the odds. Gruenwald himself was a bettor. He would occasionally wager twenty to fifty dollars with one of the bookies who swarmed over Kennedy Airport like marauding sharks, but his bets were nothing like the frightening sums that Werner was throwing away.

It was insane the way his friend bet, Gruenwald had felt for a long time, but he could offer little in the way of advice. Werner, who considered himself intellectually superior to Gruenwald (and many other people), took advice badly, especially on the subject of sports betting. He was a man, Gruenwald realized, who thought he knew all the answers.

This was a delicate area in the friendship between the two men, and by silent compact, Gruenwald refrained from proffering any advice. Otherwise, it was a smooth friendship, although those who knew both men considered them an odd couple.

In terms of background and interests, they were remarkably alike. Both were relentlessly middle class. They lived near each other in the prototypical suburb of Levittown on Long Island until Werner moved into his mother's home in Queens. They bowled together and drank together after work. They both worked at Lufthansa Air Cargo, Werner for ten years, Gruenwald for eight. By 1978, Werner was an operations supervisor, overseeing incoming shipments, while Gruenwald worked on another floor, handling outgoing shipments. Their tasks were not especially taxing, and they saw each other often during the workday. After work, they socialized together several nights a week and on weekends. The friendship had survived the marital discord that afflicted both men. Following the split between Werner and his wife, Gruenwald's wife, the daughter of a Taiwanese jeweler, left him and returned to Taiwan—citing, among other grievances, her husband's friendship with Werner, a man she thoroughly distrusted.

———

Mrs. Gruenwald was not alone in that evaluation. Many found Werner a shifty character; the combination of his constant bragging and open hunger for money induced an uneasy suspicion that he would do anything for a buck. Some felt that Werner took advantage of Gruenwald, a much milder and quieter man. But Gruenwald, a tall and husky mustached German immigrant who spoke a curious, stilted English, seemed to be captivated by Werner, whom he regarded as a misunderstood, overemotional talent who had gotten a lot of bad breaks. And he remained convinced that Werner's money-making schemes would pay off someday.

Gruenwald nurtured that thought, for as vague as Werner's plans for the future were, Gruenwald's were quite specific. They involved a dream that had preoccupied him ever since his wife had left: he would make his big score, shed his humdrum middle-class existence, and head west to the Orient. There, the newly enriched Peter Gruenwald, a glittering figure of wealth and prestige, would win back his wife. Together they would live in comfort somewhere in the Far East, far from the rat race, noise, and struggle that marked his life in New York.

Gruenwald confided this dream to no one except Werner, nor did he share even deeper secrets. One of them concerned a plan he and Werner had been discussing for several months, a scheme to rob the company for which they worked. Another was an even bigger secret: they had robbed the place once before.

"A bad day, yes?"

"Right," Louis Werner replied, as he stood beside his friend Peter Gruenwald in the employees' men's room of the Lufthansa Air Cargo terminal.

In this intimate moment, as both men stood before adjoining urinals, Gruenwald heard the note of utter defeat in his friend's voice. Werner did not elaborate on the reason for his discouragement—the $1,000 loss on a sure bet at the track that morning—but Gruenwald knew that Werner must once again be on the losing side in his struggle with the vagaries of sports betting. Given the lengthening list of losses Werner was suffering lately, there was real danger that he would be swamped by debts at any moment. The time had come.

"We should talk again about making the robbery," Gruenwald loudly whispered.

"What, are you crazy, you dumb bastard?" said Werner in a hiss, as he frantically looked around the men's room. Although they were the only ones there, Werner was furious that Gruenwald had openly mentioned their big secret.

"You better watch your mouth," Werner warned as he stepped away from the urinal and toward the sink to wash his hands. He turned the faucet on full blast, the noise allowing him to raise his voice.

"What the hell's wrong with you, talking that stuff in here? You want to get us busted?"

"Oh, Lou, I say it before to you," Gruenwald said, smiling. "And so what? No one can hear us anyway. You know, we are wasting time. If we are to make a robbery, we should do it and stop wishing about it."

"We'll talk later," Werner said loudly as another employee entered the men's room.

"Later" meant a local bar in which Werner invariably stopped after work for a few drinks—and to meet one of the bookies who hovered around, his antennae alert for working-men who thought they knew a lot about sports and were willing to bet money to prove it. The bar was one of several, equidistant from the airport and Aqueduct, that catered to horseplayers and airport workers. It had a long, curved bar; one wall was covered by a collection of horseracing photographs that served as inspiration to the patrons, who kept several pay phones busy booking bets.

As usual, Werner and Gruenwald took seats at the far end of the bar, slightly away from the steady ringing of pay phones, the drone of the television set behind the bar, and the raucous discussions among the brawny cargo handlers who clustered near the front door. It was not the first time, of course, that the two men had sat in the bar planning to rob Lufthansa, but Gruenwald was now injecting a note of urgency. He felt as if he were watching his business partner drown, with only seconds to get the combination to the office safe before he slipped beneath the waves.

"The most important part is to have a plan that will work," Gruenwald was saying, reaching into the attaché case he invariably carried to and from work, as though he were some kind of business executive.

"Right," Werner agreed, wondering why Gruenwald was bringing up this point again, an elementary decision they had jointly reached long ago.

"Because," said Gruenwald, putting a sheet of paper on the bar, "without a good plan, there is nothing."

Prepared with Teutonic thoroughness, the paper contained a sketch painstakingly drawn by Gruenwald, showing the exterior and interior dimensions of the Lufthansa Air Cargo terminal, with important rooms and exits marked. Werner's eyes were immediately drawn to the space labeled "high val room." It was a room that often dominated his imagination.

In what amounted to the central irony of his life, Werner each workday was surrounded by so much money that it made his mind spin to think what would happen if he could get his hands on it. Like a vampire in a blood bank, Werner was almost constantly exposed to the one thing in this world that was irresistible to him. It lay in sealed cartons in the "high value room," which everybody at Lufthansa called simply "high val," the place where large shipments of cash, gold, and jewels arriving from all points on the globe were temporarily stored pending further shipment.

As one of several supervisors overseeing the disposition of all this wealth, Werner spent much of his day processing paperwork—waybills and Customs forms—that afforded him some insight into how much money was lying around at any given time, mostly in the form of interbank shipments of cash. Since he was only one of the supervisors, he had no idea exactly how much money there was, but what he did see was sufficient to keep him in a state, especially lately, of frustration. Right in front of him it rested, seemingly just waiting for a man smart enough to figure how to take it out.

His supervisory position allowed Werner that rarity at Lufthansa, access to the high val room—an access that stimulated his thought processes on how to steal what was inside. It also reminded him of the fairly formidable obstacle the room represented to anyone trying to break in. No one at Lufthansa could carry anything in or out of that area without being accompanied by another employee similarly authorized to enter the area. Upon leaving the high val room, both men had to sign a log book attesting that they had both been there—or, put more bluntly, that they had kept an eye on each other while inside. The val room itself actually was two one-story rooms. To get inside, one had to insert a special key into an alarm lock on the door to the first room. A similar procedure was used to enter the inner room, where the most valuable shipments were stored. The walls of both rooms were lined with shelves on which the valuable parcels were kept, guarded by a set of hidden alarms.

As both Gruenwald and Werner realized, it would be foolhardy to attempt a frontal attack on the high val room; the only possibility would be an inside job. In other words, both men would provide critical inside information about the layout of the terminal interior and details on the security system guarding the high val room. Equipped with that information, robbers recruited by Gruenwald and Werner would be able to bypass the security system—in return for which they would receive at least half the take.

But the problem was that for this plan to work, Gruenwald and Werner needed a gang of professional robbers to carry out the actual theft. And among the gaps in the knowledge of both men was the criminal world. They simply did not know any real criminals, nor did they have the slightest idea of how to find them.

"Of course, we have to find people we can trust," Werner noted. "You know, people who'll do the job, give us our money and won't kill us."

"Naturally," Gruenwald said, for the first time considering the very real possibility that a robbery at Lufthansa might involve killing. "So where do we find such people?"

"I don't know," Werner replied. "All I know is they gotta be good people; we don't wanna be shafted."

Gruenwald considered this a moment. "I think I might be able to get some people," he said. "I know some guys who are, you know, kind of wild."

"Wild?" said Werner, squinting at him. "What's that supposed to mean?"

"I think," Gruenwald replied, lowering his voice conspiratorially, "they are people who are mixed up in some things. I will talk to them and find out if they are willing to do this robbery, using our plan. How much do you think is there to be taken?"

"Five hundred thousand, maybe a million," Werner said casually, as though he were discussing shoes or string beans.

"A lot, a lot," said Gruenwald, mentally computing how large his share would be from such a score. "All right, I will talk to these people, and we will get rolling on this."

"Fine, the sooner the better," said Werner, doing his own mental computations on how his betting debts would suddenly and miraculously melt in the glare of his share like a snowball in the sun. The more he thought about it, the more feasible it seemed—despite the fact that all he and Gruenwald had at the moment was a piece of paper. Besides themselves, there were no crooks, no discussions on exactly how the money was to be removed from the terminal, and, most important, no comprehensive scheme for dividing up the money. All Werner was certain of at the moment was that the robbery was to take place, he and Gruenwald would be enriched as a result, and under no circumstances would they repeat the mistakes of "the other thing." It was an experience neither of them wanted to relive.

———

"The other thing" had begun routinely enough on the morning of October 8, 1976, when two employees of the La Paz Money Exchange in Quito, Ecuador, signed over a package containing $22,000 in various foreign currencies to Lufthansa Air Cargo at Quito airport. The shipment was destined for La Paz's sister exchange in New York City.

Lufthansa Air Cargo at Quito followed the standard procedure for such shipments, filling out the necessary waybills and U.S. Customs forms, then packing the money shipment into the large canvas bag known around Lufthansa as a "val bag," a special bag used to transport high-value shipments. The bag was sealed with a distinctive blue chip, signifying it as a high-value shipment, packed inside a large cargo container, and shipped off to New York aboard flight 493.

It arrived at Kennedy at 9:50 P.M., and, after clearing Customs, was moved to Lufthansa Air Cargo. There, one of the employees working the four-to-twelve shift was assigned to check the cargo manifest, secure any valuable shipments aboard, and take them directly to the high val room for storage.

The employee assigned this task was Louis Werner.

It remains a small mystery why Werner decided then and there to rip off the $22,000 shipment, a loss that would be immediately obvious to Lufthansa. Also, since Werner had been told to verify its presence in the first place, its disappearance would cause grave suspicion to fall on him. Despite these considerable hurdles, Werner, on the spur of the moment, broke open the seal on the val bag, removed the contents, then calmly reported that there was no high-value shipment on board flight 493.

Sometime around midnight, when the entire cargo of flight 493 was being unloaded, the bag with the broken seal was found. By that time, an extremely nervous Louis Werner had called the home of Peter Gruenwald from a pay phone.

"I have to talk to you right away," Werner said when Gruenwald answered. "I have to come over to your place to talk about a business proposition."

"It is midnight, Lou," Gruenwald replied, somewhat testily, wondering what kind of business Werner could possibly have to discuss at that hour.

"I just stole twenty-two thousand dollars from Lufthansa. I gotta get rid of it."

"Jesus Christ, Lou," said Gruenwald, imagining Werner calling him on the run while police cars were closing in from all sides.

Actually, Werner drove unpursued the twenty-two miles from the Lufthansa terminal to Gruenwald's home. There, he showed Gruenwald a medium-sized cardboard box into which he had put the money. The cash was not, as Gruenwald first assumed, American currency, but in fact various foreign denominations: 8,000 Canadian dollars; 30,000 French francs; 30,000 Belgian francs; 10,000 Swedish kronor; 2,000 Australian dollars; and 2 million Italian lire. Its precise value in U.S. dollars was unclear, but as Werner had noted from the shipment manifest, the entire package was insured for $22,000.

"Can you hide this for me?" Werner asked, and offered his friend a share when it was exchanged for American money.

"We have to wait some time," Gruenwald said, agreeing to the basic proposition. "It is too risky now; the money is too hot. There may be people watching to see who tries to exchange it."

In truth, Gruenwald was in something of a panic. Although he and Werner had discussed robbery, the talk amounted to an abstraction. This was real, an actual robbery, and Gruenwald did not know quite what to do. First, he put the box in his car, but then, like a man acutely aware he has a vial of nitroglycerin around just waiting to be jostled, he later arose from a sleepless night and tried to figure out a safer hiding place. He suddenly thought of a nearby garbage dump, and at 1:00 A.M., walked there and hid the box under some old discarded furniture and tires.

Gruenwald's fear stemmed, in large part, from his belief that, because he was a friend of Werner, police might assume he had hidden the money. Therefore, he concluded, it was wise not to have the evidence anywhere near his house. In the cold light of dawn the following day, Gruenwald felt less concerned —after all, there were no hordes of police ripping up the floorboards—and during a clandestine meeting with Werner at a local gas station later that morning, he hit on the idea of burying the money in his back yard.

They removed the money from the box and put it into several shopping bags, which they wrapped in plastic and buried in the back yard of Gruenwald's home. Gruenwald's plan was to keep the money there for several weeks—"until the heat has blown off," in his jangled phrase—but the pressure of Werner's gambling debts soon forced a change. A week later, Werner, citing the necessity to pay off some gambling debts, convinced Gruenwald that it was now time to cash in the buried hoard. As Werner noted, although Lufthansa strongly suspected him of having stolen the cash, a number of errors in connection with that shipment (at one point, the val bag had been mistakenly delivered to the post office), had contrived to render any proof of guilt impossible.

Gruenwald, who knew something about foreign currency exchange, volunteered to handle the job, but Werner, the budding criminal mastermind, had a better plan: he would get another friend to make the exchange, in return for which the man would get "some money," presumably a percentage of the final take. According to Werner's estimate, they would each net about $8,000 on the deal.

Werner's choice for this task was an old buddy, Bill Fischetti, a fellow bowler who ran a small taxi company on Long Island and was, like Werner an inveterate gambler. The choice was odd for a number of reasons, not the least of which was the fact that Fischetti at the moment was having an affair with Werner's estranged wife, Beverly. Werner, who had separated from Beverly the previous April, was fully aware of the relationship, but he was unaffected; his friendship with Fischetti remained the same. Werner believed that more important considerations overrode any possible awkwardness in his relationship with Fischetti, chief among them his conviction that Fischetti was as crooked as Werner himself.

He was not proved wrong. One morning Werner met Fischetti in a doughnut shop and opened the conversation by asking, "How would you like to make some extra money?"

"Sure," Fischetti replied instantly. Since Werner was not known to be involved in mink farming or any other such supplemental employment, clearly he was proposing something illegal.

Werner told him how he had stolen the money from Lufthansa, then proposed that Fischetti convert the money through foreign exchanges in New York City.

"I don't know," said Fischetti, hesitating. "It sounds risky; I'm worried about it."

"Don't worry about it," Werner assured him, adding if he cashed in no more than $500 at each of several locations, there would be no danger (exchanges above that amount have to be reported to the U.S. Treasury). For his trouble, Fischetti would receive 10 percent of the total, plus expenses—although there is cause to wonder what Werner could have meant by "expenses" in a propect that involved wandering from exchange to exchange in the relatively compact Manhattan financial district.

In any event, Fischetti agreed, and after receiving the shopping bags during a subsequent meeting at a McDonald's, carried out his end of the project by the simple expedient of looking up foreign exchanges in the Yellow Pages, then cashing in the money. Two months later, he handed Werner $10,-000 in cash, explaining the total as the net, following deduction of his 10 percent and "expenses"—among which he included a trip to Canada to exchange the Canadian dollars.

"Canada?" an angry Gruenwald said when Werner handed him his $5,000 share of the enterprise. "Lou, that is a joke. You don't have to go to Canada to exchange Canadian money. You can do that right here. Let me tell you, he has fucked us, Lou."

"Nah, he didn't fuck us, Peter," Werner said, waving aside Gruenwald's anger. "He's a good guy."

"Bullshit!" Gruenwald snapped. "He has fucked us, and now we are left with this. Look, do not bother me anymore with things of this kind. I will not put my job in jeopardy because of five thousand dollars. This is no good; to do a robbery, we cannot have this sort of thing. I will get some people who will do it right, and then we will have no more to do with people like Fischetti."

"Okay, Peter," Werner said. His resigned tone suggested he agreed. But while he listened to Gruenwald recite how he would now go out and recruit a gang of professionals who would "properly" rob Lufthansa, Werner mentally toyed with the idea of using Fischetti in the scheme for the bigger robbery—a robbery, Gruenwald warned him, he would have nothing to do with unless it involved "at least a million dollars." Werner's idea was that Fischetti would enter the Lufthansa terminal during working hours posing as a customer and wearing a long coat; somehow, Werner would contrive to slip him one of the high-value packages. Fischetti would hide the package under his coat and walk out of the place. They would split whatever amount of money the package contained, which Werner estimated at somewhere between $400,000 and $800,000.

The plan was perfectly idiotic. For one thing, such glorified shoplifting could not be carried out during the warm spring and summer months when long coats are not worn. It was just another example of Werner's serious lack of talent in the area of criminal enterprise. He believed that he had successfully concealed his role in the theft of the $22,000 and that the whole thing had been forgotten. Actually, his employers, especially Lufthansa's security division, were quite convinced that he had done it, although they had no proof. So was the FBI, which investigated the theft; they also had no proof. But Werner's name was noted and filed away. As Werner was to learn later, the FBI files never forget.

Werner's theft of the $22,000 demonstrated an ineptitude that was exceeded only by his decision to use Fischetti in disposing of the money. Werner considered this a master stroke, a means of removing himself and Gruenwald from the actual disposal—as if that mattered much in the larger scheme of things—but Fischetti was inexperienced in such matters, and he was a crook to boot. Any child could have told Werner that Fischetti had ripped them off, and yet Werner intended to compound that error by trying to involve him in his "masterpiece," the big robbery of Lufthansa. All this, even though Fischetti had already demonstrated only that he was even more crooked than Werner—and about as stupid.

Sure enough, Werner no sooner began discussing "the big heist" with Fischetti than Fischetti, incredibly, revealed the plan to Werner's estranged wife. Not unreasonably, she began hectoring her husband, wondering if the money from such an enterprise would allow him to make support payments.

"You got a fucking big mouth!" Werner yelled at Fischetti, and announced that his participation in the heist was over.

"Me and Peter, we got our own plan," Werner bragged. "It's a good plan; it's gonna work."

———

Actually, the plan, as it existed, continued to lack an essential ingredient: the gang to carry out the actual heist. To that end, Gruenwald set about to round up the men who, he had told Werner, seemed "a little wild." That was about the extent of Gruenwald's insight into the world of crime, and he had no real conception of how anyone with knowledge of $1 million available for the taking actually finds the people willing to do it.

Gruenwald had considered the matter carefully, and his chosen targets for recruitment were among a group of young airline workers who hung out in the same bar in which Gruenwald and Werner drank after work. Gruenwald had heard that one of them had been in trouble with the law for some unspecified minor offense; the others, he believed, seemed very eager to get their hands on money, did not seem especially squeamish about how they got it, and seemed to have the recklessness of youth he believed necessary for the considerable risk of robbing a major airline cargo operation.

Gruenwald devoted the bulk of his attention to Brian Weremychik, a cargo agent for one of the Kennedy Airport freight forwarders. He drank occasionally with Gruenwald—whom he called "P.G."—and while they were friendly, the relationship was, at best, casual. And that is why Weremychik was taken aback one night in August 1978 when he asked Gruenwald for a loan of ten dollars and got an answer he never expected.

"Sure," Gruenwald said, in response to the loan request. He drew a ten dollar bill out of his wallet and suddenly leaned closer to Weremychik.

"Listen," said Gruenwald, his voice a conspiratorial half-whisper, "you know, there is a great deal more where this came from. I know where I can get millions."

"Horseshit." Weremychik laughed. He assumed Gruenwald was kidding.

"No, no, it is the truth," Gruenwald insisted. "I know how to get them out of Lufthansa. If I had some good people to help me, we would all be millionaires. It would be easy."

"Sure," said Weremychik, "Lufthansa is just going to let you take their money, right? Come on, P.G."

Undeterred by this initial failure, Gruenwald returned to the attack two days later in the same bar, but this time he brought some ammunition with him.

"Look at these," he said, showing Weremychik several Lufthansa Air Cargo load manifests with the insured value of several shipments clearly spelled out. Weremychik was no mathematician, but a quick estimate revealed a total well over $1 million.

"So you're not kidding around," he said, interested for the first time.

"No, of course not," Gruenwald said. "I know you are a little wild, Brian. Do you have any friends as wild as you?"

"I can ask," Weremychik said, although he was unsure what Gruenwald meant by "wild." Perhaps he wanted hell-raisers, Weremychik speculated, wondering if young guys who drank too much and drove too fast would be of any use in a major robbery.

Nevertheless, he met with Gruenwald again several days later, this time with four of his young friends in tow. Gruenwald went over his plan, which consisted, basically, of entering the building sometime during a holiday weekend, when a large amount of money and jewel shipments would be kept inside. After overpowering the skeleton crew on duty, Gruenwald said, the robbers would gain access to the high val room, using the inside information Gruenwald would provide. This information would allow them to bypass the alarm system. The specifics of how the alarms worked—and how to turn them off—would be withheld from them until the night of the robbery, Gruenwald noted in a final flourish.

In his infatuation with the genius of his own plan, Gruenwald failed to notice that although Weremychik's crew seemed to be very enthusiastic, they really had no idea what he was talking about. The results of their collective criminal experience amounted to several speeding tickets and an arrest for boosting quarters out of a vending machine. The intricacies of entering a guarded building, overpowering whatever employees were on hand, and then evading a sophisticated alarm system (not to mention getting away) were about as far beyond their ability to grasp as quantum physics was.

"Yeah, well, it's a great plan," Weremychik said at one point while he, four friends, and Gruenwald sat around in Gruenwald's Levittown home. They had just finished examining a set of sketches carefully prepared by their host of the precise layout of the interior of the Lufthansa Air Cargo terminal.

"So when can you do it?" Gruenwald pressed, reminding them that the Labor Day weekend was just eight days away.

"Too close," Weremychik said, as his friends nodded in agreement.

"Columbus Day?" Gruenwald asked.

"Maybe," Weremychik replied, taking another sip of the beer his host provided. "You know, P.G., you just can't rush into these things; it takes a lot of time and planning and all that."

"I thought that was what we were doing," Gruenwald said evenly.

"Well, we are," Weremychik said, opening another can of beer.

"What about guns?" a voice asked, and for a moment there was awkward silence. No one had thought of that before.

"Right, guns," Weremychik repeated, stalling for time. As he was aware, neither he nor any of his friends had guns. And he didn't have the slightest idea where they could get any.

"Well, we could get them at a sporting goods store," somebody suggested and it was at that point that Gruenwald realized that these allegedly "wild" men were not capable of pulling off a major robbery, much less understanding the plan for one. Even Gruenwald knew that the only guns sold in sporting goods stores in New York without a permit were rifles and hunting shotguns, hardly suitable for major armed robberies. With a sinking heart, he began to despair. The conversation turned to the question of handcuffs (Gruenwald's plan called for the thieves to handcuff Lufthansa employees during the robbery).

"Oh, I can get plenty of handcuffs," one of Weremychik's friends said. "I work in the city. I'll just go in one of them Times Square stores, you know, and get as many as we need."

"Times Square," Gruenwald repeated dully, hardly believing what he had just heard. In other words, his band of master crooks proposed buying handcuffs in one of those Times Square novelty stores, those tin jobs sold to tourists, the ones children use, testing each other on how many seconds it takes to escape from them.

———

On that note of low comedy, Gruenwald's attempt to recruit a Lufthansa robbery gang began to collapse. By Thanksgiving of 1978, convinced that he had managed to become involved with a collection of the stupidest human beings on earth, Gruenwald gave up on any further attempt to involve Weremychik and his friends. Despite constant pressure, the group found one excuse after another not to carry out the robbery, and it was clear they had no real heart for it.

"You are nothing but children," Gruenwald said to Weremychik one night in the bar, waving his hands in disgust. He angrily stomped away.

If Gruenwald was angry about the collapse of the recruitment effort, Werner was positively beside himself with rage. "What the fuck is the matter with you?" he demanded of his partner in crime as Gruenwald outlined the failure. "How come you let these guys into your house? Don't you realize you can't ever, *ever* do that? I mean, for Christ's sake, now they know who you are, where you live, all that shit. The day we pull the robbery, those guys will lead the cops right to you."

Werner had put the emphasis on "we" in that rebuke, but it was only a language habit, for he fully intended now to strike out on his own. Clearly, Peter was not up to the requirements of the task. It was time, Werner believed, for him to take decisive action; he would recruit his own gang, make his own arrangements.

Besides, Werner had no more time to delay. The gambling losses were mounting again, and one bookie, to whom he owed about $6,000, was beginning to drop strong hints about possible physical harm unless Werner made a significant dent in the debt.

"Jesus, I'm bleeding to death," Werner complained aloud to himself one night while bowling.

With a sigh, he watched his ball hook into the gutter.

PART
TWO
A NIGHT AT THE
RED BARON'S

Chapter

4

"How can you play with broken arms?"

Even the local aficionados were aware that the cavernous bowling alley just east of the invisible line that divides Queens from suburban Nassau County was not one of the great palaces of the sport. Its aging beauty was now surpassed by the slick, computerized establishments that lured a younger crowd, and the old place survived on the loyalty of the industrial leagues that had been bowling there for generations.

For Louis Werner, who bowled there regularly, the place had the kind of gritty, nostalgic charm he liked. Bowlers still used the big score sheets on which scores were entered in thick pencil—unlike those new places with elaborate computers that automatically put up the scores every time a pin fell down. And unlike the new places, with the little kids and teenage couples fooling around, Werner's place was a real old-fashioned bowling alley, with the groups of men in bright shirts, the names of their companies sewn in script on the back, razzing each other loudly as they bowled. In between frames, they drank beer out of tall paper cups and ogled the ladies' league teams on nearby alleys, especially the women in tight slacks whose buttocks moved in a minor symphony each time they bent and glided to roll a ball down the alley.

Next to gambling, bowling was Lou Werner's main diversion. He felt comfortable with the down-to-earth blue-collar workers who spent two nights a week in what was only incidentally a sport—the more important attraction of bowling was social ritual, the gathering of friends, wives, neighbors, and girlfriends. This camaraderie had only a passing relation with rolling a heavy ball down a narrow alley and knocking down as many red and white pins as possible.

Louis Werner was fairly typical of the men in bright blue short-sleeved shirts with "Lufthansa" stitched in white script on the back. He was known to most of them as "a pretty nice guy," although some were slightly put off by the fact that Werner had "a mouth"—in other words, he was a boastful man who did not hesitate to upbraid people who got in his way. He was also an inveterate gambler, but this was no mark of shame in the world of airport workers where a lot of men tried to beat the odds.

The bowlers who worked most closely with Werner detected a few subtle changes in him during the fall of 1978. He was still the boastful wisecracker, but there was a new tension in him, as though a heavy burden had been placed on his shoulders. The men ascribed it to Werner's marital problems. No one suspected the turmoil that was boiling inside him, the crushing burden of debt that was eating away at him and threatening his very life. And certainly no one knew that Werner was receiving direct threats from bookies who were tired of waiting for their money.

Even Frank Menna was beginning to exert some pressure.

———

Werner had met Frank Menna while bowling nearly twenty years before, when Werner was living in Brooklyn. Their mutual interest, not surprisingly, was gambling. Menna, an exhairdresser who in 1978 was operating a luncheonette, spent much of his time as a "runner," a go-between for bookmakers and bettors. The runner's job can be fraught with peril, for losing bettors tend to vent their frustration on the runner who is sent to collect their debt or on the runner who doesn't deliver payments for winning bets fast enough. The runner also tends to get caught in disputes between bookmakers and debtors over bets, all of which are based on oral contracts.

Menna had tried to arbitrate these occasional disputes, but Werner's certainty that he was always right soon made Menna's middleman position untenable. And it was particularly untenable in the case of a bookmaker who in late 1978 seemed to be handling the bulk of Werner's wagers and who was connected with the mob. That connection meant it was dangerous for Menna to play too active a role as middleman, so he tended to let Werner and the bookmaker fight their own battles, restricting his role simple to that of money courier.

The bookmaker's name was Martin Krugman.

"What the fuck is with this guy?" Krugman asked angrily one September morning in 1978, looking contemptuously at the $100 Menna had brought from Werner. In light of the $5,000 Werner owed to the bookmaker, it was a puny payment.

"What can I tell you?" replied Menna with a shrug. "He says that's the best he can do."

"*The best he can do?*" Krugman almost shrieked. "Listen, friend, let me tell you something. This guy keeps fucking around, he's gonna be in big trouble. What does he think he's playing with here? We're talking *blood*."

Uttered in the back room of the hairdressing salon where Krugman ostensibly worked, amid the blank-faced plaster heads wearing wigs of every conceivable hair color and style, the mention of "blood" seemed incongruous. And yet, as Menna knew, the Marty Krugman who was carefully combing out a hairpiece meant to make its wearer look like John F. Kennedy was also the Marty Krugman who hung around with the gang at Robert's Lounge. And these were people not to be trifled with. In his two decades in the world of illegal gambling, Menna had known too many men who did not believe the stories about what happened to those who did not pay their debts. They did not believe the tales until the hoods showed up, the ones who knew how to hurt a man so that he'd never forget—the ribs broken so that every breath was agonizing pain, the teeth smashed in with a steel pipe, the knees fractured with a baseball bat.

"I'll talk to him," Menna said, accepting the $50 bill Krugman occasionally proffered as a reward for running bets. Menna's concern was not so much for Werner's physical health—although he did feel an obligation to warn his old friend about the danger of offering cold cuts to a hungry lion—but the fear that the conflict between Werner and Krugman would put an end to his profitable sideline of running bets.

The look of concern on Menna's face was highly satisfactory to Krugman, for his threats were largely playacting. In fact, he was delighted when Werner sank deeper in the hole, for as Jimmy Burke had often instructed him, a man in Werner's position was like a blue-chip stock. Werner's debt represented steadily growing dividends, and the point would soon come when Werner, in desperation, would have to make a move; since he had no money, he would have to offer the only currency he did possess—information. Werner was hooked now, Krugman knew; he had to be played carefully, like a hungry but scared fish. The timing was crucial, however. The pressure had to be increased in careful increments, and at the right psychological moment, Werner himself would make the offer. What he finally would offer could not be guessed—although Lufthansa was known to handle big shipments of cash and jewels—but he would offer *something*, that was for sure.

To put an even sharper edge on Menna's warning, Krugman called Werner at Lufthansa. "Hey, how come you don't pay your debts?" the bookmaker said to Werner.

"Why the fuck did you call me at work?" Werner said angrily.

"Why don't you pay?"

"What is this shit, Marty?" Werner complained. "Why are you breaking my balls now? I know I owe. I'm good for it, you know that."

"I'm getting heat, Lou," said Krugman, dropping his voice a significant octave. "The boys want their money, and they want it now. You follow me?"

Werner certainly did, and the new edge in Krugman's voice convinced him that he had even less time than he'd thought. To get the thousands needed to pay off Krugman and whatever gorillas were lurking behind him meant that the robbery of which he had dreamed for so long would have to take place very soon. And there was no time for the kind of scheme he and Gruenwald had originally devised. Now Werner would have to play the simple role of inside man, providing the information for a quick score. It would not return as much money as the scheme in which he played the mastermind, but he was backed into a corner. So what if he would no longer get the biggest share? His take would be sufficient to get people like Krugman off his back, with enough left over to allow him to leave New York and start again someplace else.

It was time to make a move, to find a gang to pull off the robbery. No amateurs, like the fools Gruenwald had rounded up; these would be professionals, the kind of guys who would be in and out of the place just like that, the pros who could pull off the job, disappear, and make sure Louis Werner got his cut. Where would he find them?

Maybe through Menna. He knew a lot of wiseguys.

"Let me give you a piece of advice," Frank Menna said to Louis Werner. Normally it was a mistake to make such an offer to Werner, who disdained any advice, but this night, he actually seemed to be listening carefully.

"You can't screw around with these people," said Menna as the two sat at a small table in the bowling alley. It was early November 1978. While they talked, they gazed idly at the lanes, which rumbled with the noise of rolling balls and tumbling pins. The winter bowling season had begun, and the place was jammed.

"See," Menna said, "my attitude is, if you owe to people who might hurt you, you pay. That's it. Whatever you have to do, you pay; you don't fuck around. So if Marty begins throwing some muscle around, he's serious, because there are serious people behind him. What, you think Marty works the whole thing by himself? Forget it. Marty is backed by big people, and they don't tolerate people who don't pay."

"I got it," said Werner, taking a sip of his beer. "I'm having a real bad run, real bad. I know I can get back, but I gotta get the cash now, I understand that." He paused. After a minute of silence while he watched the Lufthansa and Pan American air cargo teams compete at a nearby alley, he began to speak slowly, almost as if he were reciting a memorized speech.

"You know what's funny, Frank?" he said. "Every day, there's millions of dollars pass through my hands, millions. Figure that: I can't find two nickels to rub together, and there

I am, looking at millions of dollars every fucking day. And you know what's even funnier? The goddam money is just lying there, and I know how to just take it. All I need is some help."

"Help?" Menna said, suddenly alert.

"If I had the right kind of people," said Werner, leaning closer to Menna, "I could show them how to do it. I'm telling you, it'd be so goddam easy, you wouldn't believe it."

"You gotta be kidding." Menna smiled, but Werner noticed that he was paying rapt attention.

"Listen, I'm serious, for Christ's sake," Werner said. "There's maybe two million there at any given time; I know exactly how to grab it. I planned the whole thing out." He then launched into a recitation of how he and Gruenwald had formulated a plan, how Gruenwald had failed to round up a gang of robbers, and how Werner proposed to remove the millions from Lufthansa on his own—with a little help from his friends.

"So what about Peter?" Menna asked, checking.

"Fuck Peter," Werner replied, with some vehemence. "I'm tired of waiting for him. He's out, as of right now. It's *my* plan now. Let me ask you: do you know where I can get some good people?"

"I'll see what I can do," Menna said, as the thought crossed his mind that Werner, in the process of betraying his employer, had just double-crossed his closest friend. Who else was he willing to betray?

———

"Well, if he's for real and he needs help," said Martin Krugman, as he combed a salt-and-pepper hairpiece, "I might be able to accommodate him."

"So what do I tell him?" Menna asked.

"Tell him to sit tight. I'll arrange a meeting, and then we'll see."

Krugman had said all this casually, as if barely interested. In truth, he could hardly contain his joy. The patient manipulation of Werner was about to pay off at last; the fish was ready to be gaffed into the boat. The moment Menna left the salon, Krugman called his friend Henry Hill. Immediately, Hill contacted his mentor, Jimmy Burke.

———

As an old gambler, Jimmy Burke knew that luck ran in streaks, and true to form, his own luck had suddenly and dramatically improved. Like the card player who laments a long run of bad cards, Burke had been close to despairing that anything good would come his way. But in only a week in the late fall of 1978, he was dealt a number of astonishingly good hands, almost as if he were controlling a stacked deck.

Hill then told him that a Kennedy Airport employee might be able to provide very lucrative inside information—perhaps the big score Burke had importuned his gang to look for. This promising news came on the heels of two other equally lucrative propositions, both of which, Burke noted with satisfaction, had also come from his protégé, Henry Hill.

———

During the summer and early fall of 1978, Hill had tried to interest Burke in the schemes of one Paul Mazzei, a Pittsburgh dog groomer who had turned to a life of crime, primarily narcotics sales. Hill and Mazzei had become friends in prison, where Mazzei, serving time for narcotics peddling, proposed a plan. Essentially, the plan involved a double-barreled operation: Hill and Mazzei would set up an interstate narcotics operation, which would include the exchange of Hill's heroin supplies for Mazzei's cocaine, with the promise of immense profits for both.

More interestingly, Mazzei had a secondary twist to the drug operation, one that promised even greater profit. He knew a player on the Boston College basketball team, one of the nation's most important college squads—and the subject of heavy betting throughout the country. This particular player and a teammate, Mazzei said, were willing to "do some business": in exchange for cocaine and money, they would agree to shave points.

Hill, involved for years in illegal gambling, needed no education on the potential of the plan Mazzei was proposing. The key to such gambling was the point spread, the number of points by which a particular team was favored to win. If, for example, team A was picked by the odds-makers in Las Vegas to beat team B by three points and then proceeded to win by only two points, those who had bet on team A to win by the spread would lose their bets. (If team A won by three points, it was called a "push," or tie, in which event no one won or lost.) On the other hand, bettors could "bet against the spread"—in other words, bet that a particular team would win, but by nowhere near the margin prophesied.

There were a number of variations, but this basic scheme remains the lifeblood of the multibillion dollar illegal betting business in this country. The key, obviously, is the point spread: if a bettor knows that a particular game is guaranteed to result in a a certain margin of victory, then he can proceed, as H. L. Mencken put it, with the calm certitude of a Christian holding four aces.

To Hill's disappointment, Burke was initially skeptical of the Mazzei scheme. He was uncertain that the bets could be sufficiently dispersed to avoid rousing the suspicions of book-makers around the country, he did not know if Mazzei could keep college basketball players on the take, and he doubted Hill's ability to oversee an enterprise of such scope. Moreover, the scheme required a capital outlay, and Burke was reluctant to commit his dwindling resources to a risky operation. Never-theless, as a criminal capitalist, he saw the vast potential of the deal: profits from the basketball-fixing would be reinvested in the narcotics transactions, which in turn would fuel a widen-ing sports-fixing operation, which in turn would underwrite more narcotics transactions . . . and so on.

"Keep it quiet, for now," he told Hill, stalling for time. "Before anything happens, I want to talk to Mazzei."

In early November, Mazzei came to New York to meet Burke. Accompanied by his fellow conspirators, the brothers Rocco and Anthony Perla, Mazzei met Burke in Robert's Lounge and laid out his proposal. Also present was Krugman, who nodded significantly several times during Mazzei's pre-sentation, a signal to Burke that the idea of using a network of cooperative bookmakers to conceal large bets (several hun-dred thousand dollars) was viable.

The question of how the bets would be made was critical to the scheme. They had to be made carefully, for a sudden in-fusion of bets on one side in a particular game would compel the odds-makers to shift the line in order to balance the betting. Furthermore, a huge amount of money bet one way was almost always an indicator that a game had been fixed. Bets as large as those that Burke and Hill were planning to make had to be parceled out in relatively small chunks so as not to arouse suspicion.

"I like it," Burke said when Mazzei was finished, and with that the deal was struck: Mazzei and his confederates would provide the corrupt player and the cocaine; Burke would provide the starting capital, the network of bookmakers, and his organization's muscle.

If there were any doubts in Mazzei's mind about the Burke gang's sinister reputation and willingness to use violence, they were dispelled during his visit to New York. Mazzei had spent much of his time in Robert's Lounge, the kind of place he thought existed only in the movies; he later told Hill he had never seen so many scary-looking hoods in one place, including the menacing James Burke. Hill himself proved to be pretty scary. One night, following dinner with Mazzei in a Long Island diner, Hill became enraged by an astrology machine that took two of his quarters but refused to tell his future. Hill tried to remove the balky machine entirely, even though it was chained down. When an angry diner employee, armed with a butcher knife, attempted to stop him, Hill pulled a gun on the man. Then, to Mazzei's amazement, Hill set his own car on fire.

Little wonder, then, that Burke dispatched Hill to Boston to talk with the two Boston College players Mazzei had said were on the take. Armed with $5,000 from Burke to begin the payoffs (and a sanction to commence operations from a delighted Paul Vario, Sr.), Hill was there to show the flag and to make two things perfectly clear. He was to demonstrate to the two young men—Richard (Rick) Kuhn and James Sweeney—that his "organization" had things well in hand: they would never have to fear retribution from angry bookmakers not in on the fix who might discover they had been had. Second, he was to let the players know that this was no game; he was the chosen representative of heavy hitters who were prepared to do anything to protect their investment.

"You don't have to worry," Hill told the players in what he took to be his most quietly menacing tone. "If there is any problem, the people in New York will handle it. They are heavyweights, believe me, so nobody's gonna retaliate against you. Got it?"

Kuhn, who understood both the explicit and implicit meanings of what Hill had said, haggled a bit, then settled on a deal that would give him $2,500 for each game in which he would try to ensure that a particular point spread would be maintained. Although Sweeney said almost nothing during this exchange, Hill assumed that his silence meant consent. To seal the deal, Hill gave Kuhn $600 in cash and a quarter-ounce of cocaine.

Kuhn had marked six games on a pocket schedule he brought with him. These were to be nationally televised games against major teams that were certain to attract strong betting interest. The first of the six games, on December 6, almost ended the entire deal: what was supposed to be a seven-point loss turned out to be a nineteen-point victory, and some of the big bookmakers in on the scheme began grousing about "those fucking kids."

Surprisingly, however, Burke, who had lost a modest amount of money on that first game, seemed only moderately upset—at least by his standards: he only once threatened to kill all the participants.

Hill discovered that there were nearly as many excuses as there were points in the game. Kuhn claimed that despite his best efforts, Boston College—on the strength of an outstanding performance by the team's star—simply ran away with the game. Hill warned him there were to be no further slipups, and he told Kuhn to persuade the team's star player to take part in the scheme. When Kuhn tried to offer a few more excuses, Hill made it clear that neither he nor "the organization" was interested in hearing them. "Listen," Hill snarled, "how can you play with broken arms?"

Despite his propensity for strong-arming, Burke did not participate directly in this episode. He had become temporarily preoccupied with a matter of greater concern, which was the chief reason for the relative equanimity in his disposition.

The man from Lufthansa had just delivered the key to the treasure vault.

———

Louis Werner checked his watch in the darkness inside his yellow Plymouth, waiting until the headlight beam from one of the cars entering the diner parking lot swept across him so he could read the dials. Nearly 10:00 P.M.

———

There was a frosty chill in the air that night in early November, so Werner kept his car idling. The heater's low buzz prevented him from hearing the man approach his car from the rear. Werner looked up at the sharp sound of a gloved hand rapping on the driver's side window. He rolled the window down a few inches and saw a heavyset man.

"Get in that car," the man said, pointing to a brown Buick parked just ahead of Werner in the lot. Werner got in the passenger side, and as the other man settled behind the wheel, Werner heard him gasp with effort; Werner noticed that he was quite beefy and was running to fat.

The driver said nothing for nearly a minute. Then he spoke. "Understand you want to talk to somebody about a job," he said. He did not offer his name, and Werner knew better than to ask.

"That's right," Werner said.

"So, what is it? Where is it? You know, all that."

"Lufthansa, the air cargo building; it's money and jewels and gold. A lot of it."

All this the man behind the wheel knew, for he had been dispatched by Jimmy Burke to "talk with this Lufthansa guy and see if he is for real." The man selected for that task—Joseph Manri—was the obvious choice for the job, since he had plenty of experience in robberies and hijackings and he knew his way around the Kennedy air cargo terminals. He had been inside Lufthansa Air Cargo several times and knew that its reputation for tight security was well deserved. This had made Manri skeptical when Burke first told him of the Lufthansa cargo agent's offer. "I don't buy it," he had told Burke. "From what I hear, the goddam place is almost a fortress. And this guy claims he knows how to grab what they have with no big problem? And he's got this plan that'll absolutely work? Bullshit. What is he, just some cargo man? No way."

But Burke, itching for the big score, was not about to dismiss Louis Werner so easily; he sent Manri the skeptic to find out if Werner was in fact for real. He was not impressed with the first sight of the cargo agent. Werner struck him as a low-level sneak who was probably exaggerating his own knowledge of Lufthansa's valuables in hope of getting out from under Krugman's debt. Almost certainly, Manri believed, this guy would know how to get at some stuff around the place, but it would hardly be worth the effort of the Robert's Lounge Gang; the real good stuff remained in the vaults where Werner had no real idea how to get at it.

Manri was sometimes called Buddha, partly for his ever-widening girth and partly because of his habit of sitting, hands folded across his belly, and staring inscrutably at whomever was talking to him. He was a man of few words, creating the illusion of deep wisdom.

Werner assumed he was dealing with a quietly professional crook of vast experience. Manri obviously knew what he was talking about; as Werner described his plan, the fat man interrupted with cogent questions. How could the alarms be turned off? How many guards were there, and what was their schedule? When was the best time to hold up the place?

Manri's calm demeanor masked a sense of growing excitement, for the more he listened to Werner, the more he realized that he had badly underestimated the squinting cargo agent. Werner knew the place cold and had obviously devoted a great deal of time to figuring out how to rob it. Even better, he knew precisely how the alarm system in the high val room worked—and how to get it turned off.

Still, there was the question of security, the very real possibility of armed guards shooting it out with robbers. Werner snorted when Manri asked him about it. "There's *nobody* guarding the high val room," he said. "You understand? Once you're in the high val room, that's it; it's over."

They had left the diner parking lot, and as Manri drove around Queens, Werner tried to convince him that getting in and out of Lufthansa Air Cargo was vastly easier than he or anybody else on the outside believed. "As a matter of fact," Werner said as the car pulled into Kennedy Airport for a cruise past the building, "the fucking place is a cheese box—if you know the right time to go."

Werner heard a surprised intake of breath from Manri, despite his best efforts to conceal it. "What are you talking about?" Manri asked.

"I'm saying," Werner replied, "that if you go in at a certain hour, you own the place. Listen: three A.M. everybody takes a meal break, including this security guard at the front door. You follow?"

"Uh-huh," Manri said, nervously tapping his fingers on the

steering wheel as the car slowly moved past the Lufthansa Air Cargo building. He could hardly believe what Werner was saying: Lufthansa, reputedly among the most secure air cargo facilities at the airport, had a huge gaping hole in its defenses at a certain hour—a hole so big that a gang of robbers could literally walk into the place undetected while everybody was in the cafeteria and then walk out with every nickel in the place. Impossible.

"I'm telling you," Werner insisted, "you go in there at three A.M., and you can take the whole goddam building with you if you want."

Werner had a second surprise for Manri: the amount of money, gold, and jewels in the high val room toward the end of the week, including accumulations awaiting shipment on Monday, often totaled $2 million or more. That was much more than Manri assumed was ever inside the building at one time. He realized then that, in Werner, the Robert's Lounge Gang had hit the mother lode.

"That's a pretty good plan you got there," Manri said as he drove Werner back to the diner parking lot. He tried to sound noncommittal, but Werner could see that he was excited.

"Yeah, well, I worked on it a lot," said Werner, accepting the compliment. "All along, I've been saying I just need the right guys to help me, you know, to go in and do it."

"Okay," Manri said, exhaling heavily, "we'll call you on this and let you know. Take it easy."

Werner climbed out of Manri's car. He stood there in the diner parking lot a moment, watching as Manri drove away. Not once, it now occurred to Werner, had the man behind the wheel given his name.

———

It was near midnight by the time Manri got back to Robert's Lounge, where Jimmy Burke was sitting at the bar. "So what's the story?" Burke asked as Manri took off his coat.

"It's good," Manri replied. He paused a moment, then added, as if for emphasis, "It's *real* good."

"This guy Werner got his shit together?"

"Looks that way. He looks like he's got it all—the guards, the alarms, the schedule, where the money's at, the whole thing."

Burke scowled. "How much?"

"He says about two million, maybe more."

Manri saw Burke's eyes widen slightly. "And he's saying what, that it's a cinch to go in and grab it?"

"Just about," replied Manri. He then outlined a basically simple plan to take advantage of an astonishing gap in the Lufthansa security: four or five robbers would enter the building during the 3:00 A.M. meal break on a weekend, when there was only a skeleton staff on night duty. Meanwhile, another robber would drive a van around the building to the loading dock. There, he would wait while his confederates inside got the drop on the employees and forced one of them to open the cargo bay door. Still another participant would drive the van inside and compel the Lufthansa supervisor on duty to open the high val room. The robbers would then load all valuables aboard the van, handcuff the employees, and drive away. Simple.

"You're shittin' me," Burke said, still unable to believe that a heist of that dimension could be so easy. Yet the experienced Manri, who was not prone to exaggeration, was saying exactly that. Like Manri, Burke was overcoming his own doubts and gradually becoming a convert to a heist that, incredibly, promised a bonanza for less risk than a gas station stickup.

While Manri sipped a drink, Burke scowled. He lit another of the Kools he chain-smoked and slowly blew the smoke out. "Well," he said after a while, "I guess we'll take the Red Baron for a little ride."

Manri smiled at the allusion to Lufthansa's popular advertising slogan. He also was smiling because he knew that at that moment, Jimmy the Gent Burke had made his decision: the Robert's Lounge Gang would hold up the Lufthansa Air Cargo building.

The choice of the Robert's Lounge Gang to carry out the Lufthansa heist would seem at first to be the height of folly. This was the very same gang, after all, that had managed to foul up just about everything it touched while Burke was in prison. Yet there were compelling reasons for Burke's choice.

For one thing, Burke felt that the actual heist of Lufthansa would be relatively easy. It would not require the standard procedure in such instances, the recruitment of a gang of professional stickup artists, of which there were many in the New York underworld. Second, Burke was concerned about the potential million-dollar-plus size of the haul. Such a large amount would cause all sorts of problems among crooks of low-scale intelligence suddenly confronted with a lot of money. He wanted the heist gang to comprise people he trusted and could control and discipline if necessary.

As a man who had pulled a dozen good stickups in his youth and who possessed a criminal mind of some dimension, Jimmy Burke was perfectly capable of planning a crime that would require organization and attention to details as well as order and discipline.

Burke chose Sepe, DeSimone, Cafora, Manri, and McMahon as his first-line force, the men who would carry out the actual robbery. As supporting players, Burke picked Stax Edwards to dispose of the van that would be used to move the money from the air cargo building, while his son Frank played a backup role. Burke himself would play the criminal mastermind, but would not be an on-the-scene participant.

The most important role was Manri's. He was to serve as general supervisor of the robbery crew and as a liaison with Werner. Manri and Werner held several meetings in a mob-run motel in Queens where Werner passed on further details of the security setup at Lufthansa Air Cargo, including the vital information on how the high val alarm systems worked.

Manri then passed the details on to Burke, who used them to formulate an overall robbery scheme. His plan, in the end, amounted to a refinement of Werner's, but it included a number of touches that Werner, an inexperienced crook, had neglected. It took Burke nearly three weeks to perfect the final five-phase plan:

Phase One: Three vehicles would be used—a van and two cars. One car would be the "chase car." It would trail the van as it left the Lufthansa building after the robbery and deflect the police if they took pursuit. The second car would wait at the "switch point," a spot not too far from the airport. There the robbers would transfer the loot from the van into the waiting "switch car." The van would then be destroyed to remove any traces of the heist gang and to prevent the police from broadcasting its description.

The van and chase car would go to the Lufthansa Air Cargo building at about 3:00 A.M. on a Monday morning. The chase car would remain in the parking lot, while the van dropped off the men who would enter the building by way of the front door. The van, with two other men, would then move around to the rear of the building. One of the two men would cut the lock on the chain-link fence surrounding that area and replace it with an unfastened substitute, so that anyone looking at the gate on a dark night would assume it was still secure.

Phase Two: While the van waited outside the cargo bay door, the men who had been dropped off at the front would enter the building, track down all the employees on duty, and hold them in one place, preferably in the company cafeteria. They would have to account for the ten employees Werner had said would be on duty, including two supervisors, a security guard, and a man who made runs to other airlines. The next phase could not begin until all ten employees had been rounded up.

Phase Three: The most critical phase of the operation, gaining entry to the high val room, would be accomplished by forcing the senior supervisor to turn off an alarm box in his office. In the box were several clocklike mechanisms that controlled the high val alarms; the dials had to be set to a certain series of positions to deactivate the alarms. The thieves would also use the supervisor to evade the high val room's secondary line of defense, the silent alarms. By threatening to kill his family, they would force the supervisor to show them where the hidden alarms were located.

Phase Four: They would force the supervisor to unlock the cargo bay door. The driver would back the van in and load it with whatever was in the high val room. Meanwhile, the thieves would handcuff all the Lufthansa employees. Once that had been accomplished, they would warn them to lie still for at least ten minutes.

Timing was a critical ingredient in this phase of the plan, for the Port Authority Police could seal the airport in less than ninety seconds. Thus the robbers had to get away from

Lufthansa and out of the airport before the employees raised an alarm.

The most important item linking the robbers to the scene —what the Lufthansa employees saw as they were being robbed—would be obscured by the robbers wearing dark, nondescript clothing and ski masks. The van would be a dark color, and the thieves would later replace its license plates with a stolen set.

Phase Five: Followed by the chase car, the van would head toward the switch point in Brooklyn. There the men would transfer the haul to the switch car. Stax Edwards would put a new set of plates on the van, then drive it to an auto junkyard in New Jersey, where it would be destroyed in a powerful compacter used to transform junk cars into squares of crushed steel for shipment to metal recycling plants.

All the participants—including Burke's son Frank, who would drive the chase car—would quickly leave the switch point. Later they would receive their pay. The robbers' fees ranged from $10,000 to $50,000, depending on the importance of a man's role in the robbery. The amounts were predicated on an anticipated haul of about $2 million. (Werner was to receive a flat 10 percent of the final take.)

———

"Don't forget," Jimmy Burke repeated at least two dozen times during a series of meetings with his heist crew in Robert's Lounge, "you gotta account for ten guys. Ten guys."

Burke hoped that repetition of this and other important details would help his crew remember them. The reminders seemed necessary; around a table in a dim corner of the bar, studying two large sketches Werner had made, DeSimone, Sepe, and several of the others were tense with puzzled concentration as they attempted to absorb the details of the sketches before them.

Aware of their limited intelligence, Burke tried to hammer in the important details: keep the ski masks on, say only what you have to say, get in and out as fast as possible, grab all small cartons with bank seals on them, don't exceed the speed limit when you leave the airport, and finally, don't spend your money wildly afterward—a dead giveaway to police that a man has just been enriched by a major robbery.

———

Worry over whether his gang could keep all the details straight and not commit a major error preoccupied the mind of Jimmy Burke as the fall gradually turned into winter that November and early December of 1978. He was also busy with another problem, the considerable amount of diplomacy required to make the robbery work. Paul Vario, Sr., had given his enthusiastic approval, but Burke still had to see to several important subsidiary matters. He had to negotiate with the mobster who would arrange for a suitable van to be reported stolen. Another would launder the cash taken in the robbery. Another would dispose of any gold or jewels, and still others would provide hiding places for the money, Mafia "banks" where the freshly laundered cash—bills substituted to prevent the tracing of recorded serial numbers or hidden marks—would wait to be withdrawn.

One of the more important arrangements was the negotiation with a representative of the Gambino family. Under Mafia protocol, Burke had to apprise the Gambino organization of the heist, seek its approval, and, most important, promise it a cut of the haul. In return, the Gambino organization would provide a number of necessary support services for the heist, including the Brooklyn auto shop they would use as a switch point.

The Gambino representative chosen to meet with Burke was one of the family's rising stars, a hood named John Gotti. Surrounded by a retinue of lower-ranking hoods and hangers-on, Gotti was deep into a six-course dinner on the night Burke met him in one of the Mafia's favorite Manhattan restaurants, famed for its Italian cuisine. Following the ritual hugs and kisses—Burke always felt distinctly uncomfortable with this Italian tradition—Gotti looked around the table and said to his companions, "Why don't you people take a nice walk outside?"

Alone with Burke, Gotti heard out the general outline of the heist plan. "It's good," he announced when Burke was finished and, with that imprimatur established, moved on to offer whatever services Burke might require. "You want it, you got it, Jimmy," he announced grandly, knowing it was unnecessary to mention that in exchange for this generosity, the Gambino family would be dealt a healthy percentage of the take.

Ultimately, they settled on a figure of $200,000, and although Burke assumed they had negotiated all the necessary components of the deal, he was to discover a few days later that an extra clause had been attached. It came in the form of a chilling individual named Paolo LiCastri, a thirty-year-old Sicilian immigrant who was known to be a vicious contract killer. LiCastri, Vario informed Burke, had been imposed on the job by the Gambino organization, and neither man needed to be told why: LiCastri would serve as enforcer of the mob's interests in the Lufthansa heist.

Burke disliked LiCastri from the moment he walked into Robert's Lounge to introduce himself. Short and thin, he had been convicted of murder in 1975; early in 1978 he was deported to Sicily as an illegal alien. He had been smuggled back into this country in the fall of that year—for the express purpose, Burke and Vario assumed, of overseeing the Lufthansa job. LiCastri's presence was a result of the New York Mafia's recent practice of smuggling in Sicilian Mafia hoods to fill slots in the various families. The theory was that Sicilian hoods were much more reliable and loyal than their American-born counterparts; they were less likely to turn if arrested, and they took seriously the oath of *omerta* (silence). They were also considered less greedy than the new generation of American Mafia hoods and more willing to do the various dirty jobs, such as killing, to earn higher rank.

Burke found LiCastri disturbing. An arrogant punk, he seemed untrustworthy, and he clearly enjoyed killing. When briefed on the Burke plan to rob Lufthansa, LiCastri asked, in his heavily accented English, what plans had been made to kill the security guard. Burke made it clear there were no plans to kill anybody during the robbery. Only stupid robbers did that, he said.

LiCastri snorted. "Whatsa matter?" he asked. "Not man enough for it?"

Burke went for him across a table, and it took three men to prevent him from grabbing LiCastri's throat.

The encounter marked the growing tension that surrounded the Robert's Lounge gang as they waited for Louis Werner to give the word that the right time had arrived to pull the heist. They had carried out one dry run, had stared at Werner's diagrams, and had gone over each man's role again and again. They were ready; the longer they waited, the more tension mounted. The "inside man," they were told, was watching to see when the most money would be stored over a weekend in the terminal. The time would come soon, Burke reassured his increasingly nervous crew: the Christmas shopping season was approaching. Soon the big shipments of gold and jewelry would begin flowing westward from Europe. The call should come any minute now.

———

The moment came on the evening of December 8, 1978, when Werner made a phone call to a jittery Joseph Manri. "It's gotta be this weekend," Werner said. He explained that an unexpectedly large interbank shipment of cash had been delayed at the terminal and was being held in the high val room pending delivery on Monday. Manri immediately called Burke, who responded with a one-word order.

"Go."

Chapter

5

"Your brains are gonna be on the ceiling"

The van headed along North Boundary Road, the main service thoroughfare along a strip of air cargo terminals near the northern edge of the sprawling airport. It moved quietly in the predawn darkness that Monday morning, December 11, 1978, as the great airport slumbered restlessly.

In a few hours, it would come fully awake and begin another busy work week, with the rumble of trucks and cars, the scream of the jets, the steady roar of one of the world's busiest airports. But just before 3:00 A.M. there was only the normal off-hours hum of an occasional truck or car, a few jets landing or taking off.

At one of the parking lot entrances, the van turned right. It rolled slowly into the lot in front of the large building with its yellow Lufthansa Cargo sign shining brightly in the darkness. The van stopped near the front door of the building. Two men in the front seat of the van sat quietly for a moment, scanning the cars in the parking lot and the lighted windows on the building's third floor.

"Okay," one man said after finishing his reconnaissance. The side door of the van slid open, and four men got out. All were dressed in dark slacks and dark jackets, their faces covered with ski masks. Three of the men carried pistols; the fourth held a sawed-off shotgun.

Even with the masks, they winced slightly as a cold wind blowing in from across Jamaica Bay hit them. It was a few degrees below freezing. The thickly overcast skies hinted of snow later in the day.

3:05 A.M.

The man with the shotgun stood looking around for a moment, then sharply rapped once on the side of the van. "Let's go," he said as the van moved away.

The four men entered the front door and discovered that Louis Werner was right: there was no guard at the front entrance. They paused a second, then quietly and slowly began to climb the flight of stairs leading to the upper levels of the building.

3:07 A.M.

The van moved down a driveway at the right side of the building and stopped in front of a large double gate of heavy-gauge steel mesh. The two sections of the gate were secured by a thick chain and a heavy padlock.

One of the men in the front of the van jumped out. With a pair of bolt-cutters, he snipped the lock, which fell to the asphalt with a dull thud. He pulled the gate open and the van drove through. Then he closed the two sections, looped the severed chain back through the steel mesh, and replaced the lock with another, which he drew from his pocket. Some distance behind him, he saw the late-model Buick pull into the parking lot and douse its lights.

3:13 A.M.

Inside the cargo terminal, the four masked men reached the top of the stairs, where they heard voices coming from the far end of a corridor. One man stayed behind, and the three others walked stealthily toward the voices.

Senior cargo agent John Murray was taking advantage of the meal hour by grabbing a catnap at his desk. He was not fully asleep when he became aware of the sound of rustling cloth. He opened his eyes and saw three masked men pointing guns at him.

"Don't move," one of them said, "and don't do anything stupid."

Fully awake, Murray found himself looking into the business end of a sawed-off shotgun. Gripping the gun with both hands was a man in a ski mask with bright yellow trim around the eye holes.

"Where's everybody else?" he asked Murray.

"In the lunchroom," Murray replied.

"Where's the waxer?" the shotgun-wielder asked. That question told Murray immediately that the men were equipped with detailed inside information; only a few Lufthansa employees knew that a cleaning service sent someone to the building each night at midnight to wax the floors.

"Gone home," Murray said.

The man holding the shotgun walked away from him and joined the fourth man guarding that end of the corridor. The shotgun-wielder checked two rest rooms and headed for the lunchroom, leaving two masked men to guard the cargo agent. It occurred to Murray that the masked men knew exactly where the lunchroom was.

3:17 A.M.

The driver moved the van slowly, its headlights dimmed, 400 feet to the rear of the cargo terminal. There he backed it up to a large cargo bay door, high and wide enough to accommodate a truck of just about any size.

Inside the van, the two men waited for the other four masked men to open the cargo bay from the inside. They kept the engine running, and while it hummed and the heater continued to pour out warmth, they felt perspiration running down their faces under the woolen ski masks. They pulled off the masks, intending to put them back on when the door opened.

3:19 A.M.

On the third floor, the two masked men pulled Murray to his feet. One of them ripped Murray's suit jacket from his shoulders, pulling the sleeves inside out as he took it off the cargo agent's arms.

"Keep your eyes down, looking at the floor," one of the masked men ordered. He searched the jacket, then tossed it aside. The other man put handcuffs on Murray. "Let's get him into the lunchroom with the others," he said, pushing Murray ahead of him.

In the lunchroom, Wolfgang Ruppert was sitting at a table eating his meal and gazing absentmindedly out into the corridor. Suddenly, he saw a figure carrying what appeared to be a gun. Before Ruppert could react, another man burst through the door and pointed a pistol at him.

"Raise your hands!" the gunman yelled, while another masked man, this one armed with a shotgun, rushed through another door, pointed his weapon at four other employees sitting at a table and shouted, "Don't move! Lie down and don't move!"

In a shuffle of chairs, Ruppert and the other four Lufthansa workers lay face down on the floor. "Close your eyes," one of the masked man commanded. "You move, and I'll kill you."

Seconds later, the two other gunmen prodded Murray into the cafeteria. "You lie down there, too," the gunman ordered. Murray sank to his knees and then stretched out face down on the floor.

3:24 A.M.

While three masked men patted the captives down in search of weapons, the robber with the shotgun approached Andronico Cejas, who was lying on the floor, trembling with fear. Cejas felt the gunman's foot prod his left side.

"Get up careful and come here," the gunman ordered. Rising to his feet, Cejas lifted his hands high above his head. Two of the masked men pushed him into the corridor. The man with the shotgun asked, "Where do them doors go to?" He pointed the shotgun toward a number of closed doors.

"Offices, I think," Cejas answered.

"Tell me the truth, or I'll kill you right now."

"I *am* telling you the truth," Cejas replied, growing increasingly alarmed as the masked man casually waved the shotgun around.

"If somebody comes out of one of them doors," the masked man said, "I'll kill you, you son of a bitch." He grabbed a fistful of Cejas's shirt and pushed him back into the lunchroom. Cejas reassumed his prone position.

Another masked man kicked the bottom of Murray's foot. "Stay cool and you won't get hurt," he said as Murray lifted his head. "Who else is in the warehouse?"

"As far as I know, only my supervisor," Murray answered.

"Who's that?"

"Rudi," Murray replied, referring to Rudi Eirich, the cargo traffic supervisor for the night shift. Aware that the masked men knew how many men were supposed to be on duty, Murray understood that they were now attempting to account for everybody. He was also aware that there was a real danger of shooting if the robbers became convinced that somebody was missing, possibly sending out an alarm.

"Kerry Whalen's down there somewhere, too," Murray added.

"Who's he?" the masked man with the shotgun asked.

"A transfer man," Murray replied. "He takes things to other airlines."

"If you call your supervisor, will he come up here?"

"If I give him the right story, he will."

"Okay," said the masked man, "you call him. Tell him he's got a long-distance call from Germany."

Two of the masked men pulled Murray to his feet, warned him not to take his eyes off the floor, and took him back to his desk.

"Make sure you make the right call," one of the men told him, "and you better be convincing, you son of a bitch, or else I'll blow your fucking head off."

3:29 A.M.

"What the hell is going on in there?" one of the men in the van said, wiping the sweat from his face.

"Maybe something went wrong," the other man ventured. Increasingly nervous, they glanced again at their watches. The plan was falling behind schedule; they should have been inside the warehouse by now. One of the men slipped out of the van and walked to a door next to the cargo bay. Peering inside through a small window, he saw a man, obviously some sort of supervisor, calmly seated at a desk, going over paperwork and eating a sandwich.

"There's nothing happening in there," he told the other man when he returned. They began to debate what to do when the man seated behind the wheel of the van shouted, "Oh, Jesus!"

A small Lufthansa delivery van had pulled up near the cargo bay door. Kerry Whalen, who had just made a transfer delivery to American Airlines, got out of his van and began walking toward the terminal building. Passing the black van, he assumed it had made a delivery from another airline, a not uncommon occurrence, even at that time of the morning.

As he walked past the van, a man jumped in his path. "Get in the truck," he ordered Whalen, pointing a pistol at him.

Stunned for a moment, Whalen made no move.

"I said, get in the truck," the gunman repeated, louder this time.

Whalen ran for the terminal door. The gunman tackled him and smashed him in the back of the skull with the gun. Whalen screamed, and as the gunman hit him again, a second man ran over from the black van and held him. Whalen continued to scream, and the gunman hit him on the head a third time. Jamming the gun barrel into one of Whalen's eyes, he said, "Yell again, and you're a dead man." Whalen quieted.

The two men dragged Whalen into the black van. "Lie down and shut up," the gunman commanded.

3:33 A.M.

Inside the warehouse area, Rolf Rebmann looked up from his paperwork. Hearing what sounded like shouts from outside, he walked to the door to investigate.

On the third floor, John Murray felt the sweat on his brow and the churning in his stomach as a masked man handed him the telephone. He dialed a two-digit number.

"Rudi, this is John," Murray said when Rudi Eirich answered. "There's a call up here for you from Frankfurt about our freighter. Can you come take it?"

"I'll be right up," Eirich replied, to Murray's relief. He was aware that Eirich's office, one flight down, was enclosed with glass. If he spotted the robbers from it, he might be tempted to call the police. That would mean real danger of shooting. At the same time, Murray was aware that the robbers' inside information was extensive; surely they knew that a call from the home office would bring Eirich out of his office.

Eirich climbed the gunmetal stairs to the third floor, pushed open the heavy fire door, and felt cold steel against both sides of his face. Two masked men were at either side of the door.

"Don't be afraid," a voice said. "You won't get killed if you cooperate completely."

As the robbers marched him into the lunchroom, Eirich

saw the Lufthansa employees stretched out face down on the floor. They were guarded by a masked man who, Eirich thought, appeared to be very fat.

"Who's missing?" the man with the shotgun asked.

"I can't tell for sure," Eirich replied, counting the six bodies on the floor. With a crew of nine, that left two unaccounted for. "I think Rolf Rebmann is down in the warehouse, and I think one man is outside somewhere making transfers."

"Where's the guard?" the masked man asked, aware that the normal night crew included a tenth man, a private security guard.

"I don't know."

"Look, you son of a bitch," the man with the shotgun said, "we've got your address, and we'll kill your family if you don't cooperate."

"I tell you, I don't know," insisted Eirich, by now thoroughly frightened.

The masked men began debating among themselves, and although Brooklyn accents predominated, at least one of the men spoke in what seemed to be an Italian accent. When they'd made their decision, the man pointed the shotgun at Eirich and ordered, "Okay, let's take a walk downstairs. Fuck around and I'll blow your head off."

With the shotgun wedged against his head, Eirich and the masked men slowly walked downstairs.

3:44 A.M.

After hearing the yells, Rolf Rebmann opened the door next to the cargo bay and stepped outside. He saw a van backed up to the bay. Something of an RV buff, Rebmann recognized it instantly as a Ford Econoline 150 model. He also noticed that the sliding door was open and a man was standing beside it, his back to the building.

"Can I help you?" Rebmann asked.

The man spun around and pointed a pistol at him. "Don't make a sound," the man ordered, motioning with his left hand for Rebmann to come forward. "Just do what we tell you to do and you won't get hurt. Understand?"

Rebmann nodded, noticing that the man had a mustache and what appeared to be expensively styled hair. He wore a quilted vest and blue jeans with a flared leg. His shoes were brightly shined.

"Get in the van," Rebmann was ordered. "Lay down in the back."

Inside the van, Rebmann lay face-down next to what he thought was a pile of clothing. But the clothing moved, emitting a low moan.

3:50 A.M.

With the shotgun pressed into his neck, Rudi Eirich walked through the warehouse at a funeral-march pace. He looked everywhere, but saw no sign of Rebmann, Whalen, or the security guard. The masked men surrounding him began to get restless.

"If this is some kind of a trick," one of them warned, "you're gonna get your head blown off."

"I just cannot find him," said Eirich, increasingly desperate.

They arrived at Rebmann's unoccupied desk. "Maybe we oughta just splatter his fucking brains against them goddam boxes," one of the masked men said.

Just as Eirich was sure they were about to kill him, one of the robbers suddenly stage-whispered: "There's the guard!" Pointing to the far end of the warehouse, he indicated a man in uniform making his rounds.

The robbers pushed Eirich to the floor, face down. One robber crouched on top of him, his knee pressed into Eirich's back, the shotgun pointed at the back of Eirich's head. The other three men fanned out among the boxes of cargo and loading equipment that dotted the warehouse.

The security guard, Samuel Veltre, was oblivious to the impending ambush. In only the ninth day of his employment with the Wackenhut Security Services, he was concentrating on his log book and a written list of instructions that specified his duties for the night shift. He was reading that list when someone grabbed his neck from behind and jammed the barrel of a pistol into his head. The gun then moved to a point just under his chin.

"Don't do anything stupid, old man," the gunman said to the fifty-two year-old security guard, "or your brains are gonna be on the ceiling."

Veltre nodded and held his hands aloft.

3:56 A.M.

Impatient to see what was happening inside, one of the robbers in the van put on his ski mask and went inside the

cargo bay. There he saw one of his confederates crouched behind a large box.

"Hey, what are you guys doing?" he asked.

Informed that they were looking for two missing Lufthansa
employees, the man from the van said, "We got two in the
van."

"Oh, that's gotta be them."

"We got the guard!" someone shouted.

"We got the other ones, too!" the man from the van shouted
back He went back outside and led Rebmann and Whalen,
whose black watch cap was stained with blood, into the warehouse.

"Open that door," the gunman ordered Eirich as he pulled
the supervisor to his feet and pointed to the cargo bay.

Using Rebmann's key, Eirich activated the automatic opening mechanism. The van backed into the warehouse.

3:59 A.M.

Two masked men took Rebmann, Whelan, and the security
guard upstairs to the lunchroom, ordered them to lie prone,
and then handcuffed them.

Downstairs, Eirich watched as the van backed up to the
doors of the high value room.

"Listen, we know all about the alarms and all that," one
of the masked men told him, "so you don't try any cute tricks,
right?"

Eirich, his eyes focused on the floor, answered, "I will
cooperate completely. I don't want anyone to be hurt." Further
unsettled by the blood on Whalen's head, Eirich was growing
more and more concerned as threats came at him from all
directions.

"We've got a couple of guys at your house right now," one
of the masked men told him. "You do anything to fuck us
up, we'll just blow your whole family away. You got that,
right?"

As Eirich understood, their concern centered on the lock
and alarm system for the high value room. Although they obviously had some knowledge of the system, he realized that
knowledge did not extend to any hidden or silent alarms that
Eirich might trip unobtrusively—security systems common to
such operations as Lufthansa Air Cargo, reputed to be among
the most secure at Kennedy.

The gunmen took Eirich to his glass-walled office, firmly warned him to keep his eyes on the floor, and ordered him to deactivate the alarm system for the high value room. "We're gonna turn off the whole [alarm] system now. How do you do it?"

"You can deactivate the system here," Eirich replied, his eyes downcast while imagining the guns pointed at his head.

"How?"

"With a key—a special key."

"Gimme the key," one masked man demanded, and Eirich fished it out of his pocket. Handing it over, he pointed to a panel of locks and switches on one wall of his office. Uncertain of whether the key had to be turned in a certain way to avoid setting off the alarms, the masked men briefly conferred, and then ordered Eirich to turn it, after repeating the threats against his family.

Eirich was relieved at their decision, for he knew that the key had to be turned to the precisely correct position; otherwise the alarms would go off at the vault. With the shotgun in front of his face, Eirich slowly turned the key, praying his hand would remain steady enough to avoid tripping the alarms. With a sigh of relief, he heard a slight click at the panel. The alarms had been turned off.

4:09 A.M.

Eirich's ordeal was not yet over. The gunmen shoved him toward the high value room, which was about fifty feet from his office. "Open the door," one of them said as Eirich reached the outer door. When he had done so, the masked man pulled him inside. There were several piles of small cartons.

"Where's the alarm button?" the man with the shotgun asked. Eirich pointed to a button on the wall.

"Make sure he don't get near that button," one of the men ordered. He and two others shoved a table desk out of the room. Forming a line, they passed the cartons to one another and stacked them on the table, ready to be loaded into the van.

While one man began to load the van, another pushed Eirich toward the door to the inner vault.

"Open this door," the robber ordered, pressing the shotgun against his ear. "Don't touch nothing else."

With that door open, Eirich pointed out the alarm button for the inner vault. Two gunmen then took him back to the outer vault and pushed him to the floor, while another ordered, "Keep him away from the walls. Keep him in the middle and don't let him move. There might be another hidden alarm button in here."

While Eirich lay with his face pressed to the floor, one man in the inner vault threw parcels and cartons to another masked man, who stacked them on the table and the floor near the van. One of the parcels fell on the floor right next to Eirich's face. As he stared at the package, Eirich saw the foot of one of the robbers stomp it, splitting its sides. He saw a hand reach inside the broken package and emerge with a bundle of hundred dollar bills.

"This is it!" one of the robbers shouted. "Here's the cash!" Nearly jumping with glee, he yelled into the inner vault, "Keep throwing them out here; get the ones with the seals!"

Then, after what seemed no more than a minute of sealed packages flying out of the inner vault, he said "Okay, that's enough."

A gunman jerked Eirich to his feet, shoved him out of the vault, and took him up the stairs to the cafeteria. As he left, three masked men were loading seventy-two 15-pound cartons and boxes into the van.

4:16 A.M.

In the lunchroom, Eirich saw the other Lufthansa employees stretched out on the floor, guarded by two masked men. One of them pushed Eirich to the floor and tied his wrists with plastic tape.

Meanwhile, downstairs, the two men from the van suddenly realized they needed the key to the cargo bay door to reopen it and drive the van out of the warehouse. One of them ran upstairs to get the key from Eirich. While there, he noticed Whalen lying on the floor, his cap completely soaked with blood. Remembering that Whalen had seen him without a ski mask on, the now-masked robber walked over to him.

"I want to know where you live, motherfucker," the masked man said as he removed the wallet from Whalen's hip pocket. "I hear you said anything about me, I'll come get you." He searched through the wallet and found a five dollar bill.

"This all the money you got? I oughta give you ten." He threw the wallet onto Whalen's body and went back downstairs. After he left, two other masked men handcuffed the

Lufthansa employees together, then strung a rope from one employee to another. At the end of the line, they tied the last length of the rope around John Murray's wrists.

After removing several car keys from the pockets of the employees, the masked men prepared to leave the lunchroom. "Don't nobody move for ten minutes!" one of them shouted to the prostrate forms inside. "First man that moves gets his head blown off!"

The men on the floor heard the lunchroom door close. After a minute, the door suddenly flew open, and one of the masked men screamed, "I said don't move, goddammit!" The door shut again.

4:21 A.M.

The masked men ran downstairs and out of the building as the van pulled around the front. Two got into the van, and the others climbed into the chase car. Both vehicles turned onto North Boundary Road and, keeping to the 40 mph speed limit, moved toward an airport exit.

Inside the Lufthansa building, there was total silence. The men lying on the lunchroom floor could hear no sound outside the closed door. John Murray, the only man who had not been handcuffed, began working his fingers against the rope binding his wrists. After several minutes of work, he pulled his hands free.

4:28 A.M.

Murray lay still for a few seconds, uncertain whether the robbers had actually left the building. He crept to the door nearest the stairs and knocked loudly. The sounds echoed in the corridor. Hearing no response, Murray slowly opened the door and peered down the corridor. Again, he waited; the only sound he heard was the beat of his own heart and his labored breathing.

Deciding that the robbers had left, Murray walked quickly to a telephone in the office area. He dialed the number for the Port Authority Police Department.

"We got an armed robbery that took place at Lufthansa Cargo, building number two sixty-one," Murray reported, hoping that the fear he still felt would not cause him to jumble his words.

4:30 A.M.

The first faint rays of dawn appeared in the east, promising a typical gray mid-December New York day. The van and chase car, their occupants alert for any sign of police roadblocks, exited the airport where North Boundary Road flowed into the mainstream of traffic.

They saw no indications that the alarm had gone up. Now unmasked, the men in both vehicles were silent as they drove onto 150th Street; still there was not a police patrol car in sight. The driver of the van, unable to resist the temptation any longer, pumped one fist in the air and shouted, *"Awri-i-i-ightttt!"* dragging out the last syllable in the well-known New York bellow of triumph.

The two vehicles meandered for a few blocks, then headed west toward Brooklyn. Still no sign of flashing red lights or other signs that a chase was on, and the other drivers in the sparse predawn traffic took no notice of them. After passing under Cross Bay Boulevard, the vehicles headed southwest, toward Rockaway Parkway and the Brooklyn neighborhood known as Canarsie.

On a street dotted with small factories and garages, the van and car turned into the short driveway of a large auto repair shop. As if by miracle, the large double door of the shop suddenly opened, and the two vehicles rolled inside. The door closed behind them immediately; in only a few seconds, the black van and the late-model Buick had disappeared, as though the earth had swallowed them.

Inside the garage, Jimmy Burke stood waiting. Stax Edwards, who had opened and closed the big door, walked to the rear of the van and looked at the yellow New York license plate 508-HWM that he was to replace with another stolen plate.

"So?" Burke said as Angelo Sepe stepped down from behind the wheel of the van.

"Piece of cake," Sepe replied. "No problem."

Burke grunted, then asked, "How come you guys are late?"

"We had some trouble finding all them guys in there," Joe Manri said as he left the van by the side door. "It's okay, though. No problem."

"Any shooting?" Burke asked.

"No," said Sepe, "although I had to clip some guy a little bit. That's all."

"Okay," said Burke, looking at his watch. "We gotta roll now."

They all set to work, moving the packages from the van into the trunks of the chase car and another car already parked inside the garage. Forty cartons with seals—the ones containing American currency—went into the trunk of the car that had been parked inside the garage. The men loaded the other cartons, including several shipments of foreign currency and four dozen separate shipments of unmounted jewels and gold, into the brown Buick that had been used as the chase car.

In a few minutes the van was empty. As if in a well-rehearsed ballet, each man moved silently to his task. As soon as the cars were loaded, Burke and his son Frank drove off in the auto containing the forty cartons of American money. McMahon and Manri, with DeSimone and Sepe sitting in the rear seat, left the garage in the brown Buick. Cafora walked out of the garage to be picked up on a nearby street corner by a woman driving a white Cadillac. LiCastri, for reasons no one else could quite understand, announced that he would take the subway home.

As Canarsie slowly came to life, Stax Edwards was alone in the garage. Although Burke did not know it, Edwards failed to change the rear license plate as he had been ordered—for the simple reason that he had forgotten all about it. The license plate switch had seemed an unnecessary precaution to him in any event. He was to take the van to the "chop shop" in New Jersey—a relatively short forty-minute drive across the Verrazano Narrows Bridge, then across Staten Island to the grimy port city of Elizabeth.

Then, too, it seemed a shame, somehow, to drive a perfectly good vehicle into the sprawling auto junkyard, then watch as several silent men drove it into the giant crusher. And then this beautiful piece of automotive machinery would be compressed, in a clang of crunching metal and breaking glass, into a large box of squeezed metal. In that state, it would disappear into the anonymity of a metal recycling plant.

Edwards walked around the vehicle, admiring its gleaming chrome, its tinted porthole window that allowed somebody inside to look out while no one outside could see in, the wire wheels, the expensive whitewall tires, and inside the driver's section, the nice-looking radio. What a shame to destroy this fine machine.

Edwards got behind the wheel and turned the key in the ignition. The van's well-tuned engine purred. He switched on the radio, tuned it to a local rock 'n' roll station, then turned up the volume to full blast. He slowly backed the van out of the garage, his head nodding to the noisy beat of the music. Stopping the van just outside the garage door, Edwards got out, closed the door, and drove away in a squeal of tires.

As the van roared down the street and out of sight, quiet descended on that section of Canarsie. Some hours later, the men who worked at the garage arrived to begin the day's work. If any of them realized that somebody had been in that garage before they had entered it, none would ever say; it was the kind of place where no one asked questions. Certainly the man who found what appeared to be a piece of some sort of U.S. Customs seal lying on the floor didn't ask what it was doing there, nor did he wonder aloud if it had any connection with the Lufthansa robbery that dominated that morning's news. Instead, and quite instinctively, he immediately flushed that piece of paper down the toilet.

———

Stax Edwards had planned to drive to New Jersey, a task he had reminded himself he was to perform as quickly as possible. But what was the rush? Tooling through Brooklyn in his fine machine, good music blaring out of the radio, and comforted by the thought of how he would spend his share of the heist money, Edwards found the impending task less and less compelling.

There were any number of distractions, the most interesting of which was the sudden memory of a lady friend who lived not too far away. Intending his arrival in the shiny black van as a surprise, Edwards pulled up before the woman's apartment house. After rousing her from sleep, he showed her the van, claiming it was his, then announced his newfound wealth. Aware that Edwards was strictly small-time, she wondered aloud how he had come into all the money he now claimed to have. Without saying anything directly, Edwards hinted broadly that he was involved in some sort of major criminal enterprise.

Edwards spent several hours in the woman's apartment, and the distractions of sex and a few snorts of cocaine soon erased from his mind the urgency of disposing of the van. Indeed, Edwards totally forgot the van as well as the fact that he had left it in a no-parking zone.

———

Officially, Jimmy Burke and Tommy DeSimone were nowhere near Brooklyn at that moment. According to the records of the Community Treatment Center (where Burke was still officially living) they had checked in at 10:00 P.M. on Sunday night, and although they had registered rather ostentatiously, it did not occur to the guard on duty to wonder why the two men had gone through so much trouble to make sure everybody remembered that event. More significantly, the record reflected only that both men had checked in at that hour; there was no system to ensure that they had *stayed* there all night.

Nevertheless, Burke and DeSimone were at the center bright and early Monday morning, and it may be a dash of retrospective imagination on the part of some who were there that morning that colored their recall that the two men had all the appearance of contented cats who had just swallowed a very fat canary. Perhaps, yet only DeSimone had real reason to feel contented. Scheduled to be finally released from the center the following day, he now faced the prospect of freedom, along with a nice pile of money to enjoy. Ever the big spender, he required little incentive to consider the number of women he could entertain with that kind of dough.

Burke was somewhat unsettled, and it had nothing to do with the fact he was not due to be released from the center until later the following month. His disquiet stemmed from the very thing that so cheered DeSimone: all that money.

For what Burke and only a few other people knew at that moment was that the early estimates of the robbery take— about $1 million, according to the first news reports—represented a woeful underestimate. His own quick count as the money was transferred from the van showed $5 million, not counting the jewels and foreign currency.

———

The fact that he had masterminded the greatest cash robbery in American history was of scant comfort. The enormity of this haul was bound to create all sorts of problems. First, the very size of the heist would unleash every cop and FBI agent around; they would turn over all the rocks in the underworld, looking for the evidence that could break the case and make the career of the man who solved it.

But there was a more serious problem for Burke: when news of the actual size of the haul got out, there was certain to be unrest among the participants. Who would remain satisfied with $30,000 or $50,000 from "the crime of the century" when there were all those millions? What would happen when Burke's gang inevitably began to demand a bigger cut?

———

For the moment, however, things were in a state of tense quiet; in their ignorance of how much they had really stolen, the members of the Burke gang spent the hours immediately after the robbery going about their lives pretty much as always.

Paolo LiCastri had taken the subway home, and in that dawn hour, when few New Yorkers are in the subway tunnels, he shared with a few uncaring winos a car that in a few hours would be packed. On adjacent tracks ran the clattering work trains that most New Yorkers never see—the ones hauling bargelike cars filled with garbage, and the others, staffed with armed guards, that collect the turnstile receipts.

While Sepe and Frank Burke went to sleep, Louis Cafora sat his considerable bulk down at a local diner and consumed a breakfast sufficient for three lumberjacks. Manri and McMahon had a couple of drinks, Manri at one point proposing a toast "to the Red Baron," Lufthansa's popular advertising symbol who had just made them temporarily wealthy.

———

Meanwhile, the object of everyone's affections, the cartons filled with money and jewels, rested like time bombs waiting to go off in a dozen different hiding places, carefully prepared rat holes known only to a handful of people.

Some days later, the distribution process began. The money was split and transferred to attaché cases and suitcases for disposition to a lengthy list of debtors. To John Gotti of the Gambino family went a payment for his services. To the man who had contrived for the van to be "stolen" went money for the services rendered. To Joey Beck went the money due from Vario on that abortive drug deal. Others received smaller rewards for assorted services that had made the heist work. One recipient was the owner of the Brooklyn auto repair shop, whose memory would remain forever blank about what had gone on in his place a few hours before he arrived for work.

But the bulk of the heist money was reserved for a vital cut—the one due Paul Vario, Sr. Various couriers had been assigned the task of moving the cash to those who were owed cuts, but no one could be trusted to move the nearly $2 million to Vario, a sum large enough to constitute an irresistible temptation. So the task was reserved for the man most loyal to Vario, perhaps the only man the aging don considered fully trustworthy.

Some weeks after the robbery, James Burke left for Florida in a car whose trunk contained neatly stacked piles of cash. He kept the car well within the speed limit as he headed west from Queens, then across the Verrazano Bridge, on to the New Jersey Turnpike, and south toward Florida.

Involuntarily, Burke checked his pocket to make sure he had enough money for the tolls.

Chapter

6

"See, bigmouth?"

Among other deficiencies, Peter Gruenwald had little interest
in the larger world around him and seldom bothered even to
listen to the radio news headlines. Thus he was surprised, upon
arriving at work just before 9:00 A.M. on December 11, 1978,
to see the Lufthansa Air Cargo parking lot littered with police
cars.

Inside, the place was swarming with grim-looking men in
business suits, their breast pockets bearing FBI badges or the
distinctive gold shields of New York City and Port Authority
police detectives.

"What is happening?" Gruenwald asked another employee.

"Jesus, haven't you heard?"

"Heard what?" responded Gruenwald with an air of genuine
befuddlement.

"This place got robbed last night; they cleaned it out."

If he had been told that six green men had landed from
Mars and were at that moment somewhere in the Lufthansa
Air Cargo terminal, Gruenwald's shock could not have been
greater. He stood rooted to the floor, as though he had been
struck by a lightning bolt. Then he went looking for Louis
Werner.

Gruenwald found him bustling around in the main cargo area, looking much more chipper than usual, with a light spring in his step. "Did you do this?" Gruenwald asked without any preliminaries.

"I'm real busy," Werner replied, not even looking his friend in the eye. "I don't have time to talk right now."

But Gruenwald was not to be put off so easily. "I asked you," he said through clenched teeth as he followed Werner on his rounds of the cargo area, "did you have something to do with making this robbery?"

"No," replied Werner, turning to face him. "Look, I got a lot to do. Let me alone." He walked away.

Infuriated, Gruenwald stalked off toward his office on an upper floor. For the next several hours he seethed as he heard the employees gossip about how the robbers got into the building, how they got the drop on everybody, how they forced Eirich to open the high val room, how they loaded a van, drove off, and got clean away. And the more Gruenwald heard, the angrier he got: the robbers had used *his* plan, the one he and Werner had tried to implement for nearly two years. How had they managed to get hold of it?

Gruenwald's puzzlement stood him in good stead during the early afternoon when it was his turn to be interviewed by a team of Port Authority detectives routinely questioning every employee in the building. No, Gruenwald told the three detectives staring at him, he knew nothing about the robbery, had no idea who might have committed it, and was asleep at home when it occurred.

Would he be willing to take a lie detector test?

"Certainly," Gruenwald replied. After all, he was telling the truth when he said he did not know anything about the robbery.

But he had his suspicions. Late that afternoon, he again waylaid Werner. "You have to talk to me, Lou," he said.

"Peter, get the fuck away from me," Werner shot back, thereby solidifying in Gruenwald's mind the thought that his old friend Louis Werner had somehow managed to arrange the robbery using the plan the two men had so carefully developed.

"I think you did it," Gruenwald accused as he followed

Werner around. "How did they get my plan, Lou? Did you give it to them? I want to know, Lou."

"I can't talk right now," Werner said, looking around to see if anyone could hear them. "There's a lot of shit going on here right now. I gotta work." He had tried to move away, but Gruenwald put a hand on Werner's arm and slowly tightened his grip.

"Lou," he said, staring into Werner's eyes with an intensity Werner had never seen before, "the police are asking a lot of questions. They are talking to everybody." He paused. "They are talking to me, Lou. What should I say to them when they ask me do I know anything about this thing?"

Werner got the point. "Okay, Peter," he said, "we'll talk. I'll come to your house and we'll talk about it. At your house, okay?" Gruenwald nodded. "And don't bug me no more here."

By the time Werner arrived at Gruenwald's house that evening, his friend, who'd had hours to contemplate what had happened at the air cargo terminal, already had a running start.

"You fucked me, Lou!" Gruenwald shouted, shaking a fist in Werner's face. "You stole my plan, you gave it to somebody else, and you cut me out!"

"Who said I was gonna cut you out?" said Werner with an air of outraged innocence. He then began a lengthy monologue on why he had decided to go it alone and how he planned to cut Gruenwald in for a healthy share—even though, he noted pointedly, he alone had arranged for a professional robbery gang, a task at which Gruenwald had failed.

Slowly, Gruenwald cooled off. "All right," he said, as a smiling Werner, drawing on his thin reserve of charm, worked hard to mollify him. "So how much money are we talking about?"

"Well," Werner said, "I figured to give you ten percent of what I got, because, you know, I took all the chances so far." Seeing Gruenwald's eyebrows suddenly arch, Werner quickly added, "But then I saw that you deserve much more than that, so I figure you should get sixty-five thousand. How's that?"

"It's okay," replied Gruenwald, most of his anger spent. "When?"

"End of the week. I'm gonna get some of it, and I'll make a down payment to you. When I get the rest, then you'll get what's yours."

Although he had been assuaged, it was not long before resentment began to fester within Gruenwald. If, as the early reports had it, the robbers grabbed somewhere around $2.5 million, $65,000 was a pretty paltry share—especially considering the haul he could have gotten if Werner had stuck to the original plan. Still, Werner was right: it was a pretty easy $65,000 to earn, considering he hadn't lifted a finger.

"Lou, we should act like always," said Gruenwald, concerned that any flamboyance would lead police right to them. He had in mind Werner's gambling mania. "We have to act normal, like nothing has happened. That way, no one is suspicious of us."

"Oh, sure," said Werner, a response Gruenwald found somewhat cavalier, as though Werner hadn't really thought about it.

———

And indeed he had not, for if there was one trait that marked Louis Werner, it was an irresistible urge to boast, an overwhelming desire to rub his success into the noses of all those doubters: here, take a look, I did it. So, on the day following the robbery, when the newspapers, television, and radio were devoting much of their attention to "the crime of the century," Werner called Bill Fischetti. "See, bigmouth?" Werner said when Fischetti answered, then hung up.

Fischetti did not need to be told who the anonymous caller was. Some days later he received another call, and this time Werner identified himself. "If you didn't have such a big fucking mouth, you'da been in on this," Werner said. He went on to twit Fischetti about how he would now be set for the rest of his life while Fischetti continued to struggle.

Fischetti was alarmed at the call—he feared a police wiretap—and tried desperately to shut Werner up. But Werner continued boasting until Fischetti hung up on him. Yet despite the boasting, Fischetti knew Werner was in the process of collecting a great deal of money for his role in the Lufthansa heist. How could Bill Fischetti get a piece of it?

Fischetti's proposal was simple. He wanted Werner to give him a loan (presumably at no interest) of $30,000 to expand his taxi company. The two men discussed the deal at the bowling alley while Werner periodically interrupted negotiations to bowl. He seemed amenable to the idea. Fischetti did not need to voice his implicit threat: if Werner rejected the deal, Fischetti had information that the police would find most interesting.

However outwardly calm Werner seemed to Fischetti's proposal, inside he was beginning to boil. The share he was to receive was beginning to shrink dramatically. First, there was the Gruenwald blackmail, and now Fischetti—albeit more subtly—was extorting his own slice. Those slices, combined with the bookie debts he had to pay, wouldn't leave too much. The final net might not be worth the aggravation of having to endure the pressure caused by the lengthening shadow of suspicion over himself. The Lufthansa security people had talked to him three times already about the robbery, two FBI agents had come snooping around, asking about his gambling habits, and the Port Authority Police were trying to get him to take a lie detector test. Clearly the authorities were becoming convinced that Louis Werner was the inside man in what was unmistakably an inside job.

To make matters worse, the circle of people who knew of Werner's role in the robbery was steadily widening. For example, Fischetti, sensing that Werner might be stalling on their deal, decided to turn the screw by telling Werner that his estranged wife, tired of late or nonexistent support checks, would call the FBI unless Werner came up with some money for her.

"You know, you got a fucking big mouth," an enraged Werner said and then announced that the $30,000 loan deal was off. That was perfectly all right with Fischetti, who now thought better of becoming further involved with a man who seemed determined to lead the police and FBI right to him. Among other things, Fischetti noted that Werner had purchased a new van, a vehicle he had always dreamed of possessing. To Fischetti's distress, Werner announced that he had paid cash for the van. When Fischetti wondered aloud about the wisdom of such a large cash purchase so soon after a major robbery in which he was a leading suspect, Werner waved it off with vague talk of how he would explain it away somehow.

It was Fischetti's turn to worry, for if Werner was arrested—as seemed imminent, given his gross stupidity—then Fischetti himself might become ensnared. Sensing Fischetti's concern, Werner sought to soothe him with a curious mixture of balm and threat, saying, "Don't worry. If you keep your mouth shut, everything will be okay. And let me tell you something: if Beverly opens her mouth, she might fall from a tenth-story window."

"Louie, don't give me your threats," Fischetti shot back. When Werner proposed a $10,000 payment to him "if you keep your mouth shut," Fischetti made it clear he'd had enough.

"I don't want any part of it," he said, walking away. "Do me a favor: don't call me. I don't want to talk to you, I don't want to associate with you."

———

Werner faced an additional worry: Frank Menna, the bookmakers' runner who had made the connection between the inside man and Burke's Robert's Lounge Gang. Obviously, it would not require much effort for Menna to deduce that the robbery, which dominated the front pages for weeks on end, was the fruit of his conversation with Martin Krugman.

"They were impressed," Krugman had told Menna after the first meeting between Manri and Werner, and Menna knew better than to press for details. The same day, Werner had told him, "It went fine," and had hinted he would "take care" of Menna if the robbery came to pass. Menna, aware of the problems a robbery of that size might cause, immediately told Werner he wanted no part of it. He found it unnecessary to add that a grateful Krugman would throw plenty of business his way, so he didn't need a cut of the Lufthansa robbery proceeds.

Nevertheless, Werner was concerned that Menna might now attempt to apply the same sort of squeeze performed by Fischetti and Gruenwald. He therefore tried to divine the runner's intentions. "See the papers?" he asked Menna one night in the bowling alley, pointing to the big headlines about the Lufthansa investigation in one newspaper. Smirking, Werner walked away.

When Menna did not rise to the bait, Werner later went to his home and hinted at his worry about "those who know."

Menna held up his hands like a traffic policeman stopping a line of cars. "I don't want to be involved," he said. "Listen, Lou, you have to leave now. I have to go bowling."

Werner left, still uncertain of Menna's intentions. At least he hadn't asked for money. But Werner had plenty of other people to worry about—his wife, Gruenwald, Fischetti, and that crew of stumblebums Gruenwald had originally recruited for the job. Any of them could pick up a phone and anonymously tell the police or FBI that Louis Werner was the man they were looking for.

Actually, such a call would have been unnecessary, for just about everybody who had a hand in the first hours of the investigation of the Lufthansa robbery was perfectly aware that Werner was the inside man.

"Inside job," announced Captain Henry I. de Geneste of the Port Authority Police. Three detectives with him nodded solemnly.

It did not, of course, take a deep understanding of police science to draw this deduction. Within twenty minutes after they arrived at the Lufthansa terminal on the morning of December 11, 1978, the police knew that the robbers' plan was based on inside information. That early deduction offered hope to de Geneste and his detectives, for the inside man was obviously a Lufthansa employee. It would be only a matter of time before the cops found him through the process of elimination. Then he would lead detectives to the people he dealt with on the outside. As for the money, undoubtedly the serial numbers had been recorded or the bills marked in some way, thus offering another avenue of attack. (The jewels were a different matter, but then, such items were seldom recovered anyway.)

De Geneste was in command of a group of Port Authority uniformed cops, detectives, and crime laboratory technicians. The technicians were busily dusting the high val room for fingerprints as the detectives set about interviewing Lufthansa employees while their memories were still fresh. The Port Authority cops had arrived within minutes of the call from Lufthansa and sealed the airport—a relatively simple task, since the airport has only four exits—but de Geneste assumed, correctly, that the robbers had already made good their escape.

The initial comments of the employees, some of whom were severely shaken, gave de Geneste a broad outline of what appeared to be a fairly simple robbery. Their stories also told de Geneste that the robbery had been carried out by professionals—who obviously had been equipped with very detailed inside information.

In those first moments of what would become a very lengthy investigation, the police had some cause for optimism. True, the robbers had made a clean getaway, but they had made a serious mistake: at least two of them were not wearing ski masks when they encountered two Lufthansa employees. So Kerry Whalen, the employee who had been pistol-whipped, was already giving details to a police artist even as he was having eight stitches placed in his head wound. Rolf Rebmann, the other Lufthansa employee who had seen a maskless robber, was also helping the police artist to sketch the face of the man he would never forget.

Things were moving along nicely, de Geneste concluded. Upstairs, several Lufthansa Cargo executives, looking like men who had just been run over by a truck, tried to calculate the size of the loss. At the same time, they were fielding excited transatlantic telephone calls from their superiors in Germany, who were reacting to the first news flashes.

"My God, you lost millions!" shouted one German executive accusingly, as though his subordinate in America had personally taken the money and left it on a bus.

It was from the upstairs executive offices that de Geneste and his detectives received news that severely rattled their early optimism. First, there was the question of just how much money had been stolen. Initially, Lufthansa believed that something on the order of $1 million in cash had been taken, along with about $800,000 in jewels and raw gold—a hefty enough loss, to be sure. But then, in double-checking the paperwork, the Lufthansa executives made an unsettling discovery. In fact, they reported, a very large shipment of cash had been delayed at the terminal the previous Friday and was stored temporarily in the high val room pending pickup on Monday morning. How much? About $4 million.

There was worse news to come. The packages containing the American money represented cash spent by American tourists in Europe, turned into German banks for exchange, and then shipped to this country as part of a standard interbank exchange of currencies. In other words, the money was in relatively small bills, the largest of which were one hundreds. And none of the serial numbers of the bills had been recorded, nor was the money marked in any way. De Geneste could almost hear the stomachs of the detectives drop into their shoes: the money was absolutely untraceable.

This was followed by the news that the crime lab technicians had found no fingerprints, tire marks, or other such clues. Now things began to look very bleak. The police had run into a depressing collection of investigative roadblocks, mitigated only by the possibility of identifying the two robbers who had taken off their masks—and one other interesting tidbit. The tidbit involved the large shipment of cash that had been delayed at the terminal on Friday. The story was complicated, but it centered on the fact that an operations supervisor had tried unsuccessfully to get the shipment cleared for pickup by an armored car. But the previous week, another cash shipment had turned up $2,000 short, whereupon Lufthansa security had ordered stringent new requirements for such shipments, including the presence of security agents before the money could be released. The operations supervisor could not locate any security personnel—or so he said—and the money was held at the terminal when the armored car driver had to leave for another pickup. He was scheduled to return to Lufthansa on Monday morning.

That operations supervisor was Louis Werner.

––––

"What's up?" said FBI agent Walter Yoos as he walked into the terminal and spotted de Geneste.

"Oh, just a little holdup," said de Geneste brightly. "They got a few dollars—about five million dollars' worth."

"Wow," Yoos said, an unusual reaction for a man who

customarily remained calm, no matter what the circumstances. A veteran agent, Yoos ran a small FBI office at the airport, where he spent much of his time working on skyjackings and attempted bombings. He had become good friends with de Geneste during his tour of duty, and the Port Authority cops often marveled at how unruffled Yoos remained through every crisis, including confrontations with armed skyjackers. But even Yoos was impressed by the sheer dimension of the robbery at the Lufthansa terminal. After a quick look around, he called his supervisor.

As protocol required, de Geneste had notified the FBI and other law-enforcement agencies of what had transpired at Lufthansa, and soon the terminal became a mob scene. Agents and detectives from seven different federal, state, and local law-enforcement agencies swarmed over the terminal. They were followed by television camera crews, news reporters, and photographers, creating a circuslike atmosphere. Drawn by the immensity of the crime, some FBI and police superstars arrived. De Geneste recognized Lieutenant Thomas Ahearn, commander of the detective squad of the 113th Precinct, the New York City Police jurisdiction that included Kennedy Airport; FBI Supervisor Stephen Carbone, who directed Bureau investigations of crimes at the airport; Lieutenant Remo Franceschini, head of the Queens district attorney's detective squad; and Franceschini's boss, District Attorney John Santucci.

They all made the requisite obeisance to de Geneste, who gave them a quick briefing on the dimensions of the crime and where matters stood at that point. De Geneste noted with some amusement that these field generals listened politely, then immediately began barking out orders to their accompanying phalanxes of detectives and agents, jockeying for position, seeking to dominate for their respective organizations the central role in the investigation. This was a very big crime that was spawning nationwide headlines, and its solution could not only make the career of the man who solved it but also bring resounding credit to whichever agency broke the case. Like basketball players fighting for position under the basket, the seven agencies were elbowing each other, each one hoping to solve "the crime of the century."

And in many ways, as would be clear later on, that little drama would be almost as interesting as the crime itself.

Louis Werner did not recognize any of the men who swarmed all over the Lufthansa terminal that morning, and he had no idea that they would shortly change the course of his life. Werner couldn't have cared less about their identities; what mattered to him was the sour expressions on their faces, a certain indication that they did not like what they saw.

To his glee, Werner heard the toll of the theft mount. Like an investor watching a ticker tape certify the escalation in value of his hot stock, Werner saw his 10 percent cut becoming more valuable by the moment. When it became clear that the robbery's total take would be $5 million in cash alone, Werner felt, for the first occasion in what seemed a long time, some real breathing room. Even after paying Gruenwald and the bookies, he would have plenty left over.

To be sure, Werner would not get the money all at once. In scenes straight out of a spy novel, he received instructions from Manri on how he was to begin receiving his cut. There was one instruction to go to a certain phone booth near La Guardia Airport, some miles north of Kennedy. In the booth, Werner found a key that opened a locker at the La Guardia main passenger terminal. The locker contained several thousand dollars in small bills. In another scene out of John le Carré, Werner was told to take a large suitcase to a rendezvous. Following instructions, he picked up a smaller suitcase, put it inside the larger one, and walked away. Inside the smaller case was another payment of several thousand dollars.

"We gotta launder the money first," Manri told Werner by way of explaining the reason for these elaborate rituals and for giving him his cut in dribs and drabs. Werner quietly accepted the explanation. After all, he was in no position to argue.

"Launder the money?" Gruenwald exploded when Werner handed over the relatively paltry sum of $1,500 as a down payment on his $65,000 payoff. "Lou, that is crazy; they don't have to launder the money, because it is all in small bills. Only big bills are marked. So what are they talking about? Lou, they are trying to fuck you."

"Come on, Peter," Werner replied, waving his hands. "They're not trying to fuck me, believe me. That's just the way these things have to be done." In tones that suggested he knew all there was to know on the subject, Werner then expounded at some length to Gruenwald on the art of laundering ill-gotten gains, claiming that the vast amount of money taken in the heist required careful handling in small amounts among various sources so as not to attract undue attention.

Gruenwald was only mildly impressed with this exposition, for the talk about caution struck him as a stalling tactic. With all that cash, what would prevent the robbers from simply forking over all of Werner's cut at once? Why all the mumbo jumbo—unless the thieves intended to deprive Werner (and, by extension, Gruenwald) of his rightful share?

Werner felt no such concern. By Christmas of 1978, he had received about $80,000 toward his total cut, sufficient compensation—momentarily, at least—for the darkening shadow of suspicion that clouded his employment at Lufthansa Air Cargo. Everybody in the building seemed to assume that he was the inside man. Notable among them were the Lufthansa security people, who were most curious about Werner's actions on the Friday preceding the robbery, when the big shipment was held up at the terminal. Not a man to appreciate irony, Werner seethed as the security people plowed and replowed that furrow. He alone knew that the chief piece of circumstantial evidence linking him to the heist at that point was pure coincidence. In point of fact, he had *not* deliberately held up that shipment, nor did he have anything to do with the missing $2,000 that had caused the delay in the first place.

Irony piled atop irony. Werner was now the chief suspect, not because of the two years he and Gruenwald had invested in scheming to rob their employer, not because he had provided the vital inside information to the heist crew, but because of an incident that was the result of pure chance. And it was that incident which provided the bulk of the cash proceeds and made the robbery the most successful ever.

Despite his inner turmoil, Werner tried to maintain a stoical facade to the persistent inquiries of his employer and two young-looking FBI agents. Werner observed their unsettling elaborate politeness. They often apologized for having to bother him again; however, there was this minor . . . *discrepancy*. Could he help them clear it up? Or there appeared to be a . . . *small detail*. Was it possible that he had forgotten something?

"I wish I could help," Werner answered persistently, "but I really don't know anything about it." His ability to maintain this facade was aided by a vision of the future, in which the newly flush Werner, having collected his entire 10 percent, would leave Lufthansa and begin anew someplace else. Where exactly was somewhat vague in his mind, but with the kind of money he was about to collect, Louis Werner was convinced he could do just about anything he wanted.

He never considered the possibility of an arrest, for Werner was certain no evidence existed that would conclusively link him to the heist. True, his questioners were suspicious of him because he had delayed shipment of the cash, but that was no proof of anything. Likewise, the questions about an earlier $22,000 robbery, which, they hinted, he was suspected of having commited; no proof existed there either. Indeed, as far as Werner could see, he had gotten away with it.

This conviction that however dark the suspicions, nothing would ever coalesce into proof allowed Werner to enjoy a calmness that was in some contrast with his normally tense personality. He cheerily paid off his debt to Martin Krugman, whose deadpan expression concealed his awareness of the most delicious irony of all: Werner was paying off with monies collected from a robbery that had been arranged to pay that very debt. Next Werner made an even more satisfying financial transaction: he paid $10,000 in cash for his dream van. He insisted on every possible option, including carpets and a state-of-the-art stereo system. Into this mobile living room he packed himself, girlfriend Janet Barbieri, and two of her children for a Christmas vacation in Florida.

"Nothin' to worry about," Werner told Gruenwald confidently as he handed over another payment, bringing to $10,000 the total paid to Gruenwald thus far. The steadily accumulating cash in his account somewhat assuaged Gruenwald's earlier fear that the robbery gang had cheated Werner, but he was still worried about his friend's flamboyance, especially his purchase of that flashy van.

"No sweat," said Werner, waving aside his friend's concern. "So I bought a van, so what? I won some nice bets; prove otherwise. They ain't got nothin' and they won't have nothin' as long as everybody's cool, right? Right. Everything's fine, so long as everybody keeps their mouths shut. I don't know anything, and you don't know anything, right, Peter?"

"Sure, Lou," Gruenwald answered halfheartedly, still not entirely convinced that the kind of flamboyance Werner was demonstrating in the face of all that suspicion was the wisest strategy. What would he do if the suspicion shifted to the suspect's best friend?

Lost in that thought, he hardly heard Werner promise to bring him back some oranges.

———

"So what about this guy?" Jimmy Burke said to Manri outside Robert's Lounge as an early snowstorm coated the street and sidewalk.

"Seems okay," Manri replied laconically. "I ain't had no trouble."

Burke pondered this evaluation momentarily, for the question of Louis Werner's reliability was paramount. As the leading suspect for inside man, Werner would feel a great deal of law-enforcement pressure. Could he withstand that pressure even under threat of jail? Werner was the sole link between Burke's crew and the Lufthansa robbery, and if he ever talked, he would lead the cops and the FBI right to Manri. And after that . . .

This was no idle speculation, for Burke was perfectly aware of the intellectual limitations of his crew. Given their other handicaps, including the kind of police records that made them vulnerable to pressure, there was a strong possibility that they might not be able to withstand the intense heat generated by the very size of the Lufthansa robbery. As Burke was aware, every cop and FBI agent in the city was poring over the files, planning to target anyone with a record as an armed robber—and anybody who had ever been involved in a crime at Kennedy Airport. They would come after the Robert's Lounge Gang, Burke knew, "rousting" them, as the police termed it, calling the members in individually for cozy conversations in detective squad rooms. Those favored with invitations would be subjected to a mixture of cajolery and threats. We know you did it, the cops would say, pretending they were prepared to prove a lot more than they actually could. Those who claimed not to know what the detectives were talking about would be informed of the dire consequences that awaited them. A man with your record, the cops would tell a recalcitrant interviewee darkly, can expect no mercy from a sentencing judge. Of course, if you cooperate . . .

An old hand at this game, Burke understood that all members of the Robert's Lounge Gang were susceptible in varying degrees. Worse, a flickering resentment had arisen in the gang; news of the actual amount of the heist had set off grumbling about the size of their gains contrasted with the grand total. And implicit in every resentful grumble was the possibility that any man who failed to receive satisfaction could always wreak revenge by having a conversation with a most receptive FBI agent or police detective.

Burke hoped that his reputation would forestall any such possibility. As backstop, he offered a less menacing inducement to silence: how they could make their money grow. The question of who got what out of the robbery was not the important question, Burke often lectured them. What really mattered was the kind of profits the heist proceeds could generate later. It was simple criminal capitalism: $10,000 in heist money, put back on the street in the form of investment in loan-sharking operations, might return anywhere from 500 to 1,000 percent profit. Similarly, investments in narcotics or bookmaking operations or a dozen other illegal possibilities would guarantee quick and sizable profits, which could then be channeled into other enterprises.

For those who did not quite grasp this kind of capitalist theory, Burke had a perfect working example at hand—the promising enterprise of fixing basketball games.

———

Four days after the December 11 robbery, Henry Hill flew to Boston to revive, refine, and otherwise direct the Boston College scheme. Burke was unhappy about the result of the first game, in which he and several bookmakers had lost a small pile of cash. Armed with $5,000 from Burke, Hill was to provide on-the-spot encouragement for the crooked players to shave points.

The immediate focus of Hill's attention was the next night's game between Boston College and Harvard. Favored to win by a lopsided thirteen points, Boston College was playing at home against an inferior opponent. The smart money around the country was on Boston College to win by a huge margin and easily exceed the anticipated point spread.

But Burke was betting the other way—that Boston College would win by a much *smaller* margin. Bookmakers around the nation happily took what appeared to be sucker bets: no way could Harvard stay that close to a nationally ranked team.

They were as surprised as most of the fans when Harvard not only stayed close but threatened to win the game, finally losing by only three points. Among the preppies who were urging the Harvard team on sat the distinctly non-prep Henry Hill, who cheered himself nearly hoarse. (Possibly, he was the only Harvard fan with a Brooklyn accent there that night.)

Hill had good reason to cheer. Burke would tell him later, "I got down real good," meaning that his bets had paid off, earning somewhere around $150,000 in profit, while Hill earned a somewhat smaller—but nevertheless impressive—amount. As often happened in such enterprises, the actual perpetrators wound up with a relatively small slice of the haul.

Hill went to the Boston College locker room after the game. He met Rick Kuhn outside and handed him $3,000. James Sweeney, Kuhn's increasingly reluctant partner in the point-shaving scheme, later received $500 of that amount. (Some days afterward, Kuhn received in the mail a token of Mazzei's and Hill's appreciation—a new camera filled with cocaine.)

Although Burke intended the scheme to serve as something of an object lesson on the necessity of putting money to work, he also provided insight into the vagaries that can bedevil criminal capitalism. In the case of basketball game-fixing, he discovered that although he stood to win on any one game, he also faced some risk of loss in what was fundamentally a risky operation.

That part of the lesson was driven home some weeks after the commencement of the fixing scheme. The occasion was a game between Boston College and Holy Cross, a contest of some interest to Hill and Burke, since it was to be nationally televised and would attract strong betting interest. Both men decided to bet heavily and Hill, in a talk with Kuhn, laid down the rules; Kuhn would make sure that Boston College did not win the anticipated point spread.

By coincidence, on the day of the game Hill was at Burke's home helping his mentor install brick on a kitchen wall. (Apparently, Burke had discovered an area of the house which did not contain brick, and had set about to rectify that oversight.) Before setting to work, both men got busy on the telephone, carefully spreading their bets. Hill invested $15,000, while Burke bet just over $50,000.

Curious to see how their investment was doing, they turned on Burke's television toward the end of the game. Hill wished they hadn't. To Burke's mounting fury, the Boston College team was racing up and down the gym floor, literally running away with the game.

"*What the fuck is this shit?*" Burke roared. Hill noticed the unmistakable signs of an approaching explosion of the Burke temper.

"Jesus, I told them—" Hill began, but his explanation was cut short when Burke delivered a resounding kick to the television.

"That's it, no more with these goddam kids!" Burke shouted, as Hill hoped he would not vent his fury on less inanimate objects. "I'm finished! I don't want to hear about these fucking kids anymore!"

"Okay, Jimmy," Hill said, hurriedly making his exit, hoping that Burke would not hold him responsible for the failure.

In fact, Burke did feel that Hill was to blame. But in the larger scheme of things, his temper rapidly cooled, for he had already found a number of better ways to convert his $1 million slice of the Lufthansa haul into profit-making enterprises. There was that deal in Florida with Vario, for instance: a mob-owned resort club was looking for new buyers willing to put up a modest amount of cash and pick up the place for nearly a song. And that other deal involving a $250,000 outlay for high-grade cocaine that could be peddled for profits up to fifty times that.

Yet, all of it hinged on the necessity for his crew to keep their heads straight and do exactly what he told them. Evidence was accumulating that they had paid scant attention to Burke's warnings. He'd heard reports of money being spent wildly, boasts to girlfriends, and general loose talk, all followed by hints directed Burke's way that it did not make much sense for them to have taken all that risk for so little return. The indications were unmistakable: unless Burke took action, it would all come apart.

"Things are gonna hafta tighten up," Vario informed Burke. The *caporegime* of few words had summarized the situation succinctly. The FBI and police hounds were drawing nearer. It was time to take steps to make certain there were no loose ends for them to grab.

PART
THREE
COPS AND
ROBBERS

Chapter

7

"Don't worry; everything's under control"

The city park runs like a narrow ribbon along the lower Manhattan shorefront not too far from the waterfront complex made famous by the Marlon Brando movie *On the Waterfront*. The kind of hulking hood so memorably portrayed by Brando was still very much an extant species in New York in the winter of 1978, but the breed was growing rarer; the area, increasingly, was becoming dominated by young, upwardly mobile professionals who were dramatically changing the character of the waterfront communities.

The change could be seen in that narrow park. Once a favorite gathering place for older immigrants who would stroll slowly along the shore as they watched the parade of ships sailing into New York Harbor, the park was now marked by the platoons of young and middle-aged runners in bright jogging suits.

For a large proportion of them, cardiovascular fitness was very much a fair-weather proposition, and the number of runners dropped dramatically as the cold winter arrived. The more dedicated ones, including several who were preparing for the ordeal of the New York City Marathon the following October, were still out there running despite the frigid winds off the bay, the cold, the snow, and the ice.

Few of them, however, ran at night, when the temperature during a cold New York winter often drops to unbearable levels. But among those who did was a man whose devotion to long-distance running made him the subject of some comment among his neighbors. What, some of them wondered, would possess a man to put in a long workday, arrive home, and then immediately go outside to run several miles in that abominable weather?

———

For those who asked, Stephen Carbone offered a somewhat mystical explanation: long-distance running was the ultimate test of a man's fortitude and discipline; the marathon was the goal to which all runners aspired, the standard by which they could measure themselves; runners dream of good times in the marathon, achievements that marked the culminatiin of a necessary drive for excellence; a man's reach should exceed his grasp.

And so on, until the questioner's eyes glazed over. Those who knew Carbone better realized that long-distance running was very much in keeping with his character, for he was a man marked by a certain singleness of purpose. If a brick wall could not be outflanked or climbed, they knew, Carbone was certain to try smashing through it with his head.

———

Thus they were not surprised to learn that in the bitter-cold weeks of December 1978, Carbone each night would bundle up in an outfit that made him look like something of the main character in the *Rocky* movie and head out to pound the pavement, patiently putting in his five or ten miles. His announced goal was to run the next twenty-six-mile New York City Marathon in under four hours (the professionals ran it consistently in about two and a half hours), and as he made clear, he was determined to do it.

But Carbone also used his nightly practice runs for another purpose. Like many long-distance runners, he found that the so-called runner's high helped him think through a problem. Free of the normal distractions, he could concentrate his mental energies on devising solutions, aided by the extra flow of blood and oxygen to the brain, which many runners insist is the prime benefit of the sport.

A man of medium height with salt-and-pepper hair that betrayed his middle age, Carbone had the build of an athlete. With his somewhat dark complexion, he looked like an ambitious middleweight boxer, especially when bundled up in his running clothes during the winter. He also looked mean: his penetrating gaze suggested rampant aggressiveness.

Actually, it was a more accurate reflection of his intensity, a trait underscored by his stubborn pursuit of better running times as he prepared himself that December for the marathon. How he managed to find the time to run was something of a mystery, for Carbone's job was taking up the bulk of his waking hours at that point. It was also preoccupying his thoughts as he ran, for he had been confronted in his job—as supervisor for the Federal Bureau of Investigation—with a very large problem.

Who robbed Lufthansa Air Cargo?

———

"Steve, you better come over here and take a look at this."

Carbone needed no prompting that morning of December 11, 1978, on what FBI Special Agent Walter Yoos, calling from Kennedy Airport, meant by "this." The news was dominated by somewhat breathless accounts of what had happened at Lufthansa Air Cargo some hours before, and Carbone listened with mounting interest as Yoos outlined some preliminary details.

"International shipment," Carbone said at one point in the conversation, repeating an important piece of information Yoos had mentioned—important because it immediately established clear FBI jurisdiction: theft from international shipments is covered by a series of specific federal laws.

"Well, we better get rolling on this," Carbone said, concluding the conversation. At his end of the line, Yoos heard a pronounced increase in the tempo of Carbone's speech, an unmistakable clue that he was impatient to get started.

And, as Yoos noted to himself with a slight smile, with Carbone involved, things were bound to get very interesting.

The call from Yoos had arrived at Carbone's office, part of an FBI complex that occupied one floor of a modern office building in the Queens community of Rego Park, just a few miles northwest of Kennedy Airport. Known formally as the Brooklyn-Queens Metropolitan Resident Agency of the Federal Bureau of Investigation, it served as a satellite of the Bureau's New York office, the largest in the country, and helped handle the considerable action in those two city boroughs—which, together, are more populous than most U.S. cities.

Like most of the FBI men who worked there, Carbone called the place simply "the Queens office," to avoid having to repeat its rattlingly long formal title and to distinguish it from a number of other FBI satellites in the New York area, including two others farther east on Long Island and the small FBI branch office at the airport.

The sprawling Queens office served as headquarters for a number of units that handled assorted investigations involving violations of federal law. Carbone headed a unit known as BQ5; among other things, it investigated thefts of interstate shipments from Kennedy Airport.

———

Like the half-dozen other FBI men in BQ5, Carbone knew of James Burke and the Robert's Lounge Gang. He did not, however, immediately suspect that they were responsible for the Lufthansa heist. In fact, a number of other possibilities came to his mind during his first visit to the terminal.

For one thing, the robbery was well planned and executed; it therefore seemed unlikely that a notoriously lunkheaded crew like the Robert's Lounge group would have been entrusted with a task that required such professionalism. For another, it was entirely possible that the robbery was a political act. West Germany was plagued by left-wing terrorism; perhaps the heist was the work of a terrorist squad. Moreover, there was at least the reasonable probability that the crime was the work of an an out-of-state professional crew imported by organized crime.

Which of these possibilities might turn out to be true was of small consequence to Carbone. Energized, like most of his fellow supervisors, by the prospect of working on a big case, he was intent only on sinking his teeth into what promised to be the biggest case of his career. Simply put, he wanted it.

———

At certain moments Lee F. Laster, Chief of the Queens office, reminded himself as he listened to Carbone brief him about the Lufthansa robbery, operating out of the Queens office was like working in the middle of a major highway intersection.

Laster had no sooner taken up his post in the summer of 1978 when he was hit with a rush of major cases. First, there was a major political corruption case in the suburban county of Suffolk, farther east on Long Island, followed by the beginning of the ABSCAM investigation (a case that had begun on Long Island). And then, just as the rush seemed to subside slightly, the "crime of the century" took place at Lufthansa.

Laster's arrival in Queens represented something of a culture shock. He had been assigned there after two years in the FBI's Honolulu office, a relatively quiet outpost (where, Laster discovered to his astonishment one day, television news devoted a full ten minutes to a relatively innocuous statement he made about a pending wiretap bill in the state legislature). Things were certainly different in New York: a faster pace, much more crime, and a generally unsettled atmosphere surrounding a city that pridefully demonstrated its ability to function in what many outsiders perceived as a gigantic free-floating circus.

As Laster observed, even the FBI agents who worked in the city seemed to be affected by the New York atmosphere. Because of the heavy caseload, they tended to work harder than most agents elsewhere, and in the process often acquired several New York characteristics: faster speech, sharpened cynicism, and a certain casualness of dress. It was this last point that struck Laster with some force as he reviewed the troops at his new post.

A veteran of sixteen years in the Bureau by the time of his assignment to the Queens office, Laster was an FBI traditionalist. A tall, broad-shouldered man who always dressed impeccably in conservative banker's suits, he walked with an erect military bearing and spoke, at least publicly, in an approved

FBI-speak that made him sound like a Chamber of Commerce president. He was, in fact, the very personification of the classic lantern-jawed agent of FBI legend, the mythical figure of quiet omniscience whose image the FBI had successfully promoted to the public.

It was not surprising, then, that Laster was plainly taken aback by what he first saw in the Queens office. As he noted to a friend after taking his new job, "You should see how some of them [the agents] dress. They're wearing *dungarees*." Nevertheless, Laster had a reputation for solid, sensible management, and he soon overcame his initial shock and began to concentrate on the more immediate question of just how good his agents were.

They were very good, as it turned out, and among them was a man who made a particularly strong impression on Laster—a supervisor named Steve Carbone.

———

That Laster recognized Carbone's abilities was a tribute to his perceptiveness, for although they shared common careers, there was a vast difference between the two men.

If Laster looked like the typical FBI agent, Carbone did not seem to be. He was unmistakably Italian, whose college degrees had not entirely erased the accent of his native Brooklyn, an accent that deepened when he became agitated or excited. At such times, he also gave away his ethnic background by underscoring his words with hand gestures and body English.

In an important sense, Laster and Carbone represented opposite ends of a quiet revolution then under way within the FBI. Laster, to a large extent, represented the "old" FBI, while Carbone symbolized what many within the Bureau had taken to calling the "new" FBI. Carbone had joined in 1967 during the FBI's first major attempt to broaden the ethnic base of its agents and as such, was that rarity in the Bureau, a native Brooklynite. But the significance of Carbone and his contemporaries also tended to have more street smarts than older agents, and they seemed less interested in becoming the kind of unhesitatingly obedient organization men the Bureau had preferred to develop for so many years.

Laster recognized that the change was all to the good; a new kind of agent was required for the FBI's shift away from its traditional reliance on such crimes as bank robberies and toward combating organized crime. That put a premium on undercover operations and much more work down on the street, hardly the place for a man in a conservative business suit and wingtip shoes, the classic FBI uniform for decades.

———

Possibly it was the matter of dress that first drew Laster's attention to Carbone. He was struck by the bold colors of Carbone's shirts, a sartorial habit that puzzled him. Laster soon moved beyond that, however, to a consideration of Carbone's professional abilities. A soft-spoken native Arkansan who chose his words carefully, Laster was now dealing with the type most puzzling to non-New Yorkers: a New Yorker who talked at a dazzling speed, radiated an eagerness just this side of aggressiveness, and often seemed to be straining at some invisible leash with a restless eagerness to get going.

But Laster was also impressed. Carbone had an uncommonly quick mind, seemed to know his job cold, and demonstrated an innovative flair for criminal investigation. Well liked by the agents who worked for him, Carbone had an earthy sense of humor—unusual in FBI agents—and a native shrewdness.

In short, as Laster quickly decided, Carbone was the perfect man to head the FBI's investigation of the Lufthansa robbery.

———

Criminal investigation has always been a field of somewhat indefinite requisites. Principally, that is because the profession is at once an art and a science. The work requires attention to detail (a photographic memory helps), doggedness, quickness of mind, and infinite patience. A good dose of street smarts or native common sense is also immensely valuable, along with an intense liking for the job. Carbone had a real affinity for that business. "I like to catch criminals," he would say with a characteristically disarming shrug when asked why he had decided to become an FBI agent.

As with other men who have serendipitously discovered professional fulfillment in criminal investigation, Carbone had arrived at that point in a somewhat roundabout way. Originally a schoolteacher, he attended graduate school at night and

131

joined the FBI in 1967. There followed three years in various assignments outside New York. To his delight, he was assigned to his hometown in 1970, and after eight years—an unusually lengthy stay in one spot—won promotion to supervisor.

During his first three years in the Bureau, Carbone was offered foreign language training. A man noted for his pursuit of the apparently unattainable, Carbone chose Chinese, an intimidating language whose difficulty made it a rare choice among agents. However, those who knew Carbone, although unfailingly struck by the sight of him speaking Cantonese Chinese (in what to native Chinese must have seemed a very strange accent), realized that it was a characteristic choice. Even his after-work relaxations—golf and long-distance running—reflected his curious preference for the difficult.

———

Certainly, the Lufthansa investigation threatened to be difficult, a prospect only partially connected with the circumstances of the crime itself. The real problem was the profusion of law-enforcement attention, with at least seven agencies involved in the investigation. That meant there would be problems of overlap and the kind of tensions that can completely ensnarl an investigation.

In an attempt to forestall any problems, Laster visited the chief nonfederal law-enforcement officer in that area, Queens District Attorney John Santucci, to attempt to work out a *modus vivendi* that would prevent local and federal investigators from getting in one another's hair.

The meeting was a disaster. To Laster's dismay, Santucci proposed that they create a task force of local police and FBI agents. It would be headquartered in Santucci's office, the implication being that Santucci would be the czar of the entire Lufthansa investigation.

"There is no way that is going to happen," Laster replied, evenly. He was further appalled when he heard Santucci outline what appeared to be a rather elaborate campaign to gather extensive media publicity on virtually all phases of the investigation. Like most FBI agents, Laster kept an arm's-length relationship with the press, and although he was aware that Santucci was a notorious publicity hound—a not uncommon trait among district attorneys who have to face elections every four years—there grew in Laster's mind the frightening possibility that with Santucci in charge, the FBI would have to conduct an investigation under the glare of television cameras.

"The man is a hot dog," Laster announced after he returned to his office following the meeting with Santucci. Laster had decided that there would be a task force, all right—located not in Santucci's office, but in the FBI's. Furthermore, he decreed in a subsequent meeting of all the agencies involved, each agency would share the fruits of its investigation with the others to prevent duplication. However, Laster noted, there would be two exceptions: (1) each agency would keep the names of its informants secret from the other agencies, and (2) each agency would follow up leads received from its informants without telling the others.

To police officials who attended the meeting, Laster's ground rules seemed odd. They understood the necessity for guarding the identities of informants, but why would information on leads not be shared?

Laster did not tell them that Carbone and his agents had already taken a dramatic early lead in the investigation, a secret Laster wanted to protect at all costs. But in doing so, he sowed the seeds of a very serious problem.

———

In the beginning, at least, matters were running true to form. As Carbone observed, the inevitable flood of tipsters would come, the dreaded walk-ins who plague FBI offices all over the country. Like worms emerging from their holes after a heavy rain, they surface after major crimes, eager to tell the FBI of the "real story."

They range from conventional underworld informants, seeking to curry favor by providing "inside stuff," to outright kooks, including people with steel plates in their heads through which they claim to receive radio signals conveying orders from the CIA. The Lufthansa case, because of its notoriety, attracted more walk-ins than most. Some—such as the self-proclaimed psychic who insisted he'd had a vision of the place where the robbery money was buried—could be dismissed out of hand, but others required exhaustive checking. Into this category fell those informants who claimed that the robbery had been carried out by the KGB, Cuban exiles, the Baader-

Meinhof terrorist gang in Germany, or any one of a wide range of other suspects.

And yet, just forty-eight hours after the robbery, the FBI spoke with one informant whose report had the unmistakable ring of truth, like the distinct ping of genuine crystal when struck.

That unmistakable ping was there, Carbone decided as he leaned back in his office chair, listening to one of his agents, Lewis Schiliro. But as he absorbed the details passed on to Schiliro by one of his best and most reliable underworld informants, there remained a nagging doubt. According to the informant, Schiliro reported, Jimmy Burke had masterminded the robbery, using inside information provided by a Lufthansa Air Cargo employee. The informant—whom we'll call Mr. X here—also claimed that the actual robbery was carried out by the Robert's Lounge Gang. Frankie Burke was there, along with Tommy DeSimone and Angelo Sepe, among others.

"That gang of mutts?" said Carbone skeptically. Still, as he had often lectured his own agents: assume nothing, check everything.

Carbone and agent Wayne Orrell went to the Lufthansa terminal armed with six pictures. One picture was of Angelo Sepe, and it was that one Kerry Whalen—the transfer man who had been struck on the head by an unmasked robber— lingered over. Whalen could not be positive, but he thought that might be the robber. It certainly looked like the artist's sketch that Whalen had just approved as the most accurate likeness of his attacker. Rolf Rebmann, the other Lufthansa employee who had seen an unmasked robber, also could not be positive, but the picture of Tommy DeSimone looked much like the man he had seen.

"Well, so now we know————wasn't kidding," Carbone said. "And where Sepe and DeSimone go . . ."

It was unnecessary to finish the sentence, for any FBI agent familiar with Robert's Lounge Gang knew that if Sepe and DeSimone were involved in a robbery—especially one on the scale of Lufthansa—then James Burke had sent them there.

There was other interesting news from Mr. X, including the item that one of Burke's associates, a man named Henry Hill, was probably involved with the robbery. The informant dropped a few more names, all of them from the roster of the Robert's Lounge crowd.

Through it all, as the pieces seemed to fit together, there still remained the nagging question: why would Burke, no fool, use the Robert's Lounge Gang for a multimillion dollar robbery?

———

Things had begun, Carbone noted, on a decidedly mixed note. Thanks to Mr. X, the FBI was on its way to learning the identities of the robbers. That, combined with the growing certainty that a Lufthansa employee named Louis Werner, assisted by his friend Peter Gruenwald, was the inside man, already amounted to very solid leads. But there was no physical evidence or conclusive eyewitness testimony.

"All we have to do is prove it," Carbone announced, a wry joke that underscored the small mountain of work still to be done before the FBI was anywhere near getting enough for an indictment, much less a conviction, of anybody. Nevertheless, judged overall, there was some promise.

Werner and Gruenwald, the subjects of increasingly testy interviews by FBI agents, seemed to offer the best leads. They continued to blandly deny any knowledge of the robbery, even after the agents pointed out the dramatic influx of cash both men suddenly enjoyed. Given the men's lackluster reputation as gamblers, the agents could be forgiven for laughing outright when told that the newfound wealth—including Gruenwald's sudden ability to pay off his credit card debts in one swoop—was the result of shrewd bets. Werner did not seem able to remember the name of the bookmaker involved in this extraordinary turn of fortune, another cause of merriment among the FBI men. What gambler, after making a big enough score to pay $10,000 in cash for a van, wouldn't remember the name of the bookmaker who paid him all that money?

Martin Krugman, who was ostensibly Werner's bookie, demonstrated an equally astounding lack of memory when questioned about his client. No, he just couldn't recall much of anything, but he'd certainly think about it, and he'd call the FBI if and when he remembered something. And Henry Hill, identified by Mr. X as a participant in the Lufthansa heist and a member of a gun-running operation, was the subject of the

FBI's first direct move. Armed with a search warrant, agents rummaged through his house on Long Island. They found no guns, and Hill professed to be mystified by talk of such matters as armed robbery.

Hovering over all of this, of course, was the larger question of what happened to all that Lufthansa money. True, the money was unmarked and unrecorded, but Burke and his gang couldn't be sure of that. Certainly, they considered the possibility that the money was in fact marked and that any report to the contrary amounted to disinformation designed to make them spend the money and thus lead the police and FBI right to them. So in theory, at least, it was possible that the heist money had not been circulated; it could have been stashed away, pending proper laundering and a lifting of the heat. In this connection, an old FBI rule of thumb says that stolen money has to be "sat on" (kept hidden) in the ratio of one year for each million dollars stolen. There is a corollary, however: nobody ever manages to do it.

In this early flush of reasonable, if slightly tainted, optimism, some FBI agents noted with amusement the gradual transformation in Supervisor Stephen Carbone. According to FBI protocol, supervisors are supposed to be largely desk men, handling the Bureau's incessant paperwork while overseeing the agents assigned to a particular investigation. Carbone, however, was notorious for being unable to contain himself permanently behind any desk; very much the street agent, he liked to be where the action was.

To those who had worked with Carbone before, the evolution was a familiar one: as an investigation proceeded, he grew increasingly agitated. The other side of Carbone's personality began to emerge; beneath that generally amiable exterior was a man of ruthless determination.

"Steve often doesn't know the difference between agent and supervisor," Laster noted at one point, more as a bemused observation than censure. He was quite right, for major criminal investigations seemed nearly to consume Carbone.

Carbone's wife Clara was well aware of her husband's tendency to overwork, and she often worried about the toll it would take on his health. The Lufthansa case threatened to consume her husband entirely; its demands, combined with Carbone's own feverish single-mindedness once he became involved in an investigation of that size, meant he would endure long hours of backbreaking work, and soon the strain would be etched ever deeper on his face.

The enemy was time. As in all such major investigations, the critical factor is the period between the actual crime and the development of strong leads toward a solution. Reckoned in hours and days, that meant the most important work had to be done as soon as possible, while the trail was still warm. It also meant working extra-long hours, for at such times there was no such thing as a regular working schedule; the trail had to be followed until it ran cold, no matter how long that took.

For the wives of the men involved, it means a husband may or may not be home, may or may not be there at dinner and may or may not be with his family on a holiday. When he is home, the phone may ring at 4:00 A.M., announcing an urgent development that requires his immediate presence. Clara Carbone had experienced too many nights when her already exhausted husband would groggily answer the phone, conduct a brief, muffled conversation, then announce: "I gotta go."

Carbone's wife coped with such difficulties as best she could and even tried to see some of the humor in what was at root a form of madness. Shortly after the Lufthansa robbery, for example, there was a Sunday on which her husband was not working. Carbone had selected that day to paint one of the bedrooms in their Manhattan home. He moved furniture, mixed the paint, readied the wall. Then Carbone picked up the roller and went to work.

The phone rang. One of Carbone's agents was at the other end, reporting a development. A muffled conversation. Carbone returned to his painting. He stirred the paint, readied his roller, and started to paint again. A few more strokes. The phone rang. Another muffled conversation, this time with another agent. It went on like that for what seemed like hours, until Carbone finally gave up; the paint job would have to wait for another day.

———

Clara Carbone and her husband's agents shared an inside joke. In moments of greatest stress, it was a certitude that Carbone

———

would say, at some point, "Don't worry; everything's under control." Most often uttered at the very moment when things were decidedly not under control, it was Carbone's personal touchstone.

Some speculated that it was his way of keeping his sanity at such moments, and to a large extent, they were right, for he was sometimes in the position of a man trying to juggle a lot of balls. The investigation had been split into two main sections. One concentrated on Werner and Gruenwald and the question of the inside man. This part of the investigation was chiefly in the hands of one of Carbone's younger men, a bright, up-and-coming agent named Thomas Sweeney. The second section concentrated on the Burke gang and related matters, and it was there that the real complications arose.

The problem was that Burke had a lot of "known associates," all of whom had to be kept under surveillance by FBI agents. Still more agents were needed to perform the drudgery standard to such investigations: checking telephone toll records, bank accounts, and other possible sources of clues.

But clues were sparse. Police had found the van used in the robbery—forgetfully parked by Stax Edwards—but an exhaustive search of every inch of the vehicle turned up only one curious item: a sheet of paper found on the floor in the rear of the van; one of the robbers had apparently stepped on it, for it bore the distinctive footprint of a Puma running shoe.

In Carbone's mind, a tumbler clicked into place: Sepe's former brother-in-law, Anthony Rodriguez, wore Puma shoes. Mr. X, the FBI informant, had reported seeing Sepe and Rodriguez together, both carrying guns. Carbone remembered that they had both been arrested on Long Island the year before on narcotics and illegal weapons charges and that the case was later thrown out of court because of a defective search warrant.

Equipped with much more efficiently drawn federal search warrants, Carbone's agents raided the Rodriguez home in Queens, demanding that Anthony surrender his Puma shoes.

"Did you get the shoes?" an eager Carbone asked when the agents returned.

"Sure did," replied one of them, dumping several pairs of Pumas on Carbone's desk.

"Doesn't this guy wear any other kind of shoes?" Carbone complained as he prepared to ship the shoes off to the FBI laboratory in Washington for analysis. The question turned out to be academic: the lab could not match Rodriguez's sneakers and the footprint found in the van.

The setback put Carbone in an increasingly foul mood, for it was only one among many in an investigation that had started out fairly well and was now slowing down. Like a man trying to restart a car with undetermined mechanical trouble, Carbone tried every move he could think of to get some results, but nothing seemed to work. A raid on the Long Island home of Sepe's in-laws—where Mr. X hinted Lufthansa money was hidden under the floorboards—yielded nothing. An FBI surveillance team, working out of a van parked near Burke's home, took movies of everybody moving in and out of the house—and turned up nothing except cases of near-frostbite among the FBI agents working inside the unheated van. Extensive surveillances of DeSimone and other suspects produced no evidence. Sifting through all financial records, telephone toll sheets, and other papers connected with the robbery suspects produced no solid clues. Attempts to install bugs or telephone taps at Burke's home were thwarted; the house seemed never to be unoccupied. Detailed surveillance revealed James Burke to be a model parolee, faithfully working each day in his dress business and reporting to his parole officer (Tommy DeSimone and Henry Hill observed the rules of their parole with equal faithfulness). A relative of Sepe's assured FBI agents she could provide much information, but when Carbone interviewed her, he learned to his disgust and fury that she was a heroin addict. Whatever she knew about Sepe's involvement in the Lufthansa robbery was filtered, as Carbone concluded, "through a brain made of mozzarella."

Even Werner and Gruenwald, the weakest links in the chain of conspiracy, appeared to be model citizens; they showed up for work every day. Werner appeared especially chipper. His vacation in Florida had rejuvenated him. Gruenwald acted like a man without a care in the world and Werner's major concern in life seemed to be maintaining his bowling average.

———

"We are in big trouble," one agent said matter-of-factly as 1979 began.

———

139

"I know," Carbone replied morosely, for there was no denying that after two months the investigation of the Lufthansa robbery was getting nowhere.

The immediate cause of the agent's comment had confirmed Carbone's worst fear: the Bureau had announced a $500,000 reward to be paid by "cargo interests" for any information leading to "recovered value of the stolen property." Normally, such announcements stimulate a small ocean of information, but in this case, there was barely a trickle. Carbone had detailed two agents on full-time duty monitoring the calls the FBI expected to receive on a special telephone number, but they spent most of their time twiddling their thumbs; hardly anybody called.

This was puzzling, but no more so than most other aspects of the investigation. Nothing seemed to be running to form, and worse, the investigation was getting out of control. Or so Carbone thought as he heard the agents assigned to the Burke gang preparing long lists of "people of interest," defined as anyone who was suspected of involvement, direct or otherwise, in the Lufthansa robbery. The list looked like a geneaology chart of the British royal family and its myriad interconnections. The supporting cast for the heist was over one hundred and still growing. All of the members were connected in some way: suspect X's first cousin helped out suspect Y's brother-in-law, because his sister was once engaged to this other guy, who was suspect Z's former business partner, who was connected with the Gambino family, which in turn . . .

"This is not going to work," Carbone finally announced. "We can spend the next twenty years trying to hunt all these damn people down. No; what we have to do is decide where we might have a case, and then go in and make it. Forget this other crap."

Carbone had never been especially enamored of those elaborate organization charts that the FBI and the police were fond of showing off—the ones with pictures of all the big Mafia leaders and colored lines showing the criminal interconnections. The charts were pretty, but as he had often pointed out, a pretty chart never put anybody in jail.

But his own agents—at one point, as many as 125 FBI agents were working on the case—did not have much to show for all their exertions. Despite their best efforts and the priceless tips from the informant who had pointed them in the right direction, the FBI was no closer to making a case that could be presented in court.

As one agent noted, the FBI needed the essential component of any major criminal investigation: luck. Carbone agreed, but as an old Brooklyn Dodgers fan, he subscribed to the Branch Rickey theorem that luck was the residue of design. It was time, Carbone decided, for the FBI to make its own luck.

——

It gets very cold during late January in the town of Mattituck far out on the north fork of Long Island. The prevailing northerly winds sweep down from Canada, seize the town on the shore of Long Island Sound, and hold it in an icy grip until spring.

Carbone and two other FBI agents crouched together in the front yard of an enlarged summer cottage near the water, shivering as the wind whistled through the trees. Carbone had never been this far east on Long Island and so was somewhat struck by the sight of the small rural town just a few hours from downtown Manhattan.

His focus was on the house just in front of him, the one with the late-model sedan parked in the driveway. It was 3:00 A.M., and the house was quiet. "Let's hope that son of a bitch doesn't wake up," said Carbone.

He meant Angelo Sepe, who was (they hoped) sound asleep in the house owned by his in-laws. Had Sepe been awake at that moment, he would have seen a number of FBI agents lurking around the place, including one agent in a tree and another skulking in the bushes. They were there to protect Carbone's first major gambit in the Lufthansa investigation: plant a bug in Sepe's car. The idea was based on an old truth: crooks like to talk in cars, where they assume their conversations are safe from electronic surveillance. The FBI liked to work an extra twist to the game by deliberately spreading false information—impending arrests or rumors of high-level informants—to stimulate conversations that might result in self-incrimination.

Carbone and his agents had waited weeks for an opportunity to plant the bug. Sepe's schedule was erratic ("A goddam night owl," one of the agents on the surveillance team complained), and he tended to be alert for any signs of the presence of FBI agents or police.

Now the FBI had pinned him in Mattituck. Backed by a court wiretap order, Carbone could finally plant his bug. To do that, he required the services of an FBI electronics expert, who happened to live in Connecticut, just across Long Island Sound from Mattituck. The electronics expert, who also flew his own light plane, was awakened after midnight by Carbone and asked to help. As though he was taking a walk to the corner drugstore, he casually agreed to make the hop to Long Island.

The installation of the bug—a cookie-size receiver and transceiver that picked up and broadcast conversations in the car to trailing surveillance vehicles—went off smoothly. That was a relief to Carbone. He knew his quarry was a hothead who liked to wave guns around, and he did not want Sepe to wake up and discover men fiddling with his car. A pre-dawn gun battle in Mattituck was definitely not on the schedule. Carbone was aware that Sepe liked to think of himself as a major hood. He had thoroughly rattled his in-laws during their first meeting by informing them that he was now head of the family—a dictum he accentuated by wearing a shoulder holster containing a .45-caliber pistol.

Carbone was also aware that Sepe liked to talk, usually boastfully. If anyone in the Burke gang was likely to prattle about the robbery, it was Angelo Sepe. And it was also likely that he would do his talking in his own automobile while with another hood or a girl he was trying to impress.

———

The very same thought occurred to James Burke. Aware of the FBI surveillance net around him, he moved cautiously and never used his home telephone to "talk business."

Burke was concerned about Sepe and certain other gang members who tried to impress people by bragging about their criminal activities. Burke assumed that some of them had boasted of their role in the Lufthansa heist. How else to explain the fact that everybody seemed to know immediately that Burke and his crew were involved? The odds, he feared, were growing that one of these days those fools would lead the FBI and the cops right to his door.

Ever the cautious capitalist, Burke decided to use certain investment strategies to protect his money in the event of an arrest. Accompanied by the ubiquitous FBI surveillance cars, Burke headed into Manhattan one afternoon and went into a restaurant—to eat lunch, the trailing FBI agents assumed.

They were right, but Burke also had some post-meal business to transact. He did so in a back room, out of sight of the agents, where he met one of his friends, a major bookmaker.

"Fucking FBI is all over my ass," Burke complained. "I hafta take some steps."

"Tell me what you need, Jimmy," the other man replied, assuming Burke wanted him to hold on to the money. Burke, however, had a more ambitious project in mind. He outlined plans for ten separate illegal gambling operations he wanted his friend to set up, using Burke's money. The friend was to get a percentage of the profits; the rest would go to Burke's family. Each of the operations would be administered by a Burke loyalist.

"No problem, Jimmy," the man replied breezily, "consider it done. How much are we talking about?"

Burke opened the satchel he had brought with him and began laying stacks of money on the table. When he had finished, there was $750,000 lying there.

"Jesus, Jimmy," said his friend, surprised not so much at the amount as by the fact that he was almost certainly looking at the Lufthansa heist proceeds—or at least part of them. He was too polite to mention this, of course, but he did obliquely refer to rumors in the New York underworld about how the members of Burke's gang were shooting their mouths off and demanding bigger cuts.

"It's tough," he said soberly as Burke nodded, "when you got people, you know, you can't rely on. You really gotta watch yourself in that kind of situation. When you got those kind of people, you have to protect yourself, right?"

"Right," Burke agreed. "It's worked out, don't worry."

The friend knew better than to press for any further details, but he noticed that Burke began to smile for the first time since he had come into the place. The smile told him that Burke had figured out a way to eliminate permanently the problem of the loose mouths of his gang.

And as he continued to think about it, Burke smiled even more broadly. It was the smile of a cornered lion, surrounded by baying hounds, who had just seen his opening.

Chapter

8

"That's why God made detectives"

The 113th Precinct of the New York City Police Department sprawls across sixteen square miles of some of the best and worst neighborhoods of Queens, ranging from the borough's nicest addresses to the kind of housing projects where people throw their wallets and pocketbooks into elevators before getting inside, ceding their wealth to prevent being physically injured by the omnipresent muggers.

The jurisdiction also includes Kennedy Airport, a city within a city. The airport has its own police force, the Port Authority Police, who coexist, often uneasily, with the New York City Police Department. Under a complex series of agreements, the Port Authority Police handle routine crimes at the airport while the city police are summoned for major malfeasances.

Because the Lufthansa heist was a major crime, it precipitated a development that detectives of the Port Authority had come to resent: the arrival of their bigger law-enforcement cousins, who immediately and aggressively took charge of the investigation and relegated the Port Authority cops to the supporting role of spear-carriers. But however strong their resentment, the Port Authority cops couldn't do much about it; the intradepartment agreements stipulated that the city police would play the lead in the big cases.

It all made for some delicate relations between the Port Authority and New York City police departments. Most often, the main point of contact between the two groups was the 113th Precinct whose detective squad was headed by a man who alternately fascinated, amused, and angered the Port Authority cops.

They never quite figured out Detective Lieutenant Thomas Ahearn.

Even in a police department full of singular figures, Ahearn was a pure original. A tall, trim man who bore a resemblance to the actor Keenan Wynn, Ahearn became head of the 113th Detective Squad in 1974, following a stint in the police department's feared Internal Affairs Bureau, which investigates police corruption.

His experience rooting out corrupt cops during the scandals that tore the department apart in the early 1970s had convinced Ahearn that the answer to that problem was in the attitude of supervisors and squad commanders. They had to become much more involved with their men, he was convinced. Cops became corrupt because of the pressure of personal problems. The solution was for commanders to be aware of those pressures, ready to nip in the bud any problem that would compel an otherwise-honest cop facing mortgage payments and orthodonture bills to take money. New York, as Ahearn understood, was the kind of city where the opportunities for graft were immense: drug busts in which detectives found $1 million in cash lying around were not uncommon.

When he took command of the 113th Detective Squad, Ahearn set about to create a sort of mystical brotherhood over which he would preside as the stern but fair father figure. Ahearn treated his detectives as members of a family whose personal problems were his foremost concern. It was not unusual for him to revise working schedules to accommodate individual family difficulties.

146

Young detectives assigned to Ahearn's squad encountered a boss who seemed to be an odd mixture of drill sergeant and father confessor. An ex-Marine, he spent much of the day alternately bellowing and fussing over his charges like a mother hen. A prickly personality who did not suffer fools gladly, Ahearn set high standards for his men and worked hard at boosting their morale.

"The best job in this world," he would tell detectives new to the squad, "is to be a member of the New York City Police Department, the greatest police department in the world. An even greater job is to be a detective. And the greatest job of all is to be a detective in the 113th Squad."

To buttress his case, Ahearn would pull a sheet from the pile of blue flimsies—routine reports by the uniformed force to detectives on assorted incidents within the precinct area. "See, look at this," Ahearn would say. Then he would read from the report: " 'Complainant alleges that, following a bitter dispute with ———— in their home, ———— seized complainant's false teeth and threw them outside.' Now, where are you going to find the kind of job with that sort of stuff going on? I tell you, it's better than television!"

Possibly, but Ahearn also understood the grim reality of most detective work, the kinds of cases that would have a man working seventy-two hours straight, propping his eyes open so he could type up a report. Most of the detectives harbored a deep affection for Ahearn, who, they realized, was a certifiable character of considerably more depth than he appeared.

To those who dealt with him, Ahearn was most noted for his quills. ("See if the moron can put both hands on his ass at the same time!" he would roar at detectives trying to handle a particularly doltish eyewitness). He had a volcanic temper, which seemed to erupt when he was dealing with other elements within his own department or other law-enforcement agencies. Ahearn was firmly convinced that all entities, save his own detective squad, were composed of submorons whom he did not hesitate to upbraid when he felt they had failed to demonstrate sufficient mental agility. Although liked by newspaper reporters for his honesty and directness, Ahearn did not hesitate to upbraid them either. A stickler for facts, he would point out printed errors in the soothing tones familiar to anyone who has spent time on a Marine Corps drill field.

Yet those who knew Ahearn well considered him a paper tiger, a big bear whose bluster concealed a sensitive aesthete. For evidence, they cited the time when, seeking promotion to lieutenant, Ahearn attended college at night to earn the required degree for that position. Instead of majoring in law enforcement ("I already know that field; why should I major in it?" he growled), Ahearn, to many of his colleagues' surprise, took up English. To their further surprise, Ahearn turned out to be a devoted student who demonstrated a real love for literature. He began buttonholing fellow police officers, hectoring them to read the classics.

You should try this book," said Ahearn to one detective, brandishing a copy of *Moby Dick*, by his favorite author, Herman Melville.

"It's a very . . . big book," said the detective doubtfully.

"Of *course* it's a big book," Ahearn pressed. "Many great novels are. Novelists need time to develop their ideas." Ahearn then launched into an intricate monologue on the development of the modern novel, sprinkling it with a few favorite quotations from books he especially liked.

"What's the book about, lieutenant?" the detective made the mistake of asking. Like most of his colleagues, his reading was dominated by police reports, rap sheets, and surveillance logs, along with the *Daily News*, the New York cop's favorite newspaper.

"Well, it's about whaling, but of course, it's not about whaling," Ahearn explained enigmatically, immediately dispelling any interest his listener might have had in the book.

Ahearn never gave up trying. The inveterate policeman, he compiled favorite quotations from his reading, carefully writing them out on index cards. He was apt to suddenly pull one of these cards and cite the passage as a perfect summation of the problem at hand. Detectives who knew Ahearn were alternately amused and puzzled by the practice. Suspects were even more puzzled when during an interrogation Ahearn would suddenly ask them if they knew that famous passage from Flaubert, which reminded the lieutenant of just this very situation.

"Who?" the flummoxed suspect would ask, desperately taxing his IQ of about 24 for some sort of clue.

"Flaubert, you idiot!" Ahearn would roar, reading him the

passage. He might just as well have read something in Sanskrit. "All right, let's try Joyce. . . ."

"Don't know her."

The answer would send Ahearn into a paroxysm of rage, and the suspect would be left with the distinct impression that he had been dealing with a madman.

––––––

Ahearn was not a madman, and many of these stories were in fact the result of carefully calculated rages designed to place the initiative in his hands. Above all else, Ahearn was a master psychologist at his best with suspects who thought they could outwit him.

After thirty years in the police department, Ahearn was one of its more noted legends, and there was not a detective squad in the city that did not have its share of Ahearn stories. Many cops were convinced that the fictional Lieutenant Kojak was based on Ahearn, but the similarity may have been a case of life imitating art. The more Ahearn was compared to Kojak, the more he acted like him, even down to wearing three-piece suits like those favored by the television police detective.

Ahearn's specialty was murder. "God help me, I love these murders!" he would sometimes shout, and although he was kidding, many weren't so sure. Ahearn presided over murder investigations with the avidity of a philatelist studying his choicest items. A lifelong student of the crime, Ahearn had filled several thick black notebooks with minute details about every murder he had investigated. Ever the compulsive organizer and filer, he had also prepared elaborate charts on homicides, and the result was a veritable encyclopedia of murder in the 113th Precinct. Often other detectives would test Ahearn's knowledge by asking him a technical question about a murder that had taken place ten years before. Unhesitatingly, Ahearn would recite from memory even the most obscure detail of the crime.

Thus armed, Ahearn became the most noted homicide investigator in the city. His detectives were credited with astonishingly high "clearance rates" (solutions) on homicides. While a certain percentage of them were easily solved murders that had resulted from domestic quarrels, many were really tough cases. Ahearn was always careful to give credit to the men he called "my Indians," for the purposes of newspaper accounts, but the men laughed at their boss when he told reporters, "I just sit behind a desk. Those guys do all the work."

They knew better because they had watched one day as Ahearn, infuriated by a wave of killings in Queens among a colony of Rastafarians—a Jamaican drug cult that worships former Emperor Haile Selassie of Ethiopia—decided to bring it to an end. He hung a large portrait of Selassie on the wall behind his desk, then had suspects brought to him for "a nice heart-to-heart talk." The suspects had been totally uncooperative to that point, but a confrontation with Ahearn quickly changed matters. As they sat before a picture of their divinity, in the presence of this strange character who alternately chatted and bellowed at them, their resistance melted away— especially when Ahearn began dropping references to "the emperor," conveying the distinct impression that he and Selassie were lifelong friends.

Then there was the time when the body of a woman, carefully dissected into a hundred pieces and wrapped in plastic, was found in the trunk of a car. Two sullen suspects were brought to Ahearn for a discussion of this matter.

"Oh, will you just look at the workmanship!" Ahearn said rapturously as he caressed the plastic packages containing parts of the victim's body. "What a professional job! Look at the quality of the work. Look how each part is cut out of this woman, just like a surgeon. Look how each part is wrapped just so. What an excellent piece of workmanship. You can admire really well done work." The two men smiled sheepishly, basking in the glow of Ahearn's effusive admiration. Then Ahearn exploded.

"That's right, you sons of bitches, real workmanship! And the next place you'll do workmanship is when you make license plates, because we're gonna put you away for life! You got that?" The suspects were hustled away from further wrath as Ahearn made a big show of searching furiously for what the suspects were convinced was his own scalpels.

———

Detectives Joseph Connors and John Fitzsimons of the 113th Detective Squad knocked on the door of the small dress factory in Queens, which was within shouting distance of Robert's

———

Lounge. Flashing their badges to the woman who answered the door, they asked to speak with the factory owner, James Burke.

Fitzsimons and Connors were among Ahearn's star detectives. They had come to Burke's place of business—or at least the one officially reported in his parole records—with some wariness, for they imagined themselves walking into a lion's den. They had never met Burke, but his reputation made them double-check their .38 Police Specials as they were ushered inside.

Judging by what they had heard of Burke, the two detectives imagined they would encounter a modern pirate king with a cutlass between his teeth and bandoliers of ammunition draped over his chest. Instead, they met a burly, smiling Irishman who greeted them in a raspy voice with elaborate politeness.

"What can I do for you, gentlemen?" he asked, the very picture of the typical small Queens businessman, eagerly trying to drum up some new business.

Informed that his presence was desired at the 113th Detective Squad headquarters to discuss "certain allegations" made against him, Burke didn't turn a hair.

"Oh, certainly," he said, as though they were discussing slipcovers. "I'll just call my lawyer, and he'll meet us there." He smiled broadly. "Then we can talk. How about some coffee?"

"Sure," Fitzsimons replied, not quite certain what to make of it all. This was the infamous criminal mastermind Jimmy Burke, the leader of the Robert's Lounge Gang, the reputed killer of several dozen men? Fitzsimons expected that at any moment, Burke would suddenly pull out a machine gun and mow down both him and his partner.

Burke bustled around like the good host. He prepared coffee, then asked if the two detectives would like some doughnuts. They were good, he assured the two men, adding an apology: they were not as fresh as they had been earlier.

Fitzsimons studied his attentive host carefully. Jimmy Burke had occupied his thoughts for nearly two months now, ever since the morning of December 11, 1978, when Ahearn had told him and Connors to conduct the bulk of the 113th squad's investigation of the Lufthansa robbery. From that

151

moment, Fitzsimons had operated on the assumption that Burke was the central character in the drama.

The assumption was grounded partly in Ahearn's initial deduction that the Robert's Lounge Gang was involved. The deduction was based on a number of clues, among them Rolf Rebmann's description of one of the unmasked robbers' brightly shined shoes.

"Tommy DeSimone," Ahearn told Fitzsimons. "Our boy Tommy always likes to look sharp, and he's just stupid enough to be wearing shined shoes, even on a robbery. And Tommy was at Lufthansa for only one reason: Jimmy Burke sent him there. Tommy wouldn't take a crap unless Jimmy Burke told him to."

But like the FBI agents, Fitzsimons and Ahearn were to discover that however certain they were of the identity of the "perps"—Ahearn's version of "perpetrators," New York Police officialese for criminal suspects—proving it was something else again. To Ahearn's surprise and mounting frustration, his "Indians" were unable to find the vital evidence that would clinch the case against Burke and his Robert's Lounge Gang.

The effort included the inevitable attempt at a long shot: bringing in Jimmy Burke for questioning, confronting him with the evidence the detectives would claim now proved his guilt beyond the shadow of a doubt, and then hope for the best. This was one of the more ancient police techniques, and in using it on Jimmy Burke, the police had about as much chance of success as would a Republican party fund drive plea to Mikhail Gorbachev.

Legally, of course, Burke did not have to stay even one minute in any police station; unless he was under arrest, the police had no right to hold him. Further, under the Fifth Amendment, Burke could not be compelled to utter a word— unless, of course, he decided to make a voluntary confession, an unlikely event, to say the least.

But Burke, who was very experienced at this game, really had nothing to lose by playing it. Simply by appearing voluntarily, he had scored some cheap points, which he could later cite to show that he had nothing to hide and that he had bent over backwards to help in the investigation. Burke sat beside his lawyer, who was superfluous, since his client needed no prompting on how to answer loaded questions.

Burke was very much the master of the situation. No, he said with what seemed like perfect candor, he had no idea who might have carried out the Lufthansa robbery. He was not very familiar with some of the names mentioned by detectives—Tommy DeSimone, among others—and since he was fast asleep during the robbery, he hardly could be expected to know much about it. Reports of his own involvement? Idle newspaper gossip, not worth considering. He was only a businessman now, trying to make a go of his little dress factory.

With mounting irritation, Ahearn and the other detectives absorbed this performance, carried out with the charm that had long been Burke's hallmark. Clearly, Burke was playing them for fools. He sat there casually parrying questions with the unconcerned air of a man batting away a few gnats. The cops had nothing solid on him, and Jimmy the Gent knew it.

So did Ahearn. "We might as well talk to the wall," he said on the conclusion of the fruitless exercise. A subsequent strategy session with his detectives revealed the blank wall they now confronted. Teams of detectives had worn out several pairs of shoes tracking down every possible lead, but as each of them seemed to head tantalizingly down a promising road, the trail suddenly ran cold. As if a gigantic electromagnet had been turned on, the memories of dozens of people seemed to have been mysteriously erased. Nobody knew anything, nobody saw anything, nobody remembered anything. Even the normal channels of underworld informants were mostly silent, and the reason was not hard to discern: as one of them noted, "This is a Burke thing; Jimmy kills."

In that atmosphere of fear, the detectives felt as if they were trying to clamber up mountains of loose sand; as they climbed, their progress was eroded by the sand filling in around them. They outlined the problem to Ahearn, who gave them a number of investigative tasks covering the Robert's Lounge Gang. It was a daunting list and promised only more frustration. How, the detectives wanted to know, were they supposed to gather all this evidence in the face of an almost total lack of cooperation?

They mouthed the words along with him as Ahearn gave his standard answer: "That's why God made detectives."

It was an interesting piece of theology, but of no help in solving the vast array of mysteries that surrounded the case, none of which seemed vulnerable to attack. There was, for example, the matter of the stolen van used in the heist. From the first moment, Ahearn was convinced the van had not been stolen. Why would the robbery crew have risked aborting a multimillion dollar robbery on the good possibility that the stolen van would be spotted and stopped by some alert traffic patrolman even before the heist took place? Ahearn's experience compelled him to conclude that the robbers would have played it safe and arranged for a van to be made available, a vehicle that would be reported stolen later.

Interviews with the van's owner solidified that view. The man conveyed the proper aura of an innocent public citizen unwittingly caught up in a historic robbery, yet much of his account did not ring true. The story, simply, was that he had driven the van to his mother's house, parked it on the street, and checked it every so often. At one point, he noticed that it was gone.

"Do you usually check to see if your van is still parked someplace?" Ahearn inquired gently, recalling the man's statement that he had looked out the window "every twenty minutes or so."

Not all the time, the van owner replied, shifting uncomfortably, for Ahearn was zeroing in on the one detail in his story that did not quite seem to fit: how many men spend a visit with their mothers checking to see if their vehicles are still parked outside?

And there was more. Ahearn knew that police in the Bronx recently had been called to an apartment house after a tenant complained of hearing a loud fight next door. A patrolman found two men, apparently in the midst of a violent fistfight. On a table in the room was stacked $4,000 in small bills. The two men apologized profusely, claimed the scuffle was innocent roughhousing, and vowed to cease immediately so as not to disturb the neighbors. Of course, neither man wanted to prefer charges against the other.

Suspicious, the patrolman recorded the names of the two men and the general circumstances. Equally alert detectives in the Bronx checked out the names. One turned out to be a notorious Mafia hood; the other was the owner of the van used in the Lufthansa robbery. The Bronx detectives deduced, as did Ahearn, that the patrolman had interrupted a fight over the size of the payoff for use of the van in the robbery.

But it was only a deduction, and although Ahearn tried to use it as a wedge, the van owner wasn't about to give in. He didn't remember seeing any money in that apartment, and he had gone there for the sole purpose of "having it out" with a relative concerning a dispute he could no longer remember.

"He's a liar," Ahearn told his detectives, but the van owner would not budge; he even managed to pass two lie detector tests.

The incident represented still another defeat for the police, and the new year of 1979 promised no better prospects. Clearly, the break in the case would have to come from somewhere outside the main conspiracy; either the police or the FBI would have to get lucky.

Ahearn devoutly wished that it would not be the FBI, for in his personal pantheon of demons, the Federal Bureau of Investigation was far up in the hierarchy. Not far below was Supervisor Stephen Carbone.

———

No one was quite sure why Ahearn disliked the FBI so much. To a certain extent, he reflected the traditionalist New York City Police Department view of the chief federal law-enforcement agency. There had been tension for many years between the two organizations, and on more than one occasion, FBI agents and police detectives had actually drawn guns on one another. Some cops regarded the FBI as overbearing, filled with incompetents who muddled through on the FBI's vaunted reputation among the public at large. The traditionalists' chief complaints against the FBI were that its agents lacked street smarts and that the Bureau appropriated evidence gathered by police in an attempt to hog all the publicity for itself.

On the other hand, plenty of FBI veterans held equally acid views of the police. In their view, all municipal police departments were corrupt, the average police detective squad was composed of glory hounds, and sensitive information could not be shared, because corrupt police officers would immediately run out and sell it to the highest bidder.

Interestingly, there was some element of truth in both these views. The FBI *could* be overbearing, and it *did* sometimes attempt to appropriate credit for an investigation in which much of the work had been done by local police. But it was also true that corruption was a serious problem in municipal police organizations—the New York City Police Department could attest to that, certainly—and that the question of access to sensitive information which could mean life or death to an informant was no small matter.

A large part of the problem centered on the fact that the two entities were two very different law enforcement organizations. The FBI was a rigidly structured agency, with an organizational system that had remained nearly unchanged since J. Edgar Hoover first laid it down in the 1930s. ("There's a rule for *everything* in the FBI," some of its agents would often complain.) Largely immune from political pressure and outside influence, the FBI kept its agents on short leashes and tended to micromanage them from headquarters. Nevertheless, its reputation for dogged thoroughness, aided by funds from a generally benevolent Congress, allowed the Bureau to be, when it functioned as it should, the best law enforcement agency in the world.

The New York City Police Department, on the other hand, was constantly embroiled in every form of politics known to man, for it operated in the crazypatch quilt of New York politics in which law enforcement was simply another political football. Everybody in New York City wanted to have the greatest police department in America, but nobody wanted to pay for it.

The New York City Police Department was chronically short of money, and part of the antagonism some of its officers felt toward the FBI arose from resentment. Detectives told stories about their visits to FBI offices. Like poor cousins who had just visited rich relatives, they described the expensive carpeting in those offices, the television sets with videotape machines the agents used for interrogations, the big food and drink machines in the squad rooms. Back in their own squad rooms, painted in standard-issue vomit green and crammed with furniture the Salvation Army would have thrown away, they often were pestered by superiors who demanded to know which man had made that forty-cent toll call. Outside, an unmarked car used for surveillances lay useless, still waiting for the money to fix the broken muffler without which the car announced its approach from five miles away.

Nonetheless, the New York City Police Department, particularly its Detective Bureau, remained the most famous in the country, and both its triumphs (*The French Connection, Naked City*) and its failures (*Serpico, Prince of the City*) were very much a part of popular culture. A high proportion of its detectives were brilliant, especially the freewheeling veterans of the street who were allowed some room in which to maneuver. But the city cops paid a price for their work: divorce and alcoholism rates were very high, and many detectives—burdened by awesome caseloads, long hours, and constant danger—were burned out before they had put in their twenty years and retired.

———

The agencies' perceptions of each other, however, were rapidly being rendered academic by some significant changes that were only barely obvious in 1978.

The New York City Police Department was just shaking off the effects of the worst scandal in its history, one that revealed an endemic, organized system of payoffs. The corruption had even reached the Police Property Office, where confiscated heroin worth an astounding $70 million (most of it from the French Connection case) had been smuggled out and sold to Mafia narcotics kingpins. The situation was aggravated by the refusal of honest cops to inform on their colleagues. These men would balk at being assigned to notoriously corrupt units for fear of becoming contaminated by the payoff system, but they steadfastly refused to turn in corrupt cops, a course of action that was forbidden by the unofficial "honor code" of the department.

After the scandal became public, the fallout included a top-to-bottom shake-up that turned the department inside out. A somewhat different police department emerged: the men moving up into positions created by forced retirements and departmental charges were better educated, less enamored of the unofficial honor code, and determined to wipe out the lingering public suspicion that the department was permanently stained by corruption.

Meanwhile, the FBI was undergoing its own revolution.

The so-called new breed of agent, the shift of greater resources into organized crime and political corruption cases, and the gradual relaxation of some of its sterner strictures made for a different FBI from the one that so repelled Ahearn and other police traditionalists. Not all of the results of that revolution were obvious by 1978, however, and only a very few cops noticed that the FBI was trying to establish better relations with the police. The Bureau had decided it had no hope of accomplishing anything without a working partnership.

This was, of course, a laudatory goal, but the initial meetings of the police-FBI task force, which FBI chief Laster had created, demonstrated a considerable number of kinks that had to be worked out. In what could not have been worse timing, the FBI discovered that at the very time it wanted to foster a better working relationship with the police, they felt compelled to withhold two essential pieces of information from the police. One was the installation of a bug in Sepe's car. Under terms of the federal law covering its installation, it could not be revealed to any other jurisdiction. Additionally, the FBI had to conceal the existence of the FBI informant, "Mr. X," for reasons of security. A mere whisper about him on the street would guarantee his death.

The task force meetings thus tended to resemble high-stakes poker games with cautious players. The play could be described as close to the vest. One entire meeting focused on the necessity of moving against Louis Werner, the probable inside man. That probability, of course, was already as well established as the odds on the appearance of the next day's sunrise, but in an atmosphere dominated by suspicions that everyone was holding back, it was about the only safe topic of discussion.

The episode confirmed Ahearn's worst suspicions about the FBI, despite Carbone's elaborate efforts to foster close cooperation between his agency and the police. "Same old FBI," Ahearn announced to his detectives, and went on to lecture them about the evils of the Bureau, many of which he laid at the feet of Carbone. For reasons his detectives did not quite understand, Ahearn plainly disliked Carbone from the moment he set eyes on him. The dislike struck a number of observers as curious, for both men were native Brooklynites, had equal concern for the men in their charge, were intensely loyal to their respective agencies, and were uncommonly gifted law-enforcement officers. To be sure, there were some differences: Ahearn was a blustery man who spoke his mind loudly and bluntly, while Carbone, when not preoccupied with a case, tended to be soft-spoken and judicious with his comments, sometimes giving the impression of being almost diffident.

But the problem between the police and FBI was not so much personal as structural. The Laster task force was an ad hoc attempt to impose the kind of structure critical to any important investigation involving federal and local agencies. But for such a structure to work, it had to be set in place and endowed with clearly defined responsibilities and strong leadership long before an actual event forced it into motion. To create a task force on the fly, as happened in the Lufthansa case, was to invite the kind of trouble that arose.

It was a hard way to learn the lesson, and how much impact the mutual suspicion eventually had on the course of events in the Lufthansa case cannot ever be measured. Certainly, it had an important effect on such traditionalists as Ahearn, whose suspicion of the FBI was reconfirmed.

It was a frame of mind guaranteed to induce something less than joy when Ahearn discovered that the first major break in the Lufthansa case came as a result of a stroke of luck that rebounded to the FBI—a break that stemmed from an incredibly stupid mistake committed, oddly enough, by the one participant in the robbery conspiracy who may have gained the least from it.

———

In what was apparently total unconcern (or ignorance), Peter Gruenwald during the first week of February 1979 asked his employer for the forms necessary to obtain discount standby air travel tickets. According to the form Gruenwald filled out, he intended to fly to Colombia at the beginning of his scheduled vacation on February 19. From there he would travel to the Far East, where he planned to spend some time with his ex-wife.

The plan was extraordinary for a number of reasons, not the least of which was the fact that a week before, he had been served with a subpoena to appear before a federal grand jury examining the Lufthansa robbery. Gruenwald apparently was unaware that witnesses subpoenaed before federal grand juries are not supposed to leave the country. Moreover, he had been the subject of several interviews by FBI agents, who made it clear that he was suspected of complicity with his friend Louis Werner in the Lufthansa robbery. Again, Gruenwald was apparently unaware that FBI agents tend to get upset when suspects decide to leave the country.

Gruenwald had apprised Werner of his conversations with the FBI, and although he did not know exactly how much the agents knew, he conveyed his increasing nervousness; the FBI seemed to be closing in.

"Oh, bullshit," Werner said. "Listen, Peter, if they really knew something, you think they'd keep asking you questions? Don't you get it? They're asking because they don't know. If they knew, our asses would be in jail right now, believe me."

Werner was right, but Gruenwald, like many Germans who perceived the FBI as a huge American Gestapo with files on just about everybody, was becoming convinced that the FBI agents were watching him, just waiting for the right moment to grab him. "Listen, Lou," Gruenwald said, "what if they know how we did this thing? So now they are just playing with us, you know, just waiting to see if we will run, and then they will get us."

"They're not gonna get us," Werner hastened to reassure him. "Listen, you know they've been down to talk to me, they've talked to Janet, they've talked to everybody. So what? We tell 'em we don't know anything, and that's it. See, they have to prove it, and they can't—so long as you and I don't say anything, right?"

"Right," Gruenwald replied, a modicum of self-confidence restored. It disappeared a few days later with the arrival of the grand jury subpoena, a forbidding-looking document that caused Gruenwald's imagination to run wild, he saw the grand jury as some form of Inquisition that would test his resolution just short of hot tongs.

Gruenwald's nervousness made Werner increasingly edgy. His friend Peter was a weakling, he feared, and as the FBI stepped up the pressure against him, it might be only a matter of time before he cracked and gave the whole game away. Then what? Werner had no contingency plan for such an eventuality, save to tell the grand jury, when summoned, that he had no knowledge about the Lufthansa robbery. Meanwhile, he faced additional pressure from his increasingly hysterical girlfriend, Janet Barbieri, who tearfully raised the prospect of Werner's imminent dragging away by FBI agents. Werner pooh-poohed that possibility—although he imagined that if such an event occurred, he would probably be taken away by the man he considered a total pain in the ass, Thomas Sweeney.

––––

But FBI Special Agent Thomas Sweeney, however much Werner disliked him for his constant pestering and suspicions, was in no position to arrest anybody. Although Sweeney was dead certain that Werner and Gruenwald had functioned as the inside men, he did not have a shred of real proof. Nevertheless, he had maintained constant pressure, hoping it would lead one of the men to make a mistake.

The combination of pressure and close surveillance finally paid off when Gruenwald tried to leave the country. Aware within minutes of Gruenwald's travel plans, the FBI seized a priceless opportunity. They could now arrest Gruenwald on a material witness warrant. His provable attempt to leave the country while under a grand jury subpoena would serve as the legal justification. At last the FBI was armed with the weapon for its favorite tactic, the "squeeze play." Simply, Gruenwald, his head filled with dire warnings about such things as prison terms, would be induced to cooperate. Offered immunity, he would then give Werner to the FBI. In turn, Werner, when confronted with damning testimony from his co-conspirator, would see the hopelessness of his position and lead the FBI into the heart of the robbery gang, the people with whom he had dealt.

––––

To Clara Carbone's dismay, the phone call came at a relative's house, where she and her husband, with some rare time off, had gone to celebrate a family occasion. She had a premonition of what the phone call was about and sure enough, following several minutes of muffled conversation, Steve Carbone returned to the gathering with that certain look on his face.

"I gotta go," he announced.

––––

161

Carbone headed for Levittown, a sprawling suburban housing development on Long Island. In one of the small homes Peter Gruenwald sat, shoulders slumped, surrounded by several of Carbone's agents.

"I don't know anything," he said defiantly, but Carbone noted that there was not much strength in the denial. Dazed by the unexpected arrest and clearly nervous about what was to come, Gruenwald was like a frightened animal, beaten and exhausted after a long chase; he could still growl, but it was only a reflex action. The hunt was over, and he sensed his pursuers had him by the throat.

Carbone and his agents began the familiar litany of cajolery and warning designed, as it was sometimes called, "to get a man's mind right"—to present him with a superior alternative to simply sitting there and shaking his head in denial. There was a certain prospect of a prison sentence. Prisons are terrible places; terrible things happen inside them. The federal government had better things to do than put people like Peter Gruenwald in prison. They wanted the real crooks in the Lufthansa robbery. Why should he take the rap for the really guilty ones? The FBI was fully aware of Werner's complicity, so Gruenwald would simply be telling them what they already knew. The benefits of cooperation could be pleasant: no prison term, a new identity, a way out. He should think carefully about it.

But all this, as Carbone well knew, was merely a softening-up process, the prelude to the much more significant encounter that Gruenwald was about to undergo, a process that few men of his limited intelligence and criminal experience were prepared to withstand.

He was to be turned over to the tender mercies of "The Pooch" and "The Choirboy."

Chapter

9

"I don't know whatcha talking about"

Just over the Brooklyn Bridge, on the Brooklyn side of the East River, the full might and power of the federal government's legal system reposes in an impressive six-story glass and limestone structure known as the United States District Court. Over its entranceway looms a huge gold-colored metal eagle, clutching arrows and olive branches in its talons. The motto *E Pluribus Unum* is emblazoned on the banner it holds in its beak.

The main lobby is dominated by a somewhat less traditional piece of art, a huge metal bas-relief full of writhing figures meant to suggest America's immigrant masses. But the struggle and agony seem better signified by the dozens of dramas enacted every day in the courtrooms of the United States Eastern District Court of New York, the hearing rooms of the Immigration and Naturalization Service, the offices of the Internal Revenue Service, and the offices of the United States Attorney for the Eastern District. In sometimes magnificent offices meant to suggest the majesty and power of their occupants, the federal government "interfaces" (one of its favorite words) with the 7 million people of Queens, Brooklyn, Staten Island, and Nassau and Suffolk counties.

And yet it is in a suite of some less impressive offices—a virtual rabbit warren, in fact—that many of the most significant dramas take place. What the offices of the Eastern District Organized Crime Strike Force lack in impressiveness, however, is overshadowed by the many big cases that are its daily concern. This, in other words, is where the action is.

It was here that the focus of the Lufthansa case shifted in the early winter of 1979, with results that would prove alternately ironic, unsettling, and occasionally bizarre.

On a snowy Friday late in December of 1978, U.S. Justice Department Special Attorney Edward A. McDonald was feeling quite content. As he relaxed at the annual Christmas party of the Eastern District Organized Crime Strike Force on the third floor of the federal courthouse in Brooklyn, he contemplated the prospect of a few days off, during which he planned to visit old friends in Washington, D.C. McDonald had gone to law school at Georgetown, and, as he had told his boss, he was looking forward to renewing some old acquaintances. While he was considering the pleasures that lay ahead, he noticed the boss making a beeline for him.

"You're not going on that trip," Thomas Puccio, chief of the Strike Force, announced with characteristic directness. "You're going to have to work all weekend. Lufthansa."

McDonald made a face, but he was in no position to argue. He was, first of all, chief assistant to Puccio, who decided which of his staff of fourteen prosecutors got which case. Besides, the Lufthansa case, already surrounded by tales about the Mafia and other such intriguing details, promised to be an interesting one.

Standing together, Puccio and McDonald presented an odd contrast. Grimly intense, the balding Puccio radiated nervous energy and was known as a workaholic who was reputed to devote no less than twenty hours a day to his job. His 1976 appointment as head of the Eastern District Strike Force followed several years as an assistant U.S. attorney, during which he became well known in the New York law-enforcement establishment. His celebrity stemmed not only from an extraordinary record—he was generally conceded to be the best federal prosecutor in the country—but also from his personality. Abrasive and demanding, Puccio pursued cases with a zeal that made him the Savonarola of the Eastern District—or, as others called him, "the prosecutor's prosecutor." More often, he was known by his nickname, "The Pooch," a diminutive that concealed the fate that awaited suspects and difficult witnesses who fell into his clutches.

Edward McDonald, on the other hand, appeared to be as happy-go-lucky as Puccio was grim. As Puccio was the first to realize, however, McDonald's air of calm geniality masked a razor-sharp mind and extremely determined prosecutor. Puccio had recruited McDonald for his team of prosecutors after taking control of the Strike Force, luring him away from a prosecutor's job in the Manhattan district attorney's office, itself considered the cream of the city's five such offices.

Puccio knew exactly what he was doing. Equipped with a mandate to hire anyone he wanted, he got rid of the existing prosecutors, and replaced them with fourteen of the most talented local prosecutors he could find, with emphasis on the "local". All of them had to be native New Yorkers with experience in handling cases in the city. Aside from talent, they shared disparate backgrounds—one climbed mountains in Nepal for relaxation, while another grew orchids—but they were all willing to work for a fraction ($40,000 to $50,000 a year) of what they could earn as criminal lawyers in private practice. What they got working for the government were long hours, complex cases, and the dubious privilege of trying to make a dope dealer with an eighth-grade education into a credible and articulate witness.

Like the rest of Puccio's crew, McDonald flourished in the Strike Force and repaid Puccio's confidence almost immediately, demonstrating a real flair for prosecutorial work. Like his colleagues, he bore the title "United States Justice Department Special Attorney," to distinguish him from the assistant U.S. attorneys, the federal prosecutors who handled the bulk of the government's courtroom prosecutions. The special attorneys worked at the fourteen Strike Force operations around the country. Their mandate was to put together major cases involving white collar crime, political corruption, and organized crime, using the pooled resources of a variety of law-enforcement agencies. In the case of the Eastern District Strike Force, there were twenty-two different agencies involved. They ranged from the Royal Canadian Mounted Police to the New York City Police Department although, since the Strike Force was a federal agency, it worked most often with the FBI.

———

McDonald's caseload was already heavy before Puccio added Lufthansa to it, but the assignment underscored what everybody understood was Puccio's faith in his chief assistant's abilities. McDonald was clearly being groomed to succeed his boss when Puccio left—most Strike Force attorneys spent four or five years on the job, then moved on.

A basketball player briefly during his undergraduate days at Boston College, McDonald was nearly six feet five inches tall, and he still liked to shoot baskets in the schoolyards near his Brooklyn home. He had been born and raised in that borough, but his speech was an odd hybrid of Brooklynese and the Boston accent acquired during his college days.

In a city alert to ethnic identities, McDonald was unmistakably Irish. A particular favorite of female staff members of the Strike Force because of his good looks, he had that innocent, albeit slightly devilish, look common to many Irish men. His appearance, in fact, was among McDonald's most potent weapons as a prosecutor. The innocent, almost cherubic look created the impression of total guilelessness. Contrasted with the older, more cynical and detached look of the defense attorneys who practiced in the federal court, McDonald looked the very picture of earnest young prosecutor, tilting lances with the sharpies. It was an impression that McDonald did nothing to dispel, finding it most convenient when juries were trying to decide if the case they were considering amounted to a house of cards virtually manufactured by the prosecution.

In truth, McDonald's success as a prosecutor had most to do with a solid grasp of criminal law and sound trial preparation. He was also very stubborn, with a tenacity that reminded people of Puccio. But the difference between the two men came down to McDonald's apparently unlimited reserve of Irish charm, which he could ladle out in vast quantities as the mood struck him. The combination of single-mindedness and talent for guile made him a prosecutor of striking ability, noted for his handling of reluctant witnesses and grand juries. He was often called the Choirboy because of his innocent, friendly approach, but the nickname was also a tribute to whispers around the courthouse that McDonald at the top of his form could make a jury believe *anything*.

McDonald would need these talents in full measure to find the answer to the single great question in the armed robbery of the Lufthansa Air Cargo terminal: Would anybody ever be brought to justice for it?

———

That first weekend forfeited to Lufthansa in December of 1978 turned into three months of lost weekends, for as McDonald quickly discovered, this was no ordinary robbery case. There were obvious organized crime connections, a huge amount of money in the wrong hands somewhere, conspiracies within conspiracies, and enough violations of federal law to keep an entire team of prosecutors busy.

Like many men who had come into contact with the Lufthansa heist, McDonald was gradually hooked by the various elements that made the case at once daunting and extremely alluring, the most fascinating he had ever encountered. It appealed to McDonald's fondness for unraveling the threads of a criminal conspiracy. Lufthansa was a vale of mysteries, a dark maze of false clues and deadly menace.

A cursory glance, of course, revealed nothing like that. A man who worked at Lufthansa Air Cargo had provided inside information to a gang of thieves who went in one night when the place was virtually unguarded and, in a lucky break, managed to grab an unusually large amount of money that had been stored there over a weekend. But, as McDonald quickly discovered, that was just the beginning of the story.

His chief source of information was FBI Supervisor Stephen Carbone. McDonald took an immediate liking to him. They had plenty in common: growing up in Brooklyn, Catholic schooling, and perhaps most important, similar New York rhythms and experiences, not to mention a particular liking for work in law enforcement.

And Carbone liked McDonald, whom he found to be an aggressive, bright prosecutor, the kind he liked. He was, Carbone felt, just about the perfect prosecutor to handle the Lufthansa case, for the Eastern District Strike Force's reputation as the best strike force in the country would prove helpful in this very difficult case.

Despite their mutual respect, however, Carbone and Mc-Donald did not always agree. People in the outer offices of the Strike Force could hear them on occasion exchanging angry words. Much of it arose from the tensions inherent in any such relationship. As a class, prosecutors tend to like sure bets; they prefer cases that are handed to them complete in every detail, wrapped up tightly, without any loose ends. Usually, however, cases arrive at prosecutors' desks in some disarray, often piecemeal. Frequently, they contain the seeds of doubt: Is there really any chance for a conviction in this one? Additionally, prosecutors tend to be skeptical about the claims of FBI supervisors and police officials regarding the solidity of various investigations. Intent on moving ahead toward indictment and trial, law-enforcement officers sometimes oversell a case to unwary prosecutors.

Carbone and McDonald's occasional contretemps seemed to have been sparked by the difference in their approaches. Although aggressive in such investigations, McDonald was also an extremely cautious gambler. He did not like to lose and was reluctant to proceed without very short odds that he would win. To McDonald's occasional exasperation, Carbone demonstrated the brazenness of a high-stakes gambler. He was forever coming up with ideas for bold moves in the Lufthansa investigation, most of which required search warrants and court orders. When McDonald expressed his skepticism about a particular move, Carbone would aggravate him by dropping the matter, then returning to it, a little more forcefully, later in the conversation. Then again, and again. Carbone did not like to take no for an answer, and McDonald soon realized he was dealing with a man who would not admit defeat.

"You know," McDonald said to him at one point, "there's a real possibility that you're a pain in the ass."

"Maybe," Carbone replied, "I'm just trying to do my job."

McDonald felt a twinge of guilt after such encounters, for in addition to his personal fondness for Carbone, he realized that the supervisor and his agents were working their tails off, with not too much to show for it. McDonald imagined it could not have been a pleasant experience for Carbone, boiling with frustration, to hear the U.S. Special Attorney pour cold water over his latest idea.

McDonald could appreciate that frustration, for he was beginning to feel it himself. The search warrants on Sepe and Rodriguez had turned up dry, and while the FBI had succeeded in planting a bug in Sepe's car, there was no telling when or if it would produce a solid lead. Meanwhile, the money was out there someplace, and although the FBI and the police were quite certain exactly who was involved, they still had no real evidence.

Then Peter Gruenwald made his mistake.

———

"You know, I have a great idea," Gruenwald said to Carbone as he was being taken to Strike Force headquarters.

"Oh? Tell me about it," answered Carbone, who wondered whether Gruenwald was planning to rob another air cargo terminal.

"T-shirts," said Gruenwald, smiling. Carbone stared at him, thoroughly puzzled. "Lufthansa is a very big thing with the public right now. So we could make up T-shirts that have something about the big robbery on them. People would buy them; it would be sensational. We could sell thousands and thousands."

Alarmed at the mention of "we," Carbone asked Gruenwald if he was actually proposing to manufacture T-shirts commemorating the Lufthansa robbery, with himself and the FBI as business partners.

"Sure, why not?" asked Gruenwald, genuinely puzzled as to why Carbone was not leaping at this golden opportunity.

"I think," said Carbone, measuring his words carefully, "that you ought to concentrate right now on getting your legal problems resolved. As for the T-shirts, Peter, don't ever mention it to me again."

Ignoring the rebuff and apparently still brimming with entrepreneurial ideas, Gruenwald was ushered into McDonald's presence. Despite the softening-up by Carbone and his agents, Gruenwald did not seem to appreciate the gravity of the situation facing him. McDonald brought him quickly back to earth.

———

As he often did on such occasions, McDonald began in an almost chatty fashion. Anyone watching might have thought he was discussing the weather or the pennant chances of the Yankees.

Frowning, McDonald mentioned Gruenwald's attempt to fly overseas while under grand jury subpoena. Well, it was a serious matter, but then, there was the possibility of . . . *solving* this little problem. About this man Louis Werner . . .

"I don't know anything," Gruenwald insisted, but McDonald sensed he was wavering now, considering his options.

"I would like to point out the benefits of you cooperating," McDonald said. He then launched into a lengthy monologue on the serious legal difficulties Gruenwald faced, explaining that he could redeem himself in the eyes of the federal government by providing information on the Lufthansa robbery—namely how he and Werner had cooked up the original plan for it.

McDonald was in no mood to devote a great deal of time to this matter, for in addition to other cases pressing in on him, he was trying to move his wife and two small children to a new home. And on top of that, his sister-in-law was scheduled to arrive from Boston to help with the move. (It turned out to be a memorable trip for her. She and McDonald's wife were held up at gunpoint right in front of the house. She later informed McDonald acidly that while he was busy earning front-page publicity for his pursuit of the Lufthansa robbers, *real* crooks were working closer to home.)

Among other things, McDonald used his initial session with Gruenwald to take his measure, a reading which convinced him that he was dealing with a weak-minded man of almost breathtaking stupidity—and a racist as well. That insight provided an important wedge for McDonald. He decided to have Gruenwald temporarily incarcerated in the Nassau County Jail (Gruenwald's home was in Nassau). At that particular moment, as McDonald was aware, the jail population was predominantly black.

It was a shrewd move, for an alarmed Gruenwald was shortly on the phone to McDonald, shouting "*Schwarzes! Schwarzes!* [niggers]." In quick order, he was back in McDonald's clutches, having decided that perhaps the prosecutor had a point when he mentioned the wisdom of cooperating. He wanted a deal, and McDonald was prepared to give him one, based on Puccio's "little fish, big fish" theory of prosecution. Under that theory, the prosecutors would go after the little fish in criminal conspiracies first, and there expend their considerable powers to grant immunity in return for testimony against fellow conspirators. The prospect of receiving damning testimony from these little fish would enable the prosecutors to work the same routine on the next level of fish above them, until the very biggest fish—the real targets in the first place—were drawn into the net.

Certainly Peter Gruenwald was a little fish, but he represented the only route open to the next size fish, Louis Werner. And Werner, in turn, would be used to catch the real big fish, James Burke, and the men who actually carried out the robbery.

To a fascinated audience that included Carbone and several other FBI agents, the story came tumbling out of Gruenwald—his and Werner's long-standing plans to rob Lufthansa, the nerve-racking $22,000 theft, the abortive attempt to round up a robbery gang, the split between himself and Werner, and the surprising climax when Werner himself arranged for a crew of professionals to do the job. The account was extraordinary, but Gruenwald, an essentially humorless man, did not understand why some FBI agents were smiling when he recounted details that sounded like something right out of Jimmy Breslin's novel, *The Gang That Couldn't Shoot Straight*.

The agents were doing more than smiling; they were running all over the city, rounding up more little fish. They picked up the gang of nincompoops Gruenwald had tried to enlist for the robbery, along with Werner's friends Frank Menna and Bill Fischetti. Menna, having feared the worst for a long time, took one look at the two FBI agents on his doorstep and, as they flashed their identification cards, announced, "I want a lawyer. I want immunity."

McDonald willingly granted it. These men were all easy meat for the prosecutor, who quickly emptied their heads of what they knew and put them on inactive reserve status for the moment. McDonald had a plan, and it amounted to spinning a very tight web around Louis Werner. Overwhelming evidence, including the potential witnesses he was temporarily storing on ice, would be used to form an airtight case. At the proper psychological moment, Werner would be presented with this small mountain of evidence. Seeing that any further denial was pointless, he would cave in. Then the real core of the Lufthansa heist would be entered.

There was one small problem, however. Werner was known to have made threats against several people. When he became aware of the web drawing tighter around him, he might lash out in frustration at anyone who knew of his involvement in the robbery. Such as Beverly Werner.

As this possibility was being considered, Mrs. Werner herself called the FBI to complain that her estranged husband had just confessed to her that he was the "mastermind" of the Lufthansa robbery. He had also threatened to kill her if she told anyone.

That brought an FBI squad, led by Sweeney, on the run to her apartment. As they entered the parking lot, they spotted Louis Werner.

"Oh, Christ, he's killed her," Sweeney said. As several agents guarded Werner, he and other agents raced upstairs. They found the apartment door ajar. There seemed to be no one inside, but in a bathroom Sweeney saw a sight that made his blood run cold. Lying in the tub was a large, rolled-up rug that looked as though it might contain a body.

Actually, Beverly Werner was very much alive. She was sitting quietly in another room, waiting for them, as the FBI agents, slightly out of breath and somewhat chagrined, found her.

What she had to say was not especially surprising to Sweeney, for she confirmed what the FBI already knew. Her story also confirmed the FBI's suspicion that Werner, a braggart, probably made a similar boast to his girlfriend, Janet Barbieri (as indeed he had). Because she was Werner's legal wife, Beverly Werner's testimony could not be used against her estranged husband, but Janet Barbieri found herself before a federal grand jury, where McDonald pounded away at her, finally drawing an admission that, yes, Werner had boasted to her that he was the inside man in the Lufthansa theft.

Her admission was the last gambit McDonald played, and he was now ready to make his final moves in the chess game, the inevitable mating attack against a man with three pieces down and his queen gone. The array of forces McDonald had lined up against Werner was overwhelming: the witnesses who would testify against him, the damning grand jury testimony by his girlfriend, the trail of circumstantial evidence.

Louis Werner was ready to be taken.

"Mr. Louis Werner?" Werner heard the voice coming from somewhere just behind him, slightly distorted by the icy wind that blew around the parking lot of the bowling alley. It was the night of February 20, 1979, the nadir of the New York winter, and Werner was looking forward to getting inside his warm van.

"FBI," said the voice, approaching him and showing an identification card. "You're under arrest." Werner became aware of other men who had suddenly materialized out of the darkness, taking up positions on either side of him. Almost as if in a dream, Werner found himself being searched and handcuffed while one of the men, whom he could not see, recited the litany of the suspect's constitutional rights. Inside the van, Janet Barbieri began to sob loudly.

"Hey, I'm all right!" Werner shouted to her.

He was quite wrong. Louis Werner was in very serious trouble, the dimensions of which McDonald sought to explain to him. It was really pointless, McDonald said as Werner sat sullenly in his office the next day, to continue to deny any knowledge of the Lufthansa robbery. The evidence, as McDonald pointed out, was overwhelming, so little was to be gained by refusing to cooperate. If he would cooperate and provide information against the actual robbers, McDonald noted, "something advantageous" could be worked out. On the other hand, if he decided not to cooperate . . .

"I don't know whatcha talking about," Werner replied to McDonald's lengthy exposition on the benefits of cooperation.

The prosecutor then delivered a somewhat more dramatic recitation about the suffering Werner might endure after conviction—which McDonald held to be a virtual certainty—under the Hobbs Act, which generally takes a dim view of theft from interstate commerce (about twenty years' worth).

McDonald was prepared for Werner's stubborn refusal to cooperate. He picked up a phone and dialed an interoffice number.

A few minutes later, Peter Gruenwald was led through the door and stood facing his friend Louis Werner.

McDonald let the implication of this tableau sink in for a moment, then said to Gruenwald, "I think you ought to tell him now, Peter."

"Lou, I told them," Gruenwald said. As if Werner might not understand, he added, "I told them everything, how you were the inside man, Lou. You know, the whole thing."

Werner looked as though he were about to have a heart attack. Chest heaving, face turning a bright red, he was clearly shocked.

McDonald, assuming the moment had come, pressed his advantage. "As you see, Lou," he said, "we have it all. Again, I must note the benefits of your cooperation—"

"I don't know whatcha talking about," Werner snapped.

"Lou," McDonald said, adopting a brotherly tone, "I'm not sure you understand what you're doing. You can't beat this case, Lou. Gruenwald will testify against you, and when that happens—"

Werner shook his head. "I don't know whatcha talking about."

"Can you believe it?" McDonald was almost beside himself. In still another of those curious developments that continued to afflict the Lufthansa investigation, Werner had refused to bend, despite McDonald's elaborate efforts to make that choice inevitable. Another dead end had been reached, and as he sat in his office a few nights later for another joint strategy session with Carbone, the bright promise of Werner's presumed cooperation had turned to ashes. Once again, they were stuck.

"The problem is," Carbone noted, "Werner wants to be a wiseguy. He wants to be thought of as the real mastermind, the guy who really made it all go. Here's the strange part: at all costs, Werner wants the respect of the guys he dealt with on the outside. And the only way he thinks he can get that respect is to be a stand-up guy, the man who won't talk, who won't cooperate. Besides, I suspect he really thinks he can beat this case somehow."

"The man is stupid," McDonald complained. "We've got him so cold on this there is absolutely no way he can beat it. Are you telling me that he'll take a twenty-year rap and never say a peep?"

"Probably, at least until he gets a real taste of prison life," Carbone replied. "Then it may be a different story."

"Maybe," McDonald cautioned. "Meanwhile, you people better come up with something else. Otherwise this investigation is in very deep trouble."

"Don't worry; everything's under control," Carbone said.

It was his automatic response at such moments, but Carbone also had in mind another, more modest move in the game. It had begun the month before.

———

The phone had rung at Stephen Carbone's home one night in early January. With dismay, Clara Carbone noted the time: 2:00 A.M. She knew the reason for the call even before her husband picked up the receiver.

"I gotta go," he announced after one of those maddening muffled conversations.

The call had come from one of Carbone's agents, reporting a sudden chink in the apparently impenetrable armor of the Robert's Lounge Gang. Tommy DeSimone's car had been spotted. That fact was interesting enough, but even more interesting was *where* they had found it—in the driveway of Jimmy Burke's house.

For some time the FBI had been holding a court wiretap order that would allow them to carry out another of Carbone's ideas, installation of an electronic beeper on Tommy DeSimone's car. But the car, a gaudy pink Cadillac in the Mafia tradition (usually called a "pimpmobile" in New York) had always been just out of reach. DeSimone, like Sepe and the other crooks, seemed to follow no set pattern. His random movements, combined with the fact that somebody always seemed to be around the car, rendered installation of the beeper impracticable—until an agent spotted it unattended in Burke's driveway.

Carbone wanted to install a beeper to make it easier for his agents to trail the car, the theory being that DeSimone might lead them to the rest of the gang and possibly to the Lufthansa money as well. The beeper was a small device that would be affixed underneath the car with a powerful magnet. It would send out a strong, regular electronic beep that would be monitored in the surveillance cars; the strength of the signal would tell them how close they were to the car.

To the surprise of Carbone and the other FBI agents gathered in the freezing pre-dawn darkness outside the house, it turned out that DeSimone was not Burke's only visitor. Apparently other members of the Robert's Lounge Gang had gathered with their chief for a meeting whose subject Carbone did not need to wonder about.

"What I would give to be a fly on the wall in there," Carbone said in a hoarse whisper. The other agents nodded, regretting their inability to bug the inside of the house. Deployed around the Burke property, the agents waited, shivering, as another agent—sometimes affectionately known as Dr. Bug—struggled to install the beeper. It was a somewhat difficult job in the frigid darkness, for the device had to be put on metal free of rust or grease that would cause it to fall off.

While he struggled and the agents froze, Carbone faced the back door to the house, his gun out. Locked in the classic ready stance, down on one knee, holding his pistol with both hands, sighted right on the door, he hoped that DeSimone, Sepe, or Burke—all known to use guns—would not decide to emerge, guns blazing. In a gun battle involving a half-dozen FBI agents and a like number of crooks, not too much imagination was required to envision the potential carnage. It was not the kind of scenario Carbone wanted in the middle of a crowded residential neighborhood.

"Got it," the FBI agent under the car announced, and Carbone and the other agents quickly scattered. In seconds, the Burke property was deserted again; the agents had not been spotted. Much later, DeSimone emerged, got in his car, and drove off, unaware that two unmarked cars some blocks away were following him at a long distance.

DeSimone headed toward Brooklyn. Some distance behind him, the FBI cars kept on the electronic trail. The beeper was working perfectly. DeSimone would not escape, no matter where he went.

Or so they thought.

———

The more interesting electronic device, of course, was the bug planted in Sepe's car. It had just begun to show promise when Sepe, to the FBI's consternation, decided to turn in his rented car. After a mad scramble, the agents got the bug out, but before they could wonder about the next move, Sepe provided them with an answer.

In a transaction of consuming interest to Carbone, Sepe took a step up in the world in early February 1979 and purchased a brand-new black Thunderbird. A check of the car dealer's records revealed that he had paid $9,000 in cash for the car—all in fifty and one hundred dollar bills. At about the same time, Frankie Burke purchased a new Lincoln Mark Continental for $12,000. Again, the medium of exchange was cash: fifty and one hundred dollar bills.

Carbone found the two purchases extraordinary, the kind of flamboyant actions that Jimmy the Gent Burke ordinarily would not have countenanced. Yet there was no indication that he had said a word of criticism, still another clue to an interesting side of his personality. Plainly, one of the aspects of crime that most appealed to Burke was the sheer joy of getting away with something. On certain occasions in the past he had adopted a defiantly flashy style, as if reveling in his delight at having fooled the "bad people." The car purchases struck Carbone as a clear message from Burke. Look here, we got away with it, he seemed to be saying, and just watch as we rub your nose in it.

It is generally a mistake to rub the FBI's nose in anything, for there is an old Bureau saying: "We don't get mad, but we do get even." Carbone subscribed to that aphorism, and decided that if Burke and his crew wanted to play that way, he could convert their propensity for such games into a weapon that he would later turn on them. He went quickly to McDonald's office, seeking still another warrant, this one for a bug to place in Sepe's new car.

Increasingly nervous about the precious points his office

was expending with the federal judiciary in the process of moving for more warrants, McDonald hesitated. "I hate to tell you this," he told Carbone, "but something better happen in this case, and soon. We cannot indefinitely go before the judges and get them to approve all these warrants. I mean, there's a limit, you know."

"I understand that," Carbone said, "but we really need this one. It's very important."

"Sure," said McDonald skeptically. "The FBI always says that about every goddam warrant they want. Why is it that the world is always going to come to an end unless they get something?"

The discussion ebbed and flowed for a while, each man determined to make the other understand pressures created by a case the size of Lufthansa and how each man worked under pressures unique to his own organization. In the end, Carbone got his warrant, McDonald saying that if he ever went into a life of crime, he hoped that the impossibly stubborn Carbone would not be assigned his case.

"If you commit a federal crime, we'll get you," Carbone said, laughing. McDonald sensed that he wasn't kidding.

———

Carbone hoped that the bug in Sepe's car, combined with a program of deliberate leaks of disinformation to stimulate conversations between Sepe and his more interesting passengers (a process known as "tickling the wire"), would lead to a major break in the case. He did not realize the move would cause a serious rift between Lieutenant Ahearn and himself.

"I'll tell you how you make a wire like that work," Ahearn said to him when he learned of the bug's existence. "See, you go up to the car, piss through the window, and tell that little shit Sepe, 'Hey, Angelo, we know you did it, and we're gonna prove it, you son of a bitch!' Guarantee you, you'll get some good conversations in the car after that."

Stunned into speechlessness by Ahearn's suggestion, Carbone was further irritated when Sepe decided to make things difficult for his agents.

Sepe had an annoying habit—apparently picked up from the movies—of attempting to dodge surveillance. One of his favorite tricks was to roar off at 90 miles per hour, then suddenly stop, in a screech of brakes and tires, in the middle of the road. The bug in his car recorded his hysterical giggle as cursing FBI agents were forced to keep going. The bug also recorded his growing paranoia about the FBI surveillance. He treated his passengers to a running commentary on the massive surveillance he believed the FBI had on him.

"See that fucking nigger over there?" he said at one point, pointing to an elderly black man crossing the street. "That's a fucking FBI agent." Initially impressed by Sepe's ability to spot FBI agents in cunning disguises, the passenger's confidence in that acuity would waver as Sepe pointed out other FBI agents lurking around: a man sweeping a sidewalk, an Orthodox Jew contemplating the Talmud, and two girls on bicycles.

More interesting were the discussions Sepe had with another passenger—James Burke. "We hafta get Tony to start moving the money," Burke said at one point. At another, he made a clear reference to a murder. Whose murder was not exactly clear, but he had said enough, Carbone decided, for the FBI to make the most important move yet in the investigation. Angelo Sepe would be arrested for involvement in the robbery of Lufthansa Air Cargo and for parole violation: he had associated with a known criminal, one James Burke.

This plan did not sit well with McDonald. "What prospect do we have of making a case against Sepe?" he asked.

Carbone in so many words admitted that the FBI did not at that point have a conclusive case, but was in the process of building one. It was simply a matter of time, and Sepe's arrest might compel him to cooperate. "Don't worry; everything's under control," he assured McDonald.

But McDonald was not so sure and after agreeing with Carbone's plan, spent a sleepless night. The next morning, in an agitated mood, he confronted Puccio.

"Are we crazy?" he asked, somewhat rhetorically. "We're not gonna make this case. I just know it. Comes time to indict Sepe, and we'll be standing around with egg on our faces."

"Well," said Puccio calmly, "let's consider. So the FBI doesn't wind up with enough against Sepe. Those are the breaks. The worst that can happen, you walk in to the judge and say, 'Sorry, your honor, we cannot proceed.' So what?" Puccio also noted that Sepe was already in jail anyway, on the parole violation charge.

McDonald was not mollified, for as a man who shared Carbone's dislike of losing, he was horrified at the prospect of telling a judge that he could not proceed—thus leading to a dismissal of the robbery case against Sepe. By law, he had thirty days in which to make that case (until late March), and as the days ticked by, it became clear that he would not have enough evidence to indict.

Newspaper reporters, as well as courts, keep calendars, and they began pestering McDonald: When would the government move to indict? "In due course," McDonald replied, but the moment never came. On March 23, 1979, he gave up, and the case was dismissed.

"I was a fool, a real idiot," McDonald, often his own most severe critic, told his fellow prosecutors. "I let the FBI talk me into something, and now look what happens. Just wait until I get hold of Carbone."

––––

Carbone was having his own troubles. Intent on fostering the best possible FBI-police relations in the case, he had urged elaborate measures to ensure that all law-enforcement agencies would share in the Sepe arrest scheduled for February 17. Because it was to be the first arrest in the case, it would attract strong media interest. Carbone saw to it that all other agencies were notified of the impending arrest. He also developed a plan that would allow those agencies, including Ahearn's 113th Detective Squad, to participate in the actual arrest.

Everything went wrong right from the start. Less than an hour after a "confidential" notification to the other agencies, a television reporter called Puccio's office seeking to confirm it. An enraged Puccio threatened to call the arrest off, relenting only when the FBI pointed out that the operation had gone too far to be recalled.

Then a garbled radio message on the day of the arrest led Carbone, Detective Joseph Connors from Ahearn's squad, and personnel from other law-enforcement agencies to the wrong site.

"You son of a bitch," Connors snapped at Carbone, assuming that the radio message had been deliberately garbled so that only FBI agents would make the arrest.

There was worse to come. Carbone's superiors compounded matters by deciding on a rigid procedure to announce the arrest. To the mounting fury of Ahearn, he and two detectives were ushered into the FBI's Queens office, handed a short statement that was to be released, and told that there would be no press conference. They were therefore enraged to see Laster holding his own press conference later that night on a television newscast.

"You know something?" Ahearn said to detectives John Fitzsimons and Joseph Connors. "I'm getting the funny feeling we're under house arrest." They were sitting in one section of the Queens FBI office, while in another Sepe was being softened up for his forthcoming encounter with McDonald.

Ahearn rose from his chair and walked out into the hall. An FBI agent suddenly moved into his path. "Where are you going?" asked the agent.

"I'm going to the fucking bathroom!" Ahearn roared. "You want to try and stop me?" The agent stood aside.

In the bathroom, by interesting coincidence, Sepe stood at a urinal, watched over by several agents. To their alarm, Ahearn took a position next to Sepe, and when neither man was in a position to move, Ahearn looked at Sepe and smiled. Sepe's eyes widened in alarm as he assumed he would have to deal with Ahearn as well as with the FBI.

In point of fact, Carbone did not think that this elaborate ritual in the Queens office was the right way to engender better FBI-police relations, but loyalty to the FBI prevented him from saying so when Ahearn confronted him in his office.

"What the hell is the FBI's problem?" Ahearn demanded, after reciting his grievances.

"Tom, we were afraid of leaks," Carbone said, then went on to explain that the elaborate security surrounding the arrest of Sepe was part of a policy designed for maximum security. The fewer people who knew of the plan for the arrest, he argued, the better for all concerned. At some point in this exposition, Carbone made the mistake of using the word "corruption."

Ahearn exploded. *"Are you saying my guys are corrupt?"* he bellowed. "There is *no* corruption in the 113th Squad!"

Things went downhill from there, and Ahearn stalked out, his opinion of the perfidy of the FBI newly confirmed. He was still boiling two days later when the FBI Agent Sweeney—unaware of the Ahearn-Carbone encounter—called the 113th Squad, seeking information. He had the misfortune to get Ahearn on the phone.

"Listen, Sweeney, your boss Carbone is a shit, Laster is a shit, the whole FBI is for shit!" For good measure, he threw in the names of several FBI directors, past and present.

———

Carbone was distressed by this turn of events, for although he did not like Ahearn, the goal of better FBI-police relations was now further jeopardized. The Sepe arrest had made things worse instead of better, and Carbone saw no way to immediately repair the damage. Clearly, the police were deeply suspicious of the FBI's actions, and they appeared in no mood to accept an explanation that what had happened was the result of a series of circumstances over which no one had control. (The Laster "press conference," for example. In fact, Laster had decided that there would be no press conference, but was waylaid by several television reporters outside the FBI office. He felt compelled to make a few bland and cautious remarks confirming the arrest. Broadcast in tightly edited form on the news that night, they conveyed the erroneous impression that Laster was holding a press conference.)

Carbone might have felt less upset about the course of events if there had been some compensation in the arrest of Sepe. But the carefully wrought plan for that event quickly appeared pointless. Sepe sat there in the FBI office, stubbornly shaking his head as Carbone and the agents played out their little spiel, warning him of the dire legal consequences he faced, along with the bright future that awaited him should he decide to cooperate.

"I don't know nothin'," Sepe replied to all blandishments and threats. Warned that he faced a long prison term as the result of a mountain of evidence the agents hinted they had, Sepe shrugged his shoulders. "You gotta do whatcha gotta do," he repeatedly said to the agents, daring them to do their worst.

Some hours later, Sepe was put into McDonald's hands. McDonald had no better luck, although he had the sense at one point that Sepe might be wavering. McDonald pressed on, "I would like to note the benefits of your cooperation." He went into a long exposition on how Sepe would be placed in the Federal Witness Protection Program, how the government would give him a new identity, how he would be paid a monthly stipend, and how he could begin a whole new life. All he had to do was cooperate—provide information and later testify against the others involved in the Lufthansa robbery.

Sepe asked to speak with his wife privately. Afterward, he told McDonald he knew absolutely nothing about the Lufthansa heist.

"This close," said McDonald to Carbone, holding two fingers close together. Carbone nodded, for both men understood what had almost certainly happened: Sepe had told his wife he was thinking of turning in order to avoid a long prison sentence. She then reminded him that McDonald's real target was Jimmy Burke. And to turn against Burke was to invite a certain death. McDonald and the FBI agents could talk all they wanted to about how they could protect Angelo Sepe, but if Jimmy Burke wanted to eliminate the witness who could put him behind bars, then Sepe was a dead man, no matter what. Had he forgotten what kind of a man Jimmy Burke was?

———

That night, Carbone arrived home late. He put on his winter running clothes and went out for a run along the shorefront. It was a crisp, clean night. Across the water, the bright lights of Brooklyn flickered.

As he ran, Carbone thought. He thought about the succession of disasters that had marked the day. Sepe had been arrested finally, but given his intransigence, there was no reasonable hope that it would lead anywhere. Gruenwald also had been arrested, but that move showed no indication of having the desired effect: causing Louis Werner to crumble. Then there was Carbone's unfortunate encounter with Ahearn, which seemed to have ignited further police suspicion of the FBI's role in the investigation. Everybody seemed to be growing testy and irritable, even McDonald of the easy charm. Agents reported that when they told McDonald they could not find a particular witness on whom the prosecutor wanted to serve a grand jury subpoena, he threw a telephone book at them and told them to serve a subpoena on every person by that name in the book.

A bleak vista now stretched before him, Carbone reflected. If things weren't bad enough, he had detected the most ominous development of all. Carbone felt that a plan was afoot, designed by Jimmy the Gent to prevent his gang from betraying him. A plan, now in its early stages, that in full dimension would render the entire investigation useless. There would not be even one thread of a loose end for investigators to grab and exploit.

And Carbone was convinced that this simple plan had already begun to unfold.

The full impact of that thought caused Carbone to suddenly stop running. He stood for a moment in the darkness, his breath billowing in white clouds around his head. From somewhere out on the water, he heard the horn of a passing freighter, a low, mournful sound like a funeral dirge.

Jimmy Burke would murder them all.

PART

FOUR

A PECULIAR
JUSTICE

Chapter

10

"He's keeping company with a spare tire"

Although Carbone did not know it, "the great Lufthansa slaughter" had been set in motion nearly two months before— a mere ten days after the robbery.

It came in the form of one of the more sinister-looking hoods employed by Joseph (Joey Beck) DiPalermo. The hood sat in a small Queens restaurant, while on the other side of the table a distinctly unhappy Tommy DeSimone fiddled uncomfortably with a napkin.

"You gotta do this," the hood said. It was an imperative— one that clearly permitted no alternative. DeSimone could see that, but he had a small personal problem.

"Jesus," he said, "I *know* the guy; he trusts me."

Which was precisely the point. As DeSimone's closest friend, Stax Edwards was certain to trust him enough to allow his old friend to get close—close enough to kill him.

Torn between the power of Mafia logic and his personal feelings for Edwards, DeSimone was in a rare moral quandary. He was now forced to confront an inescapable conclusion: Stax Edwards had screwed up real bad. His failure to dispose of the van used in the Lufthansa heist represented the kind of gross violation of orders that called for the supreme penalty.

The emissary did not need to explain to DeSimone that a criminal organization which did not exact the death penalty for such major derelictions would not survive very long. Stax had to go.

"Why me?" DeSimone complained, but the question was rhetorical. He knew that Edwards, aware of his own failure and the danger to his life it represented, had gone into hiding. He had rented a small apartment in Ozone Park, from which he almost never emerged. By the hour, he strummed his guitar, singing the blues, hoping the trouble would all blow over somehow. Only DeSimone, his closest friend, knew about the hideout, and only to DeSimone would Edwards open the door, hence the terrible logic that dictated DeSimone be the executioner.

DiPalermo, aware of the friendship, had set up the murder contract. Under the prevailing rules of Mafia protocol, DiPalermo's demand for Edwards's murder had to be honored. Edwards, who had dabbled in narcotics-peddling, was technically affiliated with DiPalermo's organization. Vario and Burke had been consulted, but they were not about to raise any objections; they were infuriated with Edwards anyway. Now the only remaining obstacle was to persuade DeSimone to do the job.

Despite all the emissary's arguments, DeSimone was still reluctant. But the emissary had saved his trump card for last, and finally he played it. "Listen," he said, leaning close to DeSimone, laying a hand on his arm and staring into his eyes. *"You could be made on this."*

DeSimone suddenly brightened, and the Faustian bargain took hold: he would murder his friend Stax Edwards in exchange for the strong possibility that a grateful Mafia would at last induct him into the fold. DeSimone understood that such a selfless act of violent betrayal would virtually guarantee his acceptance.

On the night of December 18, 1978, Stax Edwards heard a knock at his door, but did not answer it until he heard DeSimone's voice. After letting his old friend inside, Edwards turned his back on DeSimone to get him a drink. It was the last mistake of his life: DeSimone put a bullet into his brain with a silenced .32-caliber pistol.

"It's gone," the voice of the FBI agent on the telephone reported to Carbone.

"How did that happen?" Carbone asked irritably, but the agent, one of those assigned to track DeSimone and his car, had no idea. The car had simply disappeared. Possibly the beeper had fallen off, as often happened with such devices, or had been spotted and removed. In any event, after all the effort expended on attaching the beeper bug to DeSimone's vehicle, the car had vanished like the blip of a crashed plane erased from a radar screen. That was bad enough, but the agent had even more disturbing news. DeSimone was gone, too.

Coincidentally, on January 14, 1979, Mrs. DeSimone reported her husband missing. She told police her husband had borrowed $35 two nights before, announced that he had to go out, then left. That was the last she had heard from him. To the growing unease of FBI agents and police detectives, no one had seen DeSimone; it was as though the earth had swallowed him.

That was Carbone's greatest fear. Clearly DeSimone had met with an untimely end, and the fact that his car was also gone strongly suggested that he had suffered the relatively rare fate occasionally meted out to Mafia miscreants: he and his car had been fed together into a giant crusher at some Mafia-controlled junkyard.

Or perhaps not. On the basis of tips from their own informants, the Port Authority Police believed that DeSimone had been shot and then left in the trunk of a car in the long-term parking lot at Kennedy Airport. The Port Authority detectives hoped this was not so, for one of their more distasteful duties was the discovery of bodies in car trunks after an overpowering stench from an automobile prompted a call to police. Because of the steady urbanization of Queens and Brooklyn beginning in the 1950s, the Mafia's habit of dumping bodies in vacant lots had been replaced by the more gruesome practice of leaving bodies in automobile trunks. This led to a macabre joke among the Port Authority cops when they heard that a Mafia hood was missing: "He's keeping company with a spare tire," a play on the old Sicilian Mafia saying, "Tonight he sleeps with the fishes."

The Port Authority cops opened trunks on cars at the Kennedy long-term lot, but there was no sign of either Tommy DeSimone or his car.

Many theories circulated regarding where the body of De-Simone was located and why he had been murdered. One theory held that DeSimone's application for formal Mafia membership had opened some old wounds. Some years before, he had murdered an insignificant hood who turned out to be the personal favorite of a rising young *capo* in one of the mob families. The *capo* had quietly nurtured his resentment until later, in a display of power, he had demanded DeSimone's head at the very moment of DeSimone's greatest hope for Mafia membership. According to this theory, the *capo*'s demand ignited a complex series of Mafia politics. It was finally decided that the *capo*'s satisfaction overrode any gratitude owed to DeSimone for having disposed of Stax Edwards.

Whatever the reason, Carbone decided the important fact was that the presumed murder of DeSimone was the second involving a participant in the Lufthansa heist. The FBI, of course, had no proof that either DeSimone or Edwards had been involved, but by January, a month after the robbery, they were quite convinced that Edwards had played some sort of support role, and that DeSimone was one of the robbers.

That being the case, Carbone became convinced that there was now a plan to address what Burke and Vario must have considered their central problem: how to control the obvious susceptibilities of the Robert's Lounge Gang. And that plan, simply, amounted to killing anyone who might talk.

Carbone's deduction had horrifying implications, and they began to assume some form in the lingering matter of Louis Werner.

———

"He wants a trial, he's got one," McDonald announced snappishly to Carbone in the early spring of 1979. He was talking about the case of *79 CR 89, United States of America v. Louis Werner.* Carbone perceived that McDonald was aggravated by Werner, a man he felt was about to waste the taxpayers' money (and McDonald's time) on a trial he had absolutely no hope of winning. Like a man using a flamethrower to dispose of a moth, McDonald marshaled his artillery for the final

———

assault against Werner. Actually, McDonald needed only a portion of the vast array of evidence he had on hand. Considering just the testimony of Gruenwald, Fischetti, and Menna —all of whom had received immunity in return for their testimony—Louis Werner's defense looked hopeless.

And indeed it proved to be hopeless when the trial of Louis Werner opened on May 2, 1979. The key witness, Peter Gruenwald, outlined his and Werner's plan, the $22,000 robbery, the abortive attempt to round up a robbery gang, and the way in which the actual robbers finally used the plan on the morning of December 11, 1978. Combined with the testimony of Fischetti and Menna, Gruenwald's testimony was devastating. Werner's defense was reduced to attempting to pick holes in the witnesses' accounts, a largely fruitless exercise, for no amount of nit-picking could unravel the fabric of Werner's guilt.

Werner sat through it all, glaring at Gruenwald, apparently unable to believe he would actually be convicted. At one point, he had been temporarily released from jail to visit his teenage daughter who had been badly injured in an automobile accident. During the trip, one of his FBI escorts suddenly asked him, "Lou, how do you expect to beat this?" The agent was stunned to discover Werner had no idea.

The only dramatic moment in the trial occurred when McDonald put Werner's girlfriend, Janet Barbieri, on the stand. McDonald had anticipated problems with her, but nothing like what actually happened. In a performance that left the jurors open-mouthed, Ms. Barbieri alternately screamed, fainted, collapsed in her chair, and shook like a leaf. All of this melodrama was touched off by McDonald's persistent attempts to get her to answer a simple question: Did she or did she not tell the grand jury the previous March that Louis Werner had told her he was the inside man in the Lufthansa robbery? Apparently assuming that a yes would put her boyfriend's head in the noose, Ms. Barbieri was not inclined to answer.

McDonald suspected that her bravura performance was an act designed to help the defendant. It was not an especially bright way of accomplishing that end, for she succeeded only in concentrating a fascinated jury's attention on the specific issue of what Werner had told her. Clearly the jury did not believe her when she claimed she had admitted Werner's bragging to the grand jury only because McDonald had "confused" her. The jurors had to wonder what could have been so confusing about a question that required only a yes or no answer.

The result was inevitable. Without calling a single witness and terming the prosecution witnesses "a bunch of rats," Werner's defense rested. On May 16, 1979, following a two-week trial, the jury quickly brought in a guilty verdict. Just over a month later, the judge threw the book at Werner during his sentencing: fifteen years in jail and a $25,000 fine.

Even before he was sentenced, Werner had again demonstrated his inability to grasp the essentials. Following his conviction, McDonald took Werner before a federal grand jury, gave him immunity, and demanded that he tell them what he knew. Werner refused and was given an additional one and a half–year sentence for contempt. To further complete the picture of a man perhaps not totally in contact with reality, Werner told the sentencing judge that he did not understand why he was being sentenced to jail while "the guilty ones" were still free. For some odd reason, Werner did not include himself in this category.

The stiffness of the sentence raised McDonald's hope that, faced with the unpleasant prospect of incarceration in a federal penitentiary, Werner might still relent and cooperate. But Carbone turned out to be right: Werner, determined to show the real crooks he was a stand-up guy, entered federal prison still mute.

Four months later, however, the reality of prison life finally induced Werner to contact McDonald and offer to discuss the Lufthansa robbery.

"Your cooperation," McDonald told him in a starchy tone meant to underscore his bitterness toward the cargo agent who had given him so much trouble, "will be brought to the attention of the court." In other words, McDonald was prepared to assent to the inevitable motion by Werner's lawyer for reduction or mitigation of sentence, but he wasn't inclined to knock himself out for it. Werner's sentence was later reduced to five years.

In the late fall of 1979, Werner, now a cooperative witness, began to tell all he knew. Carbone, for one, was not looking forward eagerly to the conversation; he had a feeling that he was not about to hear anything especially revelatory. Carbone suspected that Burke had long ago anticipated Werner's betrayal—as indeed he had.

Just as Carbone predicted, Werner did not have a lot to offer. He named the only man in the robbery gang with whom he had dealt—Joseph Manri. He claimed he had no contact with anyone else in the gang.

"Mr. Werner," Carbone announced with some sarcasm, "has just given us a ghost."

———

Months before, prior to Werner's conviction, Carbone knew that Joseph Manri was certain to become a dead man soon. He was doomed, Carbone decided, because the conviction of Louis Werner amounted to Manri's death sentence.

"We have to get the word out," Carbone told his agents, as he unfolded his latest plan. The FBI would spread an alarm by way of underworld informants to the effect that certain key figures in the robbery—notably Joseph Manri—faced grave danger. The members of the Robert's Lounge Gang were being eliminated one by one, and Manri was next on the list.

Carbone held this to be a Pythagorean Theorem of criminal behavior: loose ends would be eliminated before pressure could be brought to bear on them. Manri was facing final disposition of a 1977 robbery during which a pursuing police officer had been killed. He was clearly vulnerable to heavy pressure—pressure he almost certainly could not withstand. And Manri was the only man who could prove that a link existed between Louis Werner and the robbery gang led by Burke. The risk was too great; he would have to go.

Carbone's action, of course, was not entirely a humanitarian gesture. He hoped the message would drive Manri, and perhaps others, into the sheltering embrace of the FBI. It was a long shot, Carbone conceded, for he had no real hope that Manri would defy Jimmy Burke and desert to the other side. But if Manri failed to take advantage of the FBI offer, Carbone was convinced that he would die.

A terrible confirmation of that conviction came on the morning of May 16, 1979, when a boy on his way to school in the Mill Basin section of Brooklyn passed a two-door Buick parked on the street. Inside, he saw two men who appeared to be sleeping. The boy looked more closely and saw blood all over their heads. When police arrived, they found Joseph Manri and Robert (Frenchie) McMahon slumped in the front seat. Each man had been shot several times in the back of the head.

At the very moment the bodies were discovered, a federal court jury was winding up its deliberations in the trial against Louis Werner. Several hours later, the jurors found him guilty.

"What kind of people are we dealing with here?" Lieutenant Ahearn asked as he surveyed the murder scene. A man who could read much in such mute scenes, Ahearn was appalled at the casual savagery of this one. Whoever had shot the two men, Ahearn pointed out, noting the angle of the fatal bullets, was sitting in the back seat. Obviously, he was someone both victims knew and trusted, for there was no evidence that they had turned to look at their murderer, or that either man checked him out in the rearview mirror. They had sat there in the front seat, perfectly relaxed, as the murderer brought up his gun to a point just behind each man's head and fired. Or perhaps two murderers had fired simultaneously, one at each victim.

In either case, Ahearn noted, the murderer was a pure cold-blooded killer. "Notice the car," he lectured his detectives. "It's a two-door model, which means that the perp had to climb over the bodies of the two guys he's shot to get out of the car. *He's got to climb over the bodies.* Think about that: he has to crawl over those dead bodies, blood all over the place. He kills these guys, crawls over them, getting blood all over his clothes, and just as calmly as you please, he gets out of the car and shuts the door behind him. So what are we dealing with? We're dealing here with a man who likes to kill."

A perfect description of Paolo LiCastri, but the Sicilian enforcer had already escaped conventional justice. Less than a month after the Manri-McMahon murders, his bullet-riddled body, minus shirt and shoes, was found in a garbage-strewn vacant lot in Brooklyn. It had been there awhile; maggots had already eaten away half his face.

And so the great Lufthansa slaughter had begun. In this trail of blood, police detectives and FBI agents were united by a shared sense of powerlessness. Each time they began to close in on someone connected with the robbery gang, that suspect was killed, and there was absolutely nothing they could do about it.

Certainly the FBI had tried, even to the extent of attempting to get potential victims off the street before they got killed. So had Ahearn's detectives. They had hacked away at Louis Cafora until the fat man wavered in his initially firm denial of having had anything to do with the Lufthansa robbery. He had agreed to show up the first week in March at the 113th Precinct, complete with wife and white Cadillac. But he never made it: Cafora, his wife, and the car disappeared, never to be seen again. Officially, he and his wife were carried in the police files as missing persons, but everybody knew that two more loose ends had been done away with. Perhaps they and their Cadillac wound up in the same crusher that had disposed of Tommy DeSimone, another "missing person."

Martin Krugman was another loose end. He had been missing since late January when he walked out of the hairdressing salon one morning and was never seen again. According to whispers around the underworld, Krugman had been taken up in a light plane and dumped somewhere over the Atlantic Ocean. Possibly the same plane had been used for another flight, this one to dump a small trunk containing the headless and limbless torso of a woman. In this case, however, the body eventually was carried back to shore.

What remained of the woman's body, found on a New Jersey beach just two days after the Manri-McMahon murders, required the best skills of a team of pathologists to make an identification. Eventually, through exhaustive use of X-rays and after checking the identifying marks of missing persons, the pathologists found a match. The woman was a Long Island beautician who a month before had hurriedly left her place of employment one evening after telling a friend that she had to meet someone at a nearby diner.

"If I'm not back in ten minutes, come get me," the beautician said, leaving her keys and purse behind. Mysteriously, she never reached the diner; she vanished into thin air.

Her name was Theresa Ferrara.

———

There was considerable debate among the police and the FBI over the precise motives for this wave of killing. In the view of some, many of the murders had nothing to do with Lufthansa and were ordinary gangland killings carried out for the conventional reasons: to shut up a stool pigeon forever, to eliminate malefactors of assorted description, or to remove someone who had exhibited too independent a turn of mind.

Yet, they all shared a common, scarlet thread—a connection to the Robert's Lounge Gang. No one knew how many old scores were being settled in the process, but the murders seemed to be a chilling form of insurance underwriting; those who knew too much, or were burdened by circumstances that might make them vulnerable to police or FBI pressure, were slaughtered.

Also at work was a paranoia shared by Burke, Vario, and their associates about the identity of the informant who had put the FBI on their trail. Obviously, the informant was someone closely connected with the Burke gang. The FBI had focused its attention on the Robert's Lounge crew right after the robbery. This indicated they were operating on the basis of high-level information. To Burke and Vario even the slimmest scrap of circumstantial evidence was cause for murder—witness the killing of Krugman, primarily because of Burke's suspicion about the suspended sentence he had received in that Nassau County narcotics case a year before. The sentence looked fishy; any hood knows that such judicial slaps on the wrist are often handed out to men who have made a deal with the other side.

Whatever the motives for the killings, all concerned agreed that behind them lurked the menacing person of James Burke. The extent of his culpability was a matter of opinion. Perhaps he had actually carried out some of the murders himself, arranged for others to commit them, or merely acquiesced when the decision was made that somebody had to be killed, but there was no doubt that he was involved in some way. This conviction survived even in the face of persistent underground rumors that Burke had wept like a baby when he learned of his friend DeSimone's disappearance and assumed, as did everyone else, that "Two Gun Tommy" was dead.

Yet Burke had occupied a good deal of his time before the disappearance of Marty Krugman asking underworld contacts certain interesting questions: Was Marty a real stand-up guy? Would he keep his mouth shut under FBI pressure? Informed that Krugman was stand-up but that he had a habit of telling his wife *everything*, Burke said nothing, and scowled. Krugman disappeared shortly thereafter.

Burke also asked around about Manri and McMahon, who were rumored to be pressing Burke for larger shares of the Lufthansa money. Their $50,000 fees looked puny as news of the size of the haul spread, and they made the fatal error of letting Burke know how they felt.

There was unanimity of view among police and FBI agents. All of them believed that Burke was the mastermind of the Lufthansa robbery and that he was also a murderer. He acted in the old pirate tradition, murdering all the men who had helped him bury a treasure hoard, then killing the man who had drawn the map showing its location.

"One thing I'll never understand," Carbone remarked to his agents, "is how Burke ever got the 'Jimmy the Gent' business attached to his name. 'The Gent'? With his kind of record, with all those people he's killed? I'll tell you what Jimmy Burke is. Jimmy Burke is a . . ." Carbone searched for the most baleful Brooklyn insult he could find, at last arriving at the one that in his old neighborhood connoted the lowest form of life on earth: "Jimmy Burke is a *scumbag*."

————

Carbone's increasing frustration during 1979 was worsened by a physical problem, a severe flare-up of a sciatic condition. It put a severe crimp in his long-distance running, and some weeks before the New York City Marathon in October, he was hobbling around the office with a cane. McDonald's initial sympathy turned to incredulity when Carbone calmly announced he would run all 26 miles of the marathon.

"Why not?" Carbone responded when McDonald wondered whether a man in his physical condition should do such a thing. McDonald now saw, in full flower, the trait that almost everyone who knew Carbone remarked upon: the man's single-mindedness.

"I want to run it in under four hours," Carbone said, as though this explained why he would subject himself to such an ordeal. And ordeal it was. On an unseasonably warm October day, fourteen thousand people began the race. Number 9630, Stephen Carbone of Manhattan, finished in just under four hours. Pictures of Carbone during the race showed a man in agonizing pain, his body listing to one side like a torpedoed merchant ship limping into harbor.

———

"Incredible," McDonald said, summarizing his view of Carbone's achievement—an expert opinion, since McDonald himself was no slouch at single-mindedness. And like Carbone, this concentration was centered, throughout 1979, on James Burke. McDonald shared the general perception of Jimmy Burke as Public Enemy, but he faced a very real legal problem: Where was the evidence needed to convict him?

There was no evidence in the nearly two months' worth of tapes produced by the FBI bug in Sepe's car. A number of interesting references occurred in conversations between Burke and his protégé, but nothing solid enough to make a case against him. To be sure, they provided a reason for McDonald to have Burke arrested as a parole violator—associating with Sepe, a known criminal—but McDonald was aware that Burke would not be rattled by such a low-scale charge. Still, it was all McDonald had at that point, and it brought him face to face one morning in April 1979 with the man he had heard so much about.

They were brought together by the U.S. Constitution, which gave defendant Burke the right to examine the Sepe tapes that would be placed into evidence against him. Accompanied by his lawyer, Burke sat in McDonald's office for an "interview," during which the prosecutor sought to display his wares under the general rubric of "I would like to note the benefits of you cooperating."

The lawyer might just as well have been a stick of furniture for all the need Burke had of his services in that encounter. Burke had been through this game many times and was perfectly capable of playing his end of the court without any help, even against a formidable adversary like McDonald. To anyone from the outside watching the byplay between the two men, it had the deceptive illusion of a friendly conversation between two Irishmen in a pub. In fact, there was plenty of subtle thrust and parry as Burke and McDonald each spooned out heaps of charm. Burke, like McDonald, had the "gift of words," and the prosecutor realized he was up against an opponent of no mean skill.

"Well, you can't bullshit a bullshitter," Carbone accurately summarized the encounter later. True enough, McDonald conceded, but he knew Burke was laughing at him behind that facade of unconcerned charm, for Burke had obviously enjoyed tweaking the prosecutor's nose. And he undoubtedly relished the knowledge that the prosecutor was desperate for solid evidence against the mastermind of the Lufthansa heist. Yet the best he could manage was the relatively puny charge of parole violation. To a man like Burke, that was a mosquito bite.

Two weeks later, McDonald saw Burke walking down a hall in the courthouse near his office. The prosecutor stopped abruptly and stared at Burke's feet. McDonald was certain he saw Burke smile faintly at the sight of the prosecutor staring at his Puma running shoes.

"I know what he was saying to me," McDonald later told fellow prosecutors. "He was telling me, in so many words, 'Hey, I heard about you guys grabbing those sneakers. Too bad you couldn't make a match. Somebody was wearing 'em. Maybe it was me. How do you like that, sucker? You asshole!' It was a message: 'I got away with it. Now what are you gonna do?' "

If in fact that was Burke's subtle message, the answer was: Not much. For by the summer of 1979, six months after the robbery, the investigation was completely stuck. The inside man and his confederate had been convicted, but Burke and what was left of the Robert's Lounge Gang were untouched. Now Burke seemed to be openly twitting the constabulary.

Only Burke's low-life friend and occasional co-conspirator Henry Hill, along with Angelo Sepe, Burke's other protégé, seemed to have survived the great purge—for reasons which at that moment were unclear. Sepe was in jail on parole violation and had resisted all efforts to persuade him to cooperate. As for Hill, he appeared to have remained friendly with Burke.

But appearances in this case were deceiving, for certain forces had been set in motion by the Hill-Burke relationship that would provide the final and most bizarre chapter in the drama of the Lufthansa heist.

———

"Jesus Christ, you're sick, Henry, you know that? You need psychiatric help!"

Considering the speaker—James Burke—this was an interesting piece of psychoanalysis. But then, Burke, despite a criminal record that virtually made him a textbook example of what criminologists call an antisocial psychopath, was surprisingly straitlaced on such matters as sex, alcohol, and narcotics, at least as they pertained to him personally.

So it was that Burke looked upon his protégé Henry Hill with increasing dismay in the late spring and early summer of 1979. Clearly, Hill was going to hell in a hand basket at breakneck speed. He was drinking to excess and appeared to be stoned out of his mind most of the time, often helping himself to samples of the narcotics he and his prison friend from Pittsburgh were dealing. The same dealer—Paul Mazzei—had led Hill and Burke into the basketball point-shaving scheme. Although the scheme was finally ended by one of Burke's temper tantrums, all involved had just about broken even, and Burke had been willing to forget about it.

But Hill as a degenerate was quite something else again. Visiting Hill's home on Long Island one summer's day in 1979, Burke was astounded to see that his protégé's new bedroom had been redone completely in a style that could only be described as high-tech bordello, complete with huge bed, strobe lights, mirrors, and a pile carpet in which people seemed to sink to their knees.

But it was what went on there that really got to Burke. Very much the traditionalist, Burke found Hill's household arrangements a zoo. Hill had a girlfriend, apparently with his wife's knowledge (he described the third side of this triangle as "my Christmas present"), plus a string of other girls. Into the bedroom-playroom they came, along with a circle of young people Hill had recruited into his widening drug operation. They liked to party, and Burke was shocked one day to find Hill in bed with a man and a woman, both of whom were teasing him; because he was so stoned, he did not know which one had just performed fellatio on him. To Burke's further shock, they were attempting to arouse Hill so that he could have intercourse with a man elsewhere in the house.

"This shit is sick!" Burke yelled later as Hill finally began to emerge from his stupor. "What, are you crazy?" Hill did not quite understand why Burke was so angry, and this sent his mentor into another outburst, which ended in a renewed effort to get his protégé into psychiatric treatment. "You're sick, you stupid son of a bitch!" Burke shouted at him. "You hafta get help. You need a nut doctor!"

This diagnosis may or may not have been correct, but there was a certain amount of shrewd business sense behind Burke's outburst. Burke realized that Hill was very nearly out of control, and he knew that self-destructiveness would inevitably lead to an encounter with the police. Careless about the people with whom he dealt, increasingly sloppy about security in his narcotics operation, and using too much of the stuff himself—Hill was just short of being an outright addict—he was virtually inviting the police to his door. And to Jimmy Burke, who had approved and provided initial capital for the Hill-Mazzei narcotics operation. That made Burke vulnerable to a narcotics sale conspiracy charge, a serious felony in New York.

Burke had little hope that Hill could get his head straightened out, so he decided to cut the ties that bound them together. Henceforth, Burke announced, Hill was on his own; the Gent wanted no more to do with him. With that break—taken, he thought, before the police became aware of Hill's narcotics operation—Burke hoped he would be free of whatever legal consequences Hill was sure to suffer on the inevitable day when the police would burst into Hill's house.

Burke did not know that the police were fully aware of Henry Hill and his narcotics operation.

———

From his office window, Nassau County Assistant District Attorney Richard Broder could see much of the formal landscaping surrounding the cluster of government buildings in the county seat just 25 miles east of Manhattan. It was the late fall of 1979, and the trees had turned a brilliant red and orange.

"There's something you really need to take a look at," Detective Lieutenant Daniel Mann of the Nassau County Police Department said as he walked into Broder's office.

"Sure," said Broder. "Go ahead; I'm listening." There was a certain amount of wariness in his reaction, for Broder realized he was about to enter the first phase of the often intricate relationship between police and prosecutors. It was known as the "sell" phase, the time when police attempt to convince prosecutors that the case they are working on is pure gold, a developing investigation that promises to be so airtight that the prospective defendants will immediately throw themselves on the mercy of the court when confronted by the overwhelming evidence.

Often the case turns out to be something less than that. Although Mann, head of the Narcotics Squad, was widely respected as an extremely capable police officer not noted for exaggeration, Broder remained wary. Such caution was often warranted under the best of circumstances; police officers who have worked on a case for a long time occasionally fail to see the forest for the trees.

"Not here," Mann said, looking around Broder's office. For a moment, Broder imagined that Mann meant for them to talk outside because he feared hidden listening devices in the prosecutor's office. "Downstairs." Mann motioned. "I need a blackboard."

In a conference room, Mann began drawing diagrams as he outlined an intricate narcotics conspiracy that basically involved an interstate swap of cocaine and heroin, with both sides reaping immense profits. A Mafia-connected hood named Henry Hill was at the center of the conspiracy. His main contact, Paul Mazzei, had a record for narcotics sales.

The diagrams showed the relationships between nearly a dozen people who were involved, while Mann explained how the ring operated. Then Mann began showing some of the hard evidence his detectives had gathered—including, Broder noted with satisfaction, retrieved copies of airline tickets from Hill's garbage, proving conclusively the times and dates "mules" (young women who transport narcotics across state lines) had moved. Even better, Mann's men had wiretaps operating on all known participants in the ring, and the tapes were full of references to narcotics transactions.

"Of course, they're in code," Mann noted, but went on to point out that the code was as transparent as a piece of cellophane: narcotics were most often referred to as "T-shirts." The giveaway came when someone mentioned "three-quarters" of T-shirts, obviously not the usual measuring unit for such items.

And there was something else, Mann pointed out: the tapes were full of references to "the Irishman." The police believed this person to be none other than James Burke, a known associate of Hill.

Broder did not need to be reminded who Jimmy Burke was; for months newspaper readers had been told he was the mastermind of the Lufthansa robbery. Broder also did not need more convincing that the police were onto a major narcotics operation that was grossing somewhere around $1.5 million a year.

And Richard Broder wanted to be the prosecutor.

———

Six months later he got his chance. In April 1980, police arrested Hill and four other people on charges of smuggling narcotics from Colombia up through Key West and other areas of Florida, then shipping most of them out to other areas of the country; they kept the remainder for local dealers. (Subsequently, the five were among fourteen people indicted by a Nassau County grand jury for trafficking in heroin, cocaine, amphetamines, Quaaludes, and marijuana. One of the fourteen was Hill's wife.)

In short, Hill ran a narcotics supermarket, and Broder had one of the biggest cases of his career. He also had one of the easiest. Hill and his confederates, just as Burke feared, had become so careless that they left a trail a mile wide. To Broder's surprise, they even stored narcotics in Hill's house. And Mrs. Hill had an incriminating habit of writing down telephone messages regarding narcotics transactions and then leaving them lying around.

During the raid, police found these and the narcotics hidden in Hill's house, but were so taken with Hill's bedroom that they neglected to search thoroughly under that deep pile rug, where another four ounces of heroin lay concealed. Still, they collected more than enough evidence to make a solid case, Broder decided. This judgment was rewarded when a sudden development took everyone by surprise.

Henry Hill announced that he wanted to make a deal.

Broder's first encounter with Hill was in the somewhat intimate circumstances of a strip search in the offices of the Nassau County Police Narcotics Squad. First impressions revealed a man who reminded Broder of a shrewd rat, cunning and street smart, alertly waiting for the soft spot to exploit. Henry Hill was every inch the professional criminal.

A vast world separated the two men as they sat down to discuss Hill's cooperation. Broder was an idealist, a liberal, and a great admirer of Robert Kennedy. At one point he had headed the district attorney's Civil Rights Bureau. Born in New York, he had been an assistant U.S. attorney in Wisconsin. Then, desperately homesick for New York and for his culinary passions for genuine New York bagels and pizza, he and his wife returned. Broder took a job in the Nassau County district attorney's office, working for Denis Dillon, who preceded Thomas Puccio as head of the Eastern District Organized Crime Strike Force. Dillon, after winning election as district attorney, cleaned out a politically corrupt office and recruited a whole new staff of prosecutors, vowing that political considerations would no longer play a part in the way the DA conducted the people's business. To that end he transformed his office into one of the best such operations in the New York metropolitan area.

Dillon and Broder, members of the new breed in the district attorney's office, practically oozed deeply felt liberal sympathy for the poor and downtrodden within their jurisdiction. Their sincerity stood in stark contrast to the cynical world that Henry Hill the street kid represented. A thirty-six-year-old crook steeped in the intricacies of the criminal world and its established pattern of double- and triple-cross, Hill was a conniving con man who had no sympathy for anyone except himself and—to Broder and Dillon's surprise—the women in his life.

And that concern, Broder perceived, was mainly responsible for Hill's momentous decision to become a stool pigeon. He had been in prison before and had remained a "stand-up guy." He had never betrayed his mentor and protector Jimmy Burke, or the Mafia godfather with whom he was loosely affiliated, Paul Vario, Sr. But now, in addition to the twenty-year sentence Hill faced in Nassau, he was confronted with the fact that the women in his life were in danger of going to prison for a long time.

Hill's relationships with these assorted women were so tangled that Broder never did quite figure them all out. But however complex, they remained immaterial to the main point: for whatever reason, Hill had agreed to give Nassau County information that, considering his long criminal record and known associations with members of organized crime, promised to be nothing short of sensational.

"You'll have to go the whole yard," Broder told Hill. This was the prosecutor's standard warning that Hill would have to provide solid, provable information and later testify against those he had accused. Only then would the D.A. consider wiping the current charges off his slate.

In the beginning, Hill appeared to be fulfilling the hope of both the Nassau County district attorney's office and the police that he would provide them with unparalleled insight into criminal conspiracies. As Hill began talking, he made it clear he was prepared to give them the key that would unlock the mystery of the Lufthansa case. All ears, Broder and the police listened as Hill began telling a story that was hard to believe. Not noted for mental organization, Hill rambled all over the place, maddeningly flitting from one topic to another.

But there were plenty of nuggets of gold among the worthless pebbles: stories about the fallout among members of the Robert's Lounge Gang; beatings of several men who had run afoul of the Mafia; the killing of Tommy DeSimone; the intricate pattern of betrayal among those involved in the Lufthansa heist; and, for good measure, an incredible (and untrue) story about Theresa Ferrara. Paul Vario, Sr., had been smitten by her beauty, Hill claimed, and the aging don's infatuation led him to use her as a courier to move $3 million of the Lufthansa proceeds to Florida. Later, after discovering she was an

FBI informant, Vario had her gruesomely murdered, destroying her body so that he would never again have to think of the physical beauty that had so nearly unhinged him.

Taken as a whole, it sounded like lurid fiction—Broder suspected some of it might be—but it was clear that Hill had achieved his first aim; getting the undivided attention of the Nassau County authorities. And it was also clear that Nassau County, in the person of Richard Broder, was prepared to cut a deal. If, as Hill promised, he could deliver Jimmy Burke to them on a silver platter (along with several other matters of interest), then he—and the women—would walk on the narcotics case.

Broder, listening carefully, began to detect the strong fear that permeated Hill's rambling account, a fear that seemed fixed on the figure of Burke. It was something beyond the normal trepidation many men felt about the Gent and his reputation, yet Broder could not quite figure out why Hill was so plainly terrified of the man who had been his father figure for more than twenty years.

———

Henry Hill knew what it was, but for the moment, he kept it to himself. He was not yet ready to tell Broder that he had felt the shadow of death move very close to him, the cold chill of its breath on his neck.

Chapter

11

"Oh, what a mistake
you just made"

Like many such establishments in Queens, the diner was all gaudy excess, the sort of place, its regular patrons liked to joke, where they polish all that chrome and fake marble up front, while in the back they're greasing up the spoons.

Uninterested in either the decor or the level of fat globules in the food, two men sat in a corner booth. It was a steamy day in the especially hot summer of 1980, when even the asphalt seemed to sag under the heat.

"Not good," Henry Hill said, exhaling smoke as he puffed nervously on a cigarette. The man seated next to him grunted his agreement as he read through a long document, the outline of evidence, which the prosecution was required to give defendant Henry Hill.

The more Jimmy the Gent Burke read, the more unhappy he became; he didn't require a law degree to understand that what he was reading seemed to be an airtight case. Hill had been stupid; his habit of running things like a junior high school pajama party had ultimately provided the police with all the evidence they needed.

Hill waited expectantly, like an errant son bracing himself while his father read a poor report card. Burke had vowed never to have anything further to do with his wayward protégé, but Hill was once again back on his mentor's doorstep seeking counsel and support. What did Jimmy advise? How could the case be beaten?

"Who's CI [confidential informant] two twenty-one?" Burke demanded, suddenly focusing on that reference in the document.

"I don't know," Hill replied, uncertain whether this standard police–district attorney reference meant a wiretap or one of the people involved in the conspiracy.

"Think, stupid!" Burke growled. "Who was in the room with you when you talked about this stuff?"

Hill tried to remember, but a brain dulled by narcotics was having a hard time remembering. Finally, he remembered that a hood of his acquaintance, Robert Germaine, Jr., was present when salient details were discussed. Although Germaine was not a member of the Hill drug ring, his father, Robert Germaine, Sr., was.

"That's him," Burke decided instantly. "Okay, it's taken care of."

Germaine, Sr., was a professional criminal whose main claim to fame was his involvement in the million dollar robbery of the posh Hotel Pierre in Manhattan in 1972. Soon after the meeting in the Queens diner, he received a phone call from Burke. It was a courtesy call of sorts. Burke announced that Germaine's son had to be murdered because he had served as a police informant in the narcotics case involving Henry Hill. Burke expressed his apologies, but then, he reminded Germaine, business was business.

"Do what you hafta do," Germaine said simply.

Some time later, the body of his son was found in Queens with a bullet hole in his head. (In a horrible irony, it turned out that both Hill and Burke were mistaken. Germaine was not the informant. The police brought this fact forcefully to the attention of Germaine, Sr., when they arrested him later for narcotics peddling. Germaine merely shrugged and said, "That's the way it goes.")

Burke had intended the murder of Robert Germaine, Jr., both as a favor to his longtime protégé and as a means of preempting any possible testimony against himself by the presumed informant. But it turned out to be one of Burke's few major miscalculations, for the act stimulated Henry Hill's thought processes, and he began to see clearly, more clearly than he had ever seen anything in his life, that he was a dead man.

The arithmetic was irrefutable: Burke had murdered—or contrived to have murdered—almost everybody in the Robert's Lounge Gang who had any knowledge of the Lufthansa robbery. Of those who knew the great secret, only Hill and Angelo Sepe remained alive. And now Hill faced an extremely serious narcotics charge. What would prevent Burke from killing even his old buddy Henry Hill to ensure that he did not cooperate with prosecutors?

Nothing. Hill was alarmed at the casual slaying of Germaine, Jr., on a very flimsy supposition. In no small way, it drew Hill's attention to the question of his own place in the scheme of things. In this mood, Hill arrived at the deduction that he had no choice but to opt for the lesser of two evils— cooperation with the prosecutors. There was grave danger there, too, but at least he would have a fighting chance, instead of the certainty of his own execution.

Thus it could be argued that Jimmy Burke drove Hill into the arms of the Nassau County District Attorney's office. Hill himself took the next step in the late summer of 1980 by declaring his willingness to cooperate. Nassau County was certainly interested in what he had to say about Jimmy Burke and the Lufthansa heist, but Hill guessed there were other people who would be even more interested in that subject.

In the early fall of 1980, Hill contacted his federal parole officer and announced, "I want to talk to the FBI."

———

Like a magic talisman that opens the castle doors suddenly, the mention of Lufthansa in Hill's initial discussions with the FBI produced intense interest. Plainly, the Bureau was eager to hear what Hill might have to say on this subject, but the first conversations were disappointing. To Carbone's anger, Hill rambled all over the lot, and it was difficult to tell exactly what solid information he had to impart. Carbone had the feeling the FBI was going to have trouble with this witness.

McDonald was distinctly unexcited by the entry of Hill

into the Lufthansa case, which had been virtually moribund for a while. For one thing, he was a key prosecutor in the ABSCAM case, especially the trial of Senator Harrison Williams of New Jersey, and the mountain of work was crushing him. At the moment he was in no position to become reinvolved in a case that seemed to cause him nothing but aggravation. For another, the tentative deal with Hill specified that if he provided solid evidence, he would receive limited immunity on any federal charges and the pending Nassau County charges would be dropped. That, McDonald understood, involved an intricate arrangement between federal and local prosecutors, the kind of deal that carried the seeds of its own destruction. If one of the parties felt it was not getting fair value, the entire deal would collapse.

And, finally, McDonald was not impressed by his first sight of Henry Hill.

———

Like all prosecutors, McDonald believed that first impressions of witnesses were important, since juries tend to scrutinize their appearance carefully, using it as a guide when determining such matters as credibility.

Certainly Hill looked anything but credible that day in the late fall of 1980 when he walked into McDonald's office. Shaking like a leaf from drug withdrawal symptoms, he was a wreck. Glancing at the stack of baseball bats in a corner of McDonald's office—and wondering for a moment if the bats (which belonged to the Strike Force softball team) were used to enliven interrogations—Hill introduced himself to the prosecutor and began a monologue that McDonald had difficulty following.

McDonald had seen his kind many times before—the prototypical street hustler and small-time hood. Among Hill's incoherent rambling, however, McDonald detected a few flashes of intelligence. With time and effort, perhaps this fair-skinned, sandy-haired man who looked as though he had just emerged from a washing machine could be turned into a credible witness.

Or perhaps not, for just as McDonald was musing on that possibility, Hill vomited into the wastebasket.

"Get the hell out of my office," McDonald snapped at him.

———

"Go get yourself a lawyer, straighten yourself out, and then come back to see me." As Hill left, McDonald thought aloud: "*This* is our big Lufthansa witness?"

Actually, as things turned out, Hill could not provide much in the way of evidence on the robbery. Carbone and the FBI learned, to their dismay, that Hill's firsthand knowledge was limited. He knew all about how Krugman the bookmaker had put his hooks into a supervisor at Lufthansa, and he knew that this maneuver was ultimately rewarded when the supervisor produced the critical inside information. But Krugman was dead, and Werner had already been convicted, so that information was of little value. As for Jimmy Burke, Hill said that he told the Gent about Krugman's Lufthansa contact and that Burke subsequently planned the heist. To FBI agents curious why Hill himself had not been involved in the heist, Hill claimed that Burke had wanted him along on the job, but finally decided against it because of "bad blood" between Hill and Sepe. The estrangement between Sepe and himself, Hill related, went back to their days together in the federal penitentiary in Atlanta.

One day, Hill said, another inmate deliberately shoved him. Hill did not retaliate, leading Sepe to call him a "fag," among other epithets. Since then, the two men could not even be in the same room. At any rate, Hill claimed, Burke appreciated his help in setting up the Lufthansa heist and later gave him $10,000 for his trouble.

All very interesting, but it amounted to a very thin case against Jimmy Burke. So thin, in fact, that McDonald was distinctly unenthusiastic. The only thing linking Burke with the Lufthansa robbery was Hill's claim that he told Burke about Louis Werner and later received $10,000 as a reward. Without any other corroborative evidence, it wasn't enough to bring before a grand jury.

If McDonald and the FBI were disappointed in what Hill had to say, the authorities in Nassau County were astounded. What Hill was now saying to the federals was at some variance with what he had told Broder and the Nassau County Police. For example, Hill previously had not mentioned his participation in the Lufthansa plot. Even more curious was the fact that Hill, although obviously aware of the FBI's interest in Burke, failed to repeat what he had said in the confines of the Nassau County District Attorney's office—that Jimmy Burke was a participant in the Hill-Mazzei narcotics scheme, and was, in fact, "the Irishman" mentioned in the wiretaps.

Broder began to get a gut feeling that all was not well with the Nassau-federal deal on Hill. Was it possible that Hill, having decided that he liked life as a federal witness, had no intention of fulfilling his agreement with Nassau County? He was busy helping the FBI and the Drug Enforcement Administration to make several cases, including delivery of Paul Mazzei, his former partner in crime. As long as the federals were grateful for that, Hill had little incentive to extend himself for Nassau County. Plainly put, he had become a federal witness, and if he remained helpful to them, he could enjoy the considerable power of the federal government to protect him.

So much for Broder's perception. In fact, what was happening amounted to a dangerous communications gap between the federal government and Nassau County. It all turned on the operating definition of the word "cooperation." In the federal view, Hill would "walk" on the narcotics charges against him if he "fully cooperated" with the Nassau DA. In other words, "cooperate" was defined as "provide all the information he had." Whether Nassau could make a prosecutable case based on that information was another question entirely; that was not Hill's problem, for he could not be held liable for the vagaries of the jury system.

Nassau County, on the other hand, equated "cooperation" with "conviction." In other words, if Hill provided enough information for the county to indict and convict Jimmy Burke as the ringleader of the narcotics operation, then Hill's "cooperation" would then be adjudged satisfactory. Anything less than a conviction would be considered unsatisfactory.

There were political reasons for Nassau County's attitude. A politically conservative area with predominantly Republican enrollment, the county was sensitive to the crime issue. Since 1980 was an election year, the district attorney's office was not about to risk the wrath of voters by releasing professional criminals in a highly publicized, major narcotics case without getting something substantial in return—such as an equally highly publicized conviction of somebody else.

Possibly it was the political consideration that moved Nassau District Attorney Dillon to tell McDonald the deal was off. Henry Hill would be indicted in Nassau County for narcotics peddling. McDonald and Puccio were almost beside themselves with rage. Their honor as prosecutors—exemplified by the promises they had made to Hill if he cooperated—was now in danger of being undercut. It was not hard for them to imagine the effect such a development would have on any future attempts to get criminals to testify against co-conspirators.

The Eastern District Strike Force decided to fight, and when Hill was indicted in Nassau County in early 1981, a nasty brawl broke out between the two jurisdictions. The battleground was a court hearing in Nassau held to determine whether Hill had fulfilled the terms of his understanding with the county. The hearing amounted to an extraordinary display. Lawyers from both sides snarled and scratched at each other in polite legal language while Hill sat there like a wallflower who is stunned to discover several handsome beaus fighting over her.

Obscured in the flurry was the most telling legal point of all, a critical one made by McDonald. It was absurd, McDonald argued, to talk of convicting Jimmy Burke in Nassau County on a narcotics charge. Since Hill was an accomplice in the scheme, under New York State law the prosecution would have to come up with a corroborating witness, someone who was not an accomplice and who could buttress Hill's testimony against Burke. But Nassau County did not have such a witness and had no hope of getting one. So what was the reasonable prospect of ever making a prosecutable case against Burke?

The final decision in that court hearing, however, centered on the question of whether Hill had in fact fulfilled his agreement to provide information to the best of his recollection and ability. The court ruled that he had and that Nassau County had no right to indict him. The decision, which sharply rebuked Nassau DA Dillon, did not confer much credit on anyone involved, least of all Hill. In the aggregate, Hill had precipitated the whole thing by trying to trump his deal with Nassau County by reaching out to the FBI. In the view of many, Hill in effect had shrewdly played off the two jurisdictions against each other; in both cases, the coin of the realm was mention of two names that had the power to cloud men's minds: Burke and Lufthansa.

Hill, of course, was the only real winner in the resulting controversy; when the dust finally settled, he emerged unscathed. He no longer faced a major felony conviction, and he had been granted limited immunity from any federal charge. In the process, he had been transformed from the low-level street rat who had first walked into McDonald's office some months before into professional witness.

After Hill was enrolled in the Federal Witness Protection Program—which provides new identities, relocation, and a monthly stipend for witnesses who testify in cases involving organized crime—he spent most of his time in debriefings with a wide range of law-enforcement organizations, particularly the FBI. He also testified at various trials and before grand juries while wrapped in a cocoon of tight FBI security.

Most of the cases concerned relatively low-level stuff, except for an interesting parole violation case prosecuted by McDonald's office. To Hill's immense satisfaction, it involved Burke. This was the second time in as many years that the government had sought to keep him behind bars by charging him with violation of the conditions of his parole. In August 1980, Burke was charged with leaving the state in early 1979 without his parole officer's knowledge or approval—namely, as Hill testified, to visit Paul Vario, Sr., in Florida. (Burke's lapse was understandable, since the purpose of the trip was to deliver Lufthansa proceeds to the Lucchese *capo*. It would have been difficult to secure permission to deliver the loot from the biggest cash robbery in American history.)

Since this amounted to a technical violation of parole, Burke's remanding to prison was not expected to last long. Still, McDonald noted, at least he was in jail, no picnic spot for anybody, even as tough a man as the Gent.

"Don't kid yourself," said a New York City Police detective assigned to the Strike Force. He began an imitation of a weasely convict seeking to curry favor with a man of Burke's connections: "Cigarette, Jimmy? You want the top bunk, Jimmy? No problem, whatever you like. Can I get you some candy, Jimmy? Anything else I can do for you, Jimmy? Just say the word, you got it, my friend."

214

A minor exaggeration? Two detectives who transported Burke from prison to a court hearing were dismayed to hear a guard call out cheerfully, "Good luck, boss!"

———

The central issue, then, was Burke. There was no question that he would be back on the street shortly, and no one in the New York law-enforcement establishment wanted him to be there. On the streets, Burke was like an uncaged lion with a toothache; his criminal cunning, propensity for violence, and certified willingness to kill made him an extremely dangerous presence indeed. Moreover, there was the simple issue of justice. His role as mastermind of the Lufthansa robbery was only one of many major crimes for which he had not received due punishment.

But, as McDonald pointed out, there was nothing at hand that would even begin to form a major case against Burke. McDonald was still smarting over what he considered his gross humiliation in failing to indict Sepe for the Lufthansa robbery. Taking similar action against Burke seemed even more pointless. McDonald was not about to go through the Sepe experience again. If the FBI wanted to put Burke on trial, they would have to provide clear evidence of his part in the heist.

That is precisely what the FBI did not have. Hour after hour with Henry Hill emptied his brain of everything he could recall about Jimmy Burke, but he provided nothing of great substance. Hill was trying hard, for as Carbone and the other FBI agents were aware, he was greatly afraid of Burke, the man he was convinced would somehow arrange to have him killed at any moment. This fear of Burke clearly had become an obsession with Hill. He was intent on putting Burke away.

Hill had not yet recalled his every memory. Still unremembered were two long-forgotten pieces of information that would finally and utterly destroy his mentor.

For ease of reference, they can be called the Frozen Corpse and the Night in Boston.

———

In Brooklyn, it is known as The Pit, an appropriately named section near the waterfront that is mostly marsh grass, abandoned automobiles, and a few derelict shacks. It is not a cheerful place at any time of the year, but on the morning of February 18, 1979, with icy winds and gray skies, it was especially desolate.

"Hell of a place to die," observed Detective Robert Kohler as he crouched beside the body of a man lying on the floor of an abandoned tractor-trailer. Above him, through a large hole in the roof, the wind whistled. Through that hole some schoolchildren, playing in the junk-strewn lot, had spotted the body. They called police, and two homicide detectives—Kohler and his partner, Detective Sergeant James Shea—of the 11th Homicide Zone were dispatched to try to determine how the body had come to be in that particular vacant lot.

The two sixteen-year veterans of the force (sometimes called "Kohlershea" because, like many police partners, they had become extremely close) were considered among the smartest of the detectives in Brooklyn. As was often the case in such duos, there were sharp contrasts. Kohler was a large, brawny man who reminded people of a stern Dutch uncle. Generally very serious, Kohler pursued cases with a rigid avidity that made him the perfect homicide investigator. He often accentuated his points by tapping a large, bony finger on any flat surface like a gavel while saying, "I'm tellin' ya, it's *dere!*" Suspects being interviewed by Kohler could find the experience unsettling, as he would make his points while the finger tapped away in a counterpoint: "Look, don't gimme— *whap, whap*—no shit. Get me straight—*whap, whap*—you little fuck. We're gonna—*whap, whap*—getcha good, understand? We got da evidence—*whap, whap*—and you're goin' ta jail!"

Shea, on the other hand, looked quintessentially Irish, with a beet-red face and a look that suggested leprechaun. Where Kohler used the frontal assault, Shea relied on a quiet, sympathetic charm in which he enveloped suspects before they quite knew what happened to them. He and his partner had the requisite contrasting personalities to play the classic game of good-cop-bad-cop deftly; as a team, they were devastatingly effective.

———

The body in the trailer presented them with questions they had confronted many times before: Who was this person? How

———

did he wind up in the trailer? Was he murdered? If so, why was he murdered? Who murdered him?

Shea and Kohler were adept at reading crime scenes. In this case, they immediately deduced that the body had been there for a while (it was frozen stiff), had been dragged into the trailer (scrapings and other marks on the back), had been murdered (apparent strangulation marks around the throat, arms and legs bound), had been murdered someplace else (no bloodstains or other such markings anywhere in the trailer), and had been beaten before being murdered (lacerations on the scalp, abrasion marks on the nose).

The two detectives deduced a lot more as they carefully examined the body of a man they estimated at somewhere around forty years old. His body was wrapped in a yellow blanket and shaggy bathroom mat, with a blue towel around the throat, suggesting that he had been killed in a bathroom.

"They were in a hurry," Kohler observed as he searched the victim's clothes. He found no wallet or other identification, indicating that whoever murdered the victim had tried to strip the body clean to make pinpointing his identity difficult. But Kohler, in carefully examining the seams of the clothes, suddenly felt some sort of flat object. Cutting open a jacket seam, he pulled out an address book.

The find told the two detectives that the victim was probably "dirty" (crooked), since law-abiding citizens do not sew their address books into the lining of their clothes. But there was something even more interesting about that book, for as Kohler began to scan its pages, his eyes suddenly fastened on a listing under "B." It was the address and telephone number of James Burke of Howard Beach, Queens.

"Well, well, isn't that interesting," Shea observed.

"Sure as hell is," Kohler murmured. He looked toward the northeast, where Burke lived. "Oh, what a mistake you just made," he said, as if warning The Gent that he and Shea were now on his trail.

———

As experienced Brooklyn detectives, Shea and Kohler were fully aware of the criminal career of James Burke, one of the more notorious figures in the world of New York crime. Indeed, Kohler had a quiet obsession about Burke and had been tracking him for years without ever getting close to making any kind of case against him. Burke was unbelievably cunning, Kohler conceded, and he was also ready to kill at any time to protect himself, which provided him a form of double insulation. But Kohler now held in his hands one of the few clues he had ever seen connecting Burke to a crime. True, it was a clue virtually molecular in dimension and possibly would never develop into anything, but it was a lead nevertheless. Both he and Shea were convinced, based on all they knew about Burke, that the Gent had murdered the man in the trailer. Why or how were among the more important things they did not know yet—along with whether they would ever be able to prove it.

But they were determined to try. First step was to talk to a dentist whose name they found in the book. He turned out to be a busy Manhattan practitioner who remembered his patient very clearly. There was, however, a small discrepancy. After some time the police managed to identify the body as that of one Richard Richards, former manager of a Greenwich Village restaurant. Yet the dentist said the man he treated was named Richard Eaton. Was he sure?

"Of course I'm sure," the dentist replied. "I could never forget Mr. Eaton and his girlfriend." He explained that Eaton came to his office accompanied by his striking blond girlfriend who often wore a long fur coat, which she removed in the waiting room, revealing that she was naked underneath. To the further astonishment of patients sitting there, she would then prance around.

"That'd make you remember her, all right," Shea commented.

The dentist agreed to go to the morgue to make a positive identification. Upon seeing the body, he burst into tears. The show of grief was puzzling, for as Shea and Kohler had already discovered, Eaton had visited the dentist a grand total of four times. Why should he be so upset? A discreet check on the dentist revealed the answer. Though his office was fairly nondescript, the dentist lived like a Saudi prince. His lifestyle stood in contrast to his modest income tax returns; obviously, he was hiding a lot from the IRS. It also bespoke a greed, and Shea and Kohler concluded (correctly, as it developed) that Richard Eaton was probably a con man. The dentist's grief was related not so much to the death of a patient as to the loss of whatever money he had decided to invest with Eaton.

Kohler and Shea quickly established that Richard Eaton was not only a con man, but one who belonged somewhere in the first rank of all-time hustlers. Like archaeologists peeling away layers of an old civilization, the two detectives discovered that each stratum was full of still more surprises. Richard Eaton was a very interesting "ordinary" murder victim.

And, more important, it was discovered that Eaton had played an important role in the criminal career of James Burke, notably the capstone of that career, the robbery at Lufthansa Air Cargo.

———

The detectives' superiors were not at all enthusiastic about the matter of Richard Eaton, aka Richard Richards. In fact, they were downright scornful of the "crackpot theories" advanced by ordinarily cautious investigators.

"I'm telling you, Eaton was murdered by Jimmy Burke," Shea insisted during one meeting. Asked for proof of this assertion, Shea and Kohler admitted they didn't have any, but they were convinced they could find it, given the time and support.

Admittedly, the detective commanders were intrigued by what the two investigators had discovered so far. Eaton, they reported, was a character straight out of fiction. A sober middle-class citizen from upstate New York, with a wife and three children, Eaton had decided five years before—for reasons which went with him to the grave—that he'd had enough of respectability. He left his family, took up with a girlfriend, and moved into the fast lane. And in the world of con men, hustlers, and general ne'er-do-wells, Eaton found his true calling.

Eaton became a hustler on a grand scale, Shea and Kohler were to discover as they worked back through his life. Eaton was a born con man. Possessed of an easy charm and the ability to lie outrageously and get away with it, he pulled off a number of scams that were just short of awesome. One involved a big movie production company which, Eaton convinced its executives, needed a large infusion of investment capital—several million dollars' worth. Eaton further convinced them he was a mover and shaker with access to "major investment capital." Assuming they had nothing to lose, the movie executives happily signed a contract promising Eaton a certain percentage of the capital if he succeeded in attracting it.

Eaton arrived on the day he was scheduled to deliver the cash (from people about whose identity he had been studiously vague). He then announced that the briefcase he was carrying contained several million dollars in cash from the investors— who, Eaton suddenly informed them, were Mafia godfathers. Alarmed, the executives said they wanted no part of the deal and no further part of Eaton. He shrugged and left. Later, Eaton sued the company for breach of contract and won a hefty out-of-court settlement.

The briefcase, of course, was filled with newspapers.

———

All very interesting, but what did it have to do with Jimmy Burke? A great deal, Shea and Kohler found out. Their investigation of Eaton's last known job, running a Greenwich Village restaurant, revealed a number of provocative items.

The restaurant's owner, deeply in hock to the mob and unable to meet his state tax payments, had walked away from the place. The mobsters who arrived to claim the restaurant were affiliated with an organized crime group led by a man named Thomas Monteleone, a Canadian from Montreal who had formed a partnership between his organization and the American Mafia. Monteleone ran an extensive smuggling operation that funneled narcotics and Sicilian hoods (among them Paolo LiCastri, the killer assigned to the Lufthansa robbery gang) into the United States by way of Montreal.

Among other things, Monteleone owned a place called the Players Club, near Fort Lauderdale, Florida. It had seen better days, and Monteleone ruined what was left of its reputation by converting it into a mob hangout. The regular patrons included Paul Vario, Sr., and Jimmy Burke.

It was in Florida, Kohler and Shea discovered, that the Eaton connection began to get really interesting. Eaton, claiming to be a Notre Dame graduate (he wasn't) and financial genius (maybe), throughout 1978 slowly insinuated himself into the Monteleone circle. He became aware that Monteleone wanted to sell the Players Club and that Vario, who lived not too far away, wanted to buy. Having seen his opportunity, Eaton later artfully worked his way into an acquaintanceship with Vario and an associate named James Burke.

Amazingly, for two extremely shrewd criminals, Burke and Vario were completely charmed by Eaton, who dazzled them with talk about his stunning financial coups, most of them crooked. The tenor of his ethics established, Eaton then somehow convinced Vario and Burke that he, Richard Eaton, was in fact the real owner of the Players Club, but out of friendship for Vario, he was willing to work out a "good deal" for him on the place. (Whereupon Eaton lit his candle at the other end by telling Monteleone he had found a buyer, although the price was considerably less than Monteleone had hoped to get for the club.)

Enriched by the Lufthansa proceeds, both Vario and Burke were seeking investment opportunities, and Vario—who had always dreamed of running his own nightclub-restaurant—thought the Players Club was just about right. As for Burke, Eaton beguiled him with a number of interesting lures, among them a major cocaine deal which, Eaton whispered, could return undreamed-of profits; he happened to be connected with a vast cocaine-selling operation. A mere $250,000 would put Burke in the picture, with profits up to fifty times that. Burke jumped at it.

———

In recounting all this to their fellow police officers, Kohler and Shea discovered that mentioning the name Lufthansa caused a dramatic change in the way people regarded their investigation. Suddenly it was the number one priority, and Shea was astounded to discover that his superiors were willing to assign up to a dozen other detectives to pursue leads he and his partner had developed.

In Kohler's view, however, there was too much emphasis on the question of the money; it was a ridiculous investigative target, he felt, for the money was long gone. A close friend of Lieutenant Thomas Ahearn, Kohler shared Ahearn's tendency to confront what he perceived as stupidity with an explosion of temper. "You stupid fucks!" he fulminated one day. "Forget the goddam money! It's gone! Let's make a case we can prove."

That case, Kohler argued, involved the robbery's mastermind, Jimmy Burke. Obviously, he pointed out, there had been a connection between Burke and Eaton. The odds were getting progressively stronger that there had been a falling-out between the two men. Ergo, Burke undoubtedly had killed him. The only real question was why.

———

Kohler and his partner were to find the answer split between Manhattan and Florida. In Manhattan, they located the former manager of the restaurant in which Eaton had worked briefly. She had a number of tales to tell, including one about how Eaton—whom she knew as "Richard Richards"—walked into the place one fall day in 1978 and announced he was now running it. He was accompanied by two other men. One of them, who bore a resemblance to a gorilla, described himself as a "restaurant consultant" and "bodyguard for Mr. Richards." The second man, charming and elaborately polite, introduced himself as James Burke. He did not describe his function in the new management, but she later discovered he was being paid $300 a week for duties that seemed somewhat obscure.

Eaton, she observed, seemed to have an odd theory of running a restaurant. Except for employees' salaries, he paid no bills and simply took whatever money was in the till. At the same time, he was busily supervising extensive renovation in an upstairs apartment whose doorway had been replaced by a vaultlike steel door. (Much later, she found out that Eaton was converting that apartment into a bordello.)

The Florida end of the investigation is where the detectives collected the most significant evidence. Kohler had discovered Burke's connection with the Players Club, and one look at the place was enough to make him understand why Vario, Burke, and other *Mafiosi* seemed to like it so much. The detective attempted to enlighten local sheriff's deputies who had never paid any attention to the place.

"It's got an underground garage," Kohler told them. When the Florida police did not appear to catch on, he added, "So the cops can't just ride by and write down the license plate numbers of wiseguys in the place." Kohler also reminded them that the place was on the water and that it had a small dock; the mind reeled at the possibilities *that* represented.

Kohler became a sort of guru of organized crime to the sheriff's office, whose deputies were endlessly amused by the sight of this big Brooklyn detective and his partner stomping around their county, hot on the trail of a man they had never heard of. The deputies and Kohler made a decidedly odd mixture, but by early 1981, Kohler had the broad outline of why Jimmy Burke had murdered Richard Eaton. The real story was nothing so exotic, as the superiors of Shea and Kohler assumed, as a falling-out over division of the Lufthansa spoils, nor—to cite another prevailing theory—that Eaton served as the money launderer for the Lufthansa robbery millions and was killed because he knew too much.

In fact, Kohler and Shea reported, a more prosaic reason lay behind Eaton's murder. He had made the mistake of hustling Jimmy Burke. He took Burke's $250,000, then refused to pay it back when his cocaine operation proved nonexistent. Eaton's scam greatly displeased The Gent. Few men had ever scammed Jimmy Burke and lived to tell about it. (At the same time, Vario was displeased to learn that Eaton, contrary to his claim, did not own the Players Club. Vario was another man whose dislike of being scammed ran to murderous retribution.)

Then, when Burke found out that Eaton was also looting the Manhattan restaurant, the con artist's fate was sealed. Shea and Kohler were now quite sure that Eaton was waylaid in that upstairs apartment, hit over the head, wrapped for transport in whatever was available in the bathroom, then prepared for shipment on his journey into the next world.

From the physical evidence at hand, Kohler and Shea had devised a plausible theory of how it happened. Burke and two other mobsters confronted Eaton, beat him up, then decided to kill him. They smashed him on the head, then carried the unconscious Eaton out of the restaurant and put him into a car. The plan was to store him temporarily in a desolate area of Brooklyn and later, when the ground thawed out, bury him.

Kohler conjectured that during the ride, Eaton regained consciousness. What went through his mind when he awakened

223

and saw the three men who were plainly intent on killing him, can only be imagined. One of the men hit him on the head again; then the trio dragged him into the abandoned tractor-trailer in Brooklyn. Hurriedly, because of the bitter cold, one of the killers stripped his identification, but missed the small book hidden in the seam of the victim's coat.

——

But although Kohler and Shea were fairly certain of all this, they had no court case. Obviously, neither Burke nor Vario was about to help them, and Thomas Monteleone was in no position to do so: a few weeks after Eaton's death, Monteleone's bullet-riddled body was found in Connecticut.

"I know—*whap, whap*—it's *dere*," Kohler said. The investigation had taken months without producing tangible results. He had talked to enough other detectives and FBI agents to realize that this failure to connect Burke with the heist was part of the consistent pattern in the overall Lufthansa case; a thread had begun to play out hopefully, only to be snipped just as it got promising.

Shea and Kohler had a purely circumstantial case, and a thin one at that. They needed just one piece of corroboration, something—anything—that would tie up the case against Jimmy Burke.

——

That final piece of evidence would come, but not before an even more dramatic act in the drama was played out. And to just about everybody's amazement, it was Henry Hill who provided all the excitement.

——

Chapter

12

"So what's the big deal?"

The first week of June 1980 arrived in New York with almost breathtaking beauty, a rush of warm, mild weather that bathed the city in a glow and made people forget about the summer steam bath to come.

Steve Carbone took little notice of the weather, for he was absorbed in the daunting task of trying to make sense of the jumble inside Henry Hill's head. It was a job of considerable difficulty, for as Carbone and a group of FBI agents discovered, Hill obviously knew a great deal, but seemed incapable of putting it into any coherent order.

"Anybody like to spend a nice weekend away?" Carbone had asked his agents just prior to the previous Memorial Day weekend. The agents who volunteered had some sense of what they were in for: the complicated task of moving witness Henry Hill to an FBI safe house in the Pocono Mountains of Pennsylvania. They would also have to figure out the logistics of transferring his entire family.

Hill, as the FBI men discovered, was a typical street hustler, alternately demanding, recalcitrant, expansive, and charming. Above all, he was difficult, and Carbone quickly realized he was dealing with the most aggravating witness he had ever handled. Endlessly Hill beseeched him for assorted favors and bombarded him with complaints about his treatment at the hands of the federal government (money seemed to be a dominant theme), and Carbone found his often moody witness quite a handful.

But then, most such witnesses tended to be difficult, and Carbone and his agents settled down to the task of finding out what of value resided in his memory. The FBI agents were invariably polite during these sessions, although privately, many of them began to think up horrendous tortures to inflict on Hill. What he had to say was an odd mixture of fact, supposition, rumor, thirdhand gossip, and on occasion outright misstatement. Finding what was true in all this was like trying to discover pieces of gold in a slag pile.

The problem, fundamentally, was that Hill had existed too long in a world where truth was relative and could be used or abused as events dictated. Worse, Carbone decided, Hill had the mentality of an eight-year-old; he was seemingly incapable of keeping the most basic details straight. Often, he would contradict himself in the space of minutes, then profess not to understand when an FBI agent pointed out the discrepancy.

That was bad enough, but Hill then passed into the phase that Carbone and the others dreaded: the one which followed that inevitable moment when informants begin to see themselves as colleagues of the agents. The tipoff came when the word "we" crept into Hill's conversation. As if he weren't exasperating enough, now the agents had to listen to Hill talk as if he were a fellow agent.

Hill began to put forth suggestions designed, he claimed, to clean up the Lufthansa case and put Jimmy Burke behind bars. Founded partly on his exaggerated belief in the size and powers of the FBI—"Hey, you guys can do *anything*," Hill liked to say—the schemes had a number of disadvantages. Among them, Carbone noted quietly, was their illegality. Patiently, he explained to Hill such important technicalities as the necessity for the FBI to obtain warrants and court orders.

"Well, you guys can work that out," Hill would reply, rubbing his hands together like a man who had just built the house and now expected the FBI to paint it.

There were some compensations for the agents, however, chief among them the meals. Accustomed to a diet of fast food, especially in the midst of a major investigation, the FBI men had little opportunity to eat decent meals. Hill, it turned out, had an even greater distaste for take-out cuisine, for he was a trained cook with genuine culinary talent.

He demonstrated it one day after announcing that he would prepare a grand dinner for "us." While Carbone and his agents waited, Hill bustled around the kitchen, frenetically preparing what he promised would be a multi-course masterpiece.

"You know, this is surreal," Carbone remarked, as he watched Hill, humming like a contented little housewife, buzz around the kitchen. At last, dinner was ready: lobster *fra diablo*, with all the trimmings. Carbone took a bite; it was exquisite.

"I was worried about the sauce," Hill fretted.

"Oh, this is fabulous!" Carbone assured him, while the other agents added their compliments. "Really good, Henry, the greatest."

———

But dinners of three-star Michelin Guide quality were footnotes to the chief business at hand—the relentless debriefing of Henry Hill. The agents began to unearth a few gems, not the least of which was the matter of Martin Krugman. According to Hill, Burke had murdered the bookmaker on suspicion that he was about to cooperate with the FBI. He later buried Krugman underneath Robert's Lounge.

"*Underneath?*" one agent asked incredulously, for of many fantastic things Hill had told the FBI up to that point, this was among the most remarkable.

Hill was adamant: Burke had buried Krugman and two of his other murder victims beneath the cellar floor of Robert's Lounge.

Passed on to the Queens district attorney's office, Hill's story led to a court order allowing the police to dig up the cellar, followed by a highly publicized excavation that preoccupied New York City newspaper readers for an entire week. It was the kind of bizarre development New Yorkers love—"Only in

New York," as the saying went—and even Jimmy Burke couldn't resist joining the fun. In the sort of gesture that infuriated the FBI and the police, Burke announced through his attorney that, to prove his innocence, he would be willing to pay for a bulldozer to completely excavate the bar's cellar. The offer was declined, and another black mark was entered against Burke's name: wiseass.

In his own way, Carbone couldn't resist the lure of the excavation either. On a Saturday night he was watching a Broadway play with his wife, but he wasn't really concentrating. As she was aware, his mind was a few miles to the east, in the cellar of Robert's Lounge. He could not wait to find out what the diggers had found. At intermission, he got on the phone. The call was followed by "I gotta go."

Figuring that if she couldn't beat them, she might as well join them, Mrs. Carbone accompanied her husband to Queens, there to confront a media circus. Under the glare of klieg lights, a crowd of reporters, camera crews, and curious citizens had gathered behind police lines to gawk at what the diggers hoped would be a disinterment.

Carbone went downstairs into the basement where he saw several men working in a chest-deep hole. They were optimistic about finding something, for, as they told Carbone, their first sight upon entering the place was a large, deep hole in the basement floor, covered by a cardboard carton—along with signs of recent digging.

But, as had happened so often before, the promising development turned out to be nothing more than an empty hole. Hopes were raised when the police diggers found some bones, but laboratory tests later revealed them to be animal bones, probably from a cow (Robert's Lounge was built on land occupied years before by a farm).

There was some media carping about the waste of taxpayers' money in this exercise, but even police detectives who did not particularly like the FBI—Robert Kohler among them —leaped to its defense. "There *were* bodies buried in the cellar," he said to his colleagues. "But, you see, the minute Burke found out that Hill was talking, he made sure the bodies were moved."

Kohler was probably right, but it was of scant comfort to

Carbone and everybody else involved. Once again, a promising thread had been snapped.

———

But there was a silver lining in the incident. The digging, which involved the cooperation of the FBI, the Queens district attorney, and the New York City Police, revealed the continuing effort by senior FBI and police commanders to foster what both sides described as a "new spirit" of cooperation. The effort appeared to be succeeding, but there were a number of doubters, among them Lieutenant Thomas Ahearn.

Ahearn's open skepticism was a source of some concern to Edward McDonald, the U.S. special attorney. McDonald, who as a prosecutor in Manhattan grew to like and admire many cops, felt the same way about many of the FBI agents with whom he had worked in his federal job. He had long urged closer cooperation between the two law-enforcement organizations and was therefore appalled to hear Ahearn—whom he greatly admired—complain about Carbone and the FBI.

Ahearn's complaints—that Carbone had slighted his detectives, that Carbone was intent on promoting the FBI's image at all costs, that Carbone attempted to amass all investigative power for the FBI, and so on—stemmed from his belief that the FBI supervisor was a figure of Machiavellian cunning, an evil genius whose capacity for duplicity was virtually inexhaustible.

McDonald was astonished. "Oh, come on, Tom," he said, that's not the Steve Carbone I know." McDonald went on to list the qualities about Carbone that he found most appealing (omitting his occasional reference to Carbone as a "pain in the ass"). In tones he normally used to persuade juries, McDonald attempted to convince Ahearn that he had badly misunderstood Carbone. By the time he finished, Carbone sounded like a cross between Mother Theresa and J. Edgar Hoover. To buttress his argument, McDonald even included a tribute to Carbone's personality. He ended his pitch with "He's such a *nice* guy, Tom; you really ought to try to know him better."

Ahearn was unmoved, nor was he much impressed with a lengthy article that had appeared at that time in the *New York*

Times. The article quoted FBI officials as having expressed gratitude for the aid of the 113th Detective Squad, among other police organizations, in the Lufthansa investigation.

With a lawyer's propensity for negotiation and compromise, McDonald arranged a meeting in his office between Ahearn and Carbone, during which he hoped they would work out their differences. The two men sat there as the federal prosecutor tried to encourage a dialogue. He felt like a marriage counselor trying to mediate between a hopelessly divided couple. Ahearn, who would not even deign to look at Carbone, began by saying, "Mr. McDonald, would you kindly inform Supervisor Carbone . . ." Shortly thereafter, McDonald gave up.

At that point in the Lufthansa investigation, however, it hardly mattered. The plain truth was that everybody—FBI and police alike—was stuck. After nearly two years, the expenditure of thousands upon thousands of man-hours, the running down of every possible lead, and the spending of no one knew how many tax dollars, the investigation seemed to have gone nowhere. The asset side of the ledger was quite short: the conviction of the "inside man," and the holding of an important witness. The debits, aside from all the missing money and the freedom enjoyed by the men who organized and planned the robbery, included a dozen murders, none of them anywhere near solution.

The increasing irritability of Ahearn and everyone else involved in a case whose solution always seemed to be maddeningly just out of reach was a function of their frustration. Indeed, some of the investigators seemed to become nearly consumed by it.

Among them was a police detective who perhaps was the greatest expert on the Robert's Lounge Gang: Robert Hernandez, Burke's old nemesis. But despite his intimate knowledge of the gang members, the detailed insight he had into the "gang of mutts" (as Carbone called them) seemed of little use in cracking the Lufthansa case. The problem, Hernandez discovered as he became involved in the Lufthansa case, was not knowledge, but proof.

Hernandez was regarded by his colleagues as the ideal type for a case like Lufthansa. He was a man who pursued cases with a zeal that Ahearn might have compared to that of Javert in Victor Hugo's *Les Misérables*.

At the time of the Lufthansa robbery, Hernandez—to his fury—was bedridden, recovering from a gall bladder attack. Then assigned to the Queens district attorney's detective squad, Hernandez had been shifted from his old post in the Safe, Loft and Truck Squad when that unit was atomized by the corruption scandal that swept through the police department. Out of sixty detectives assigned to that unit, only Hernandez and twelve others were found to be honest. The unit was disbanded and the remaining "clean" detectives were reassigned.

Hernandez was looking forward to his new assignment on the Queens DA's detective squad, for it promised to put him in close quarters with the Queens-based gangs he had been chasing for years, notably the infamous Robert's Lounge Gang and its progenitor, James Burke.

A few days after the Lufthansa robbery, Hernandez returned to work. He was immediately confronted by his boss, Lieutenant Remo Franceschini, commander of the Queens DA's squad. "So who did Lufthansa?" Franceschini asked.

"Burke," replied Hernandez unhesitatingly.

Franceschini made a face. "You've got a hard-on for Burke."

"Maybe," replied Hernandez, feeling his hair-trigger temper rising. "But I'm telling you, it's Burke. There is absolutely no way anybody could carry out that size robbery without Burke being involved. He's the guy with the intelligence setup there, and there's no doubt that if somebody was selling information on how to grab all that money at Lufthansa, that information went to Burke."

"Maybe not," Franceschini countered. "We hear that it was some gang from New Jersey who pulled it off."

"You believe what you want, Lieutenant," Hernandez replied, irritably. "I'm telling you it was Burke and that gang of his. No doubt whatsoever."

The more Hernandez heard during the following weeks, the more he became convinced he was right. His stoolies began to whisper increasingly detailed stories about how Burke and several of his associates had carried out the heist. The informers also told of Mafia *capos* expressing dissatisfaction over the relatively small amounts of money they had received for their aid. Other reports were equally intriguing, among them one demonstrating anew the truth of the old adage that success has a thousand fathers: Mafia drug kingpin Joseph (Joey Beck) DiPalermo was allegedly seen tapping a newspaper whose front page carried a banner headline about the Lufthansa heist. "Them's my boys," he is supposed to have said.

More significantly, it was reported that Antonio (Tony Ducks) Corallo, godfather of the Lucchese family, bitterly rebuked one of his *capo*s, Paul Vario, Sr., for failing to give a sufficiently large proportion of the Lufthansa loot to his mob family.

Hernandez gradually brought Franceschini around to that view, mostly because of some interesting tidbits picked up by other detectives. There was, for example, the news that Gambino family *capo* John Gotti, whom police wiretaps revealed to be a man chronically short of money, had suddenly become flush after the robbery. So flush, in fact, he decided to set up a large illegal gambling operation in Manhattan. Using Gotti's newly enlarged bankroll, the gambling operation was to lure high rollers to high stakes roulette and dice games, where the law of probability would ensure a tidy profit for the organizers. (The police wiretaps heard Gotti's associates bitterly complain that he had become so engrossed in the games that he lost $80,000 of the money.) And another *capo*, likewise not noted for wealth, had been spotted hanging around with Burke just before the robbery; after the robbery, he was seen driving a brand-new Lincoln Continental.

Assuming that the Queens DA squad would certainly want to jump on the biggest robbery case it had ever seen, Hernandez on his own time began to hang around Robert's Lounge, checking up on the names familiar to him from his years on the street. Even a preliminary look convinced Hernandez that the Robert's Lounge Gang was the place to start solving the Lufthansa robbery. The approach, Hernandez argued to Franceschini, would be classic police work. Detectives would continually "sit on" (carry out surveillance on) everybody connected with Robert's Lounge. The police would apply unremitting pressure at all times; they would drag Burke's crew in for questioning, stop them for committing traffic violations —anything to keep up the pressure until somebody cracked.

But Franceschini did not think much of the idea. To Hernandez's anger, he announced that the bulk of the investigation would be left to the FBI, with the Queens squad providing whatever help was required. Meanwhile, the squad would carry out a number of "subsidiary" investigations connected with Lufthansa.

"What, are you saying," an infuriated Hernandez asked, "that with the biggest fucking robbery in history, we're not going to do anything?"

"Well, they're [the FBI] better equipped to handle this sort of thing," Franceschini replied. "Our strength is street crime."

"That's crazy, Lieutenant," Hernandez argued. "If we really wanted to, we could bust this case in a couple of days."

"Possibly," Franceschini said.

Hernandez argued further, but to no avail. He did not know that Franceschini was taking his cue from his boss, Queens District Attorney John Santucci, who had decided to let the FBI take the case. Santucci's action was somewhat puzzling, considering that for some time after the robbery, he had maneuvered to take over direction of the case. Indeed, the DA's detectives had assumed they would be devoting most of their time to Lufthansa, having heard on the grapevine that Santucci had proclaimed his office the natural headquarters of the investigation. "After all," Santucci was supposed to have said, "I am the chief law-enforcement officer in Queens."

True, but once Santucci changed his mind, no argument Hernandez could muster would have made a difference. A frustrated Hernandez fell into a foul mood, which worsened when he saw what "subsidiary investigations" meant.

In one instance, Franceschini and several detectives visited a New Jersey psychic who had a reputation as a finder of lost children. During her meeting with the Queens detectives, she claimed that she saw a vision of an abandoned firehouse near a silverware factory. And in the basement of that factory, she went on, she could see the Lufthansa money hidden. She followed that up by predicting a rosy future for Franceschini and several others.

Several detectives tried to track down the vision, but they had no success. Other detectives were sent to check out reports of people spending $100 bills. Hernandez was appalled by all this, and his growing estrangement from Franceschini—they very nearly came to blows—was a symptom of the angry frustration he and other detectives felt at not being able to work on the biggest case of their careers in the style and method they thought would work best.

———

Something similar to that frustration also began to break out in Ahearn's 113th Detective Squad, for slightly different reasons. One of Ahearn's acolytes, John Fitzsimons, began to suspect that the FBI was plotting against the police. One night, he told his boss, he and his wife went to the movies (ironically, the movie was *The Brink's Job*), where he spotted FBI Special Agent Thomas Sweeney and his wife.

"Sweeney lives five towns away from that movie theater," Fitzsimons noted. He went on to tell Ahearn that after the movie, he and his wife had gone to a local restaurant, where he again spotted the Sweeneys. Was it possible that the FBI man and his wife were following him?

Actually, they weren't, but in an atmosphere increasingly fraught with tension, it didn't seem unreasonable for Fitzsimons to think so. He was an extremely frustrated detective by the fall of 1979; even his own boss seemed unreceptive to some of his theories on how to get the Lufthansa investigation off the ground.

His central theory concerned Theresa Ferrara. Fitzsimons insisted that his own investigation into the circumstances of her life and death raised the strong possibility that she was a much more important character in the drama than believed. Consider, Fitzsimons argued: the man who secretly bankrolled her beauty salon was a notorious major bookmaker with connections all over the mob; the man she once lived with was a notorious Mafia thug known to be mixed up in narcotics smuggling; two of her relatives were convicted cocaine smugglers; Jimmy Burke at one time was the landlord of the building in which she lived; she was a close friend of Tommy DeSimone; there were strong indications she had been an important informant for the Nassau County Police, especially its Narcotics Squad; she could have known a great deal about the Lufthansa heist; and—in a special flourish aimed at Ahearn's well-known dislike of the federal agency—she might have been an informant for the FBI.

But Ahearn was not moved. "So what have we got?" he counterargued. "Some indications, that's it. Suppose she was simply a small-time dope dealer who got in over her head? What do we have that suggests she didn't pay up when she was supposed to at some point, so they killed her? Another narcotics killing—what does that have to do with Lufthansa?"

"But, Lieutenant," Fitzsimons pointed out, "look at the way she was killed. They went through an awful lot of trouble to kill her. You mean to tell me they'd go through all that just to knock off a dope dealer who didn't pay? Come on."

Fitzsimons tried to spur Ahearn's interest by showing him an interesting exhibit of nude photos of Ferrara.

"Interesting," Ahearn said detachedly although, Fitzsimons noticed, he had carefully adjusted his glasses before looking at the pictures.

In the end, Ahearn would not budge. He did not see the connection between Ferrara and Lufthansa, and he could not agree to the all-out investigative effort Fitzsimons wanted. During their conversation, Fitzsimons confessed that he had been haunted by the image of Terry Ferrara and had dreamed of meeting her alive.

"Oh, God help me," Ahearn proclaimed. "What the hell is happening around here? On top of everything, I've got a detective now with this Ferrara thing. You know what it is, Jack?"

"Not really," answered Fitzsimons, puzzled.

"It's like something out of *Laura*," Ahearn said in a rare cinematic reference. "I think this case is beginning to drive us all crazy."

———

Ahearn was not alone in his opinion: Steve Carbone was beginning to think the same way. Henry Hill was still chattering, but the task of making sense out of his ramblings was not getting any easier. Hill still tended to confuse details and dates. He would casually mention something important, then immediately careen over to another subject. Carbone began to wonder if he was losing his mind.

In the hope of obtaining information from the star witness, Carbone was patient with Hill, even in the face of Hill's repeated insistence that the FBI didn't understand the first thing about organized crime. He, Henry Hill, would enlighten them. The FBI agents did not feel particularly enlightened, however, and they were not pleased to discover that Hill believed he was smarter than the agents, whom he would occasionally patronize.

"I think I'm going to strangle him," Carbone told McDonald, adding his opinion that the prospect of getting anything of substance from Hill was growing dimmer with each passing moment.

McDonald counseled patience. Although Hill seemed to be downplaying his own role during a criminal career that stretched back over two decades—almost all of it in association with Paul Vario, Sr., and Jimmy Burke—it was only a matter of time before he would remember something of great interest. Of this, McDonald seemed certain.

Sure enough, a short while later, during early July, Hill was escorted into McDonald's office, where the prosecutor was attempting to get the cooperation of Judith Wicks, Hill's friend and co-conspirator in the Nassau narcotics operation. Finding Wicks somewhat reluctant, McDonald wanted Hill to persuade her that cooperation was the best route. Sweeney of the FBI, Hill's guardian, sat in on what seemed to be a routine session.

Hill was able to convince Wicks to turn herself over to McDonald, who then began checking some dates. At one point, Wicks said she couldn't remember where she was on a particular day.

"Aw, you know where we was," Hill told her, "we was up in Boston, fixing basketball games."

McDonald reacted as though someone had just punched him in the stomach. Behind him, on his office wall, was a framed engraving of the Boston College campus.

"When?" McDonald asked.

"Nineteen seventy-eight," replied Hill. He went on to list several players from "Boston University" whom he had bribed to shave points. Hill added that he was acting in behalf of Jimmy Burke. Palpably disappointed, McDonald realized Hill was confused, as usual; in fact, the names he mentioned were Boston *College* players.

McDonald stared at Hill for what seemed a long time. At last, he said, "Henry, did the FBI put you up to this?"

"What, are you kidding, Ed?" Hill answered, demonstrating a common New York habit of answering a question with a question. "No, I wouldn't do that, you know that."

"Okay," said McDonald, who noticed that Sweeney looked almost stricken. Like McDonald, Sweeney instantly grasped the significance of what Hill had so casually revealed. If it was true, Hill and Burke were involved in interstate racketeering, far more weighty than anything that could have been dredged up in connection with the Lufthansa case.

McDonald dared not believe it. That night, he reviewed an old Boston College yearbook and put together a list with pictures of ten names, including those of Rick Kuhn and James Sweeney. The next day, he showed the list to Hill. Unhesitatingly, Hill picked the names and pictures of Kuhn and Sweeney as the two players he had bribed.

————

"He said *what?*" Carbone was nearly livid with rage when Sweeney told him what Hill had revealed in McDonald's office.

"You mean to tell me," Carbone fumed, "that this guy talks to us for *two months* and never bothers to mention this little detail? Terrific. I wonder what else he's forgotten to tell us."

Carbone was further angered when preliminary checking by his agents turned up unmistakable evidence—hotel receipts, telephone records, and so on—that Hill was telling the truth. Still, Carbone was bothered: Why had Hill waited so long to reveal this?

"So we fixed a few basketball games, so what?" Hill replied when an annoyed Carbone questioned him. "So we gave them a few bucks, and we made some bucks. So what's the big deal?"

"So what's the big deal," Carbone repeated evenly, trying to control his temper. "Henry, do me a big favor. If you remember any other things like sports bribery, let us know, won't you?"

"Oh, I sure will, Steve," Hill replied brightly, missing Carbone's sarcasm.

Slowly, it all began to come together, a large jigsaw puzzle that piece by piece was assuming the shape of the most significant sports bribery scheme since the infamous college basketball fixes of 1951. McDonald, accustomed to being disappointed by anything that showed promise in the long hunt for Jimmy Burke, hoped that this promising thread would not be snapped like all the others. But there was Carbone, bursting into his office almost every day with still another piece of paper—a hotel record, a toll call slip, a Western Union receipt—proving the unbelievable: Hill was right.

Buoyed by what he now believed to be a major criminal case, Carbone was again on the prowl. This time, he spent more time behind his desk, for the investigation was essentially a hunt along a complicated paper trail. And as the trail grew in length, so it did in breadth. For instance, to Carbone's astonishment, his agents discovered that the ring leaders had sent some money to Rick Kuhn through Western Union. And Western Union keeps records: people receiving money have to sign for it.

One of Carbone's agents, Edmundo Guevera, known for his passion for detail and organization, was assigned the task of making sense out of all the paper other agents were collecting. Hunched over a computer, Guevera tried to detect patterns that would point unmistakably to a criminal conspiracy.

Carbone had one worry: increasing amounts of evidence proved the involvement of Hill, Mazzei, and some others, but there was little to prove that the real target of the investigation, Jimmy Burke, had played a role in the point-shaving plot. Hill's testimony, without some backup, would not be quite enough.

"The telephone records!" Carbone suddenly shouted. In a fortuitous flash of memory that turned out to be most significant, Carbone recalled that some time after the Lufthansa robbery, the FBI had subpoenaed Burke's telephone toll records. Agents had pored over them, but the records made no sense, for the numbers called seemed to have no relation to the Lufthansa conspiracy. They were put aside in the thin hope that someday they might be of some use.

Now they were. Hill had provided the Rosetta Stone, and the mysterious pattern of calls, fed through Guevera's computer, suddenly made sense. What emerged was a distinctive pattern of calls to major bookmakers, timed perfectly with the games Hill had claimed were fixed.

"So we finally got lucky," Carbone said, reminding his agents that the telephone company destroys its records of toll calls after six months. Had the FBI tried to get them in 1980, nearly two years after they were made, there would have been nothing to feed into Guevera's computer.

The FBI's luck got even better, and this time, it was Special Agent Thomas Sweeney who scored. On the morning of September 8, 1980, Sweeney was in Pittsburgh, where, with Special Agent James Byron of the Pittsburgh FBI field office, he was to visit the home of Rick Kuhn in the suburb of Swissvale.

It was 6:30 A.M., and Sweeney was about to employ one of the FBI's favorite techniques, the early morning interview. At that time of day, most people, having just arisen, tend not to be at their most alert.

Kuhn, just awakened, did not seem especially surprised by the appearance of the two FBI agents in his parents' home, nor did he react when they told him they wanted to talk to him about "your basketball activities" at Boston College in 1978.

"You don't have to talk to us," Byron said. With those words Kuhn had been warned; anything he said subsequently was purely voluntary—and admissible.

Kuhn agreed to discuss the matter, and all three adjourned to the FBI car parked outside. There Kuhn demonstrated appalling ignorance, including a lack of familiarity with the Constitution. He could have declined to say a word to the agents, and they could not have done a thing about it. Or he could have demanded that a lawyer be present during any conversation.

As it was, Kuhn put his head in the noose. After a few minutes of idle chit-chat, Byron got to the point: there have been "allegations of wrongdoing on your part" involving point-shaving What did Kuhn have to say about those allegations?

"Do I have to talk about it?" Kuhn asked.

"No," Sweeney said, and again told him that he was perfectly within his rights to leave the car and go back into the house.

But Kuhn stayed, and to Sweeney's surprise not only discussed the matter, but admitted his role. Kuhn confirmed Hill's account in almost every detail. Sweeney, who was taking notes, could scarcely believe his luck.

In twenty minutes of conversation, Kuhn provided the heart of the case: Hill, acting in concert with Paul Mazzei and Mazzei's friends the Perla brothers, had conspired with James Burke to fix at least six college basketball games.

The Kuhn admission overcame the last bit of hesitation on McDonald's part. Added to FBI Special Agent Edmundo Guevera's computer printouts showing the damaging pattern of Burke's long-distance calls, the admission meant that the case was ready to move forward into the courts.

And just as McDonald was about to proceed in the case that he was certain would put Jimmy Burke away for a long time, the wild card nearly destroyed it all. Henry Hill decided to play his own game.

———

With mounting anger, McDonald, telephone receiver pressed to his ear, could hardly believe what he was hearing. A reporter for the *Washington Post* was calling to inform him he was writing a story about a major college basketball game—fixing operation run by a man named Henry Hill. Did Mr. McDonald care to comment about it?

Mr. McDonald did not, for he and Carbone had been extremely careful during the several months of the investigation to keep its secrets. Yet here was a newspaper reporter who seemed to know all about it. Where was the leak? The answer came quickly enough: *Sports Illustrated* magazine was about to publish a major piece about the fix scheme. The co-author and main source was Henry Hill.

McDonald stood in the center of his office wanting to punch a wall. "I am going to kill Henry Hill!" he announced loudly.

———

A short time later, an angry-looking Carbone burst through the front door of the safe house in which Hill was staying.

———

"Hey, Steve, howya doin'?" Hill said in the standard Brooklyn greeting.

"Hello, Henry," Carbone replied. "I am going to kill you."

"What?"

"I said I am going to kill you," Carbone said, speaking slowly. "I am going to kill you in ways you can't imagine. I am going to kill you so that you are out of my life forever. Do you understand that?"

"Hey, Steve, what's your problem?" Hill asked, looking around in some alarm. The other agents were not smiling. One of them stage-whispered to him, "Please don't get him mad."

"What's this?" Carbone snarled, throwing a copy of *Sports Illustrated* at him.

"It's a magazine," Hill said.

"I *know* it's a magazine," said Carbone, almost beside himself with fury. "What about the article in there? Did you tell them all about the fixing?"

Hill confessed that he had, and explained that his lawyer had arranged a deal in which the magazine had paid him $10,000 for the story.

Carbone's concern, like McDonald's, centered on what Hill had said in the article, much of which was at considerable variance with what he had been telling the FBI.

"Tell ya what we're gonna do," said Carbone, lapsing into the form of pure Brooklynese he adopted when he wanted to establish direct communication with Hill. "We're gonna sit down, and we're gonna go over the whole thing, and we're gonna figure out exactly what the truth is. You got it?"

"Sure, Steve, anything you say," a chastened Hill replied.

———

The resulting two-day session was a distinctly unpleasant experience for all concerned. In the sort of casual acquaintance with the truth that had so often infuriated Carbone and McDonald, Hill professed to see no problem with the account he had given to *Sports Illustrated*—an account, he breezily admitted, that contained gross distortions and untruths. He did not seem to understand that the magazine account would come back to haunt him during the upcoming trial. Defense lawyers, Carbone pointed out with some asperity, would drag him through the story word by word and hang him with the contradictions. And with that, there was a good chance the whole case would go out the window.

Hill not only failed to grasp that central point but also seemed unable to understand that his testimony had to be precise; he could not treat the facts casually. Carbone and McDonald devoted two solid weeks to the considerable task of readying Hill for trial, and the process reminded Carbone of training an especially thick-headed dog not to urinate on the rug. With growing edginess, Carbone watched as Hill, just as he seemed certain of one aspect of the case, would forget it a few minutes later and claim something else altogether.

McDonald was worried: his star witness demonstrated an inability to keep things straight. He would have to be used carefully. Meanwhile, trial date was approaching, and the main defendants (there were five including Burke) had been hauled in. Burke's arrest in July of 1981 was a source of immense satisfaction to FBI agents, who, acting under strict instructions from McDonald, were to play the prosecutor's longest shot—they would point at the benefits of "cooperating" and would assure Burke that there was still time to save himself. Burke heard out this standard spiel with a smile, then responded in the way McDonald assumed he would.

"You tell Ed McDonald," Burke said quietly, "to go fuck himself."

———

On October 27, 1981, the trial opened in one of the cavernous courtrooms in the Brooklyn federal courthouse. Even in a room that size, things seemed a little crowded. Present were five defendants and their lawyers, McDonald and his prosecution team, and a packed house of spectators. The room also contained a series of large charts the FBI had drawn up showing, in organization chart style, how all the defendants interconnected. The jury could not fail to notice that a box marked "James Burke" occupied a prominent place in the center of the largest chart. McDonald intended to make his points graphically whenever he got the chance.

Defendant Burke, attired in an expensive three-piece suit that made him look like a union delegate attending a fancy wedding, was the focus of attention, for he had become at that point the most publicized criminal in the entire city. Legally, Burke was in that courtroom for a trial addressed to the question of whether he and his four co-defendants (including Paul Mazzei and the Perla brothers) had conspired, as the United States government charged, to engage in the fixing of basketball games.

But most people regarded the proceeding as "the Lufthansa trial." Mentioning the name Lufthansa was strictly forbidden on the grounds that it might prejudice the jury against the defendants, but the popular perception was that the government, having failed to get Burke in connection with the Lufthansa robbery, was settling for the fix case as consolation prize.

That was not quite true, of course, but there probably was not a single prospective juror who had not read some of the extensive newspaper stories during the previous three years openly accusing Burke of being the Lufthansa robbery mastermind. And they had almost certainly heard of Henry Hill, one of the FBI's most highly publicized informants—the man, according to the newspapers, who knew the secret of the robbery. So in an important sense, the trial threatened to amount to a showdown on the question of credibility between two professional criminals named James Burke and Henry Hill.

Which was precisely what worried Carbone and McDonald. "First time out of the chute," Carbone told the prosecutor as the trial was about to open, using still another of the animal metaphors he adopted when discussing Hill. Even after all those weeks of pre-trial preparation, there remained grave danger that Hill might not get it straight.

And he didn't. The defense attorneys were on him like hungry dogs, and Hill revealed himself to be muddled, contradictory, and uncertain of the facts that were staring at him from the charts. Worse, he conceded that facts in the *Sports Illustrated* article differed from the facts he had revealed to the FBI, then claimed that the magazine had lied. It went downhill from there, including the defense's recitation of Hill's criminal record and capacity for untruth. Hill's first appearance as a witness at a major trial was an unmitigated disaster.

Carbone was livid. Joining Hill and McDonald in the prosecutor's office during the lunch break, he exploded.

"*You stupid son of a bitch!*" he yelled at Hill. "What *are* you an idiot? The chart's right in front of you, and you can't even get dates straight!"

McDonald's relative calmness during this session had everything to do with a shrewd tactical maneuver he was playing out. He had made Hill the first major witness, and as he anticipated, the defense lawyers eventually exhausted themselves against that obstacle. In truth, there was no real cross-examination of Hill, as lawyers commonly understood the term. Since there were so many contradictions, and since Hill was so completely confused, the defense was trying to nail pudding to the wall.

And when the defense lawyers had finished pounding away at Hill, to no particular effect except that he appeared very confused, McDonald played his high card. He called to the stand one James Sweeney, the Boston College player and friend of Rick Kuhn who had been a reluctant participant in the fix scheme. Much like a father getting his son to admit that he had broken the upstairs window while horsing around, McDonald led Sweeney through the whole scheme. Since Sweeney was not testifying under a grant of immunity and had not asked for any consideration from the prosecution, his account, recited with quiet sincerity, was devastating. The jury ate it up.

The rest was anticlimax. On November 23, 1981, after nearly four weeks, the trial ended. Through it all, Burke sat calmly at the defense table as though the proceedings concerned a zoning dispute. In his prison cell when the trial was not in session, however, he demonstrated his infamous temper. "That little cocksucker!" Burke fumed to an audience of fellow convicts on the subject of Henry Hill. "That lying, sneaking son of a bitch! I give him five thousand dollars to make a few bets, and this is what happens."

Not surprisingly, Burke's cell mates agreed with this defense. But the jury did not: after twenty-two hours of deliberations, it found Burke and his four co-defendants guilty as charged.

On January 23, 1982, Burke, dressed in bright orange federal prison uniform, stood before a judge who sentenced him to twenty years in prison. Burke demonstrated not even the slightest reaction.

Back in prison, Burke went on another temper tirade. His rage arose from the circumstances in which he now found himself— imprisoned, not for the Lufthansa robbery of which everybody knew he was the mastermind, but for a betting operation he had long forgotten.

In his fury about Hill and the fix trial, Burke may have forgotten a number of other matters in his past that might come back to haunt him. Perhaps he even assumed that everybody else who knew about them had forgotten also, leaving him in no further danger.

But Henry Hill was beginning to remember other things.

EPILOGUE

THE BUG IN
THE JAGUAR

Chapter

13

"You gotta do
whatcha gotta do"

On a warm and sunny spring day in 1984, Detective Robert
Kohler passed the time during the long drive to federal prison
by chatting with his prisoner.

The chatter was not entirely idle, for Kohler's duty escort-
ing the prisoner provided him with an opportunity to study the
man he had been pursuing relentlessly for nearly three years.
The prisoner, James Burke, was charming enough, talking as
though he and his escort were taking a ride to the beach, but
Kohler began to detect something else. It was an air of menace,
a distinct atmosphere of danger that surrounded Burke like
an aura.

Jimmy Burke, Kohler decided, was the most dangerous
man he had ever encountered. Even sitting handcuffed in the
back seat of a police car, he exuded death and violence. The
charm he was now lavishing on the detective could not entirely hide the malevolent force that lurked within the man,
always near the surface and straining to get out.

"Lunchtime," one of the other detective guards announced,
looking at his watch.

As the police car came to a halt in front of a highway

diner, a posse of state police cars quickly circled it like a wagon train protecting valuable cargo against Indian attack.

"Jesus!" Burke exclaimed. "What the hell is all that for?"

"Why, didn't you know, Jimmy?" Kohler said, smiling. "You're a dangerous criminal. We don't want to take any chances."

Burke guffawed loudly, and in that moment, Kohler began to understand. Jimmy the Gent honestly did not regard himself as a criminal—certainly not the dangerous master criminal the police, FBI, and the newspapers had proclaimed him to be for so many years. That was the reason, Kohler decided, why Burke was always so polite; he actually thought of himself as some sort of gentleman highwayman. He was straight out of Regency England, when the profession had only a limited social stigma.

———

Kohler did not dwell on this thought for long, for his immediate objective was to prove that Jimmy Burke had murdered Richard Eaton. The case had preoccupied him and his partner Detective Sergeant James Shea for quite some time, and they now had the final connecting link of evidence in hand.

It had come from Henry Hill, who during his continuing conversations with the FBI, mentioned Jimmy Burke's custom of murdering people who got in his way. One of the examples Hill cited was a man named Richard Eaton, whom Hill knew casually. Hill also knew that Eaton had attempted to cheat Burke in a big cocaine deal. He was therefore not surprised, upon inquiring in March of 1979 about the whereabouts of Eaton, to hear Burke's answer: "I whacked [murdered] that lying fuck out."

Hill had felt a twinge of concern at the time, but in the New York underworld, murder was not an uncommon occurrence. Besides, by the moral standards of that world, Burke was perfectly justified in committing the murder, in view of Eaton's gross violation of business ethics. And since it was a relatively trivial matter, Hill forgot about it until he suddenly recalled it some time after he began cooperating with the FBI. McDonald was astounded by still another example of how Hill would rack his brain for months trying to remember something incriminating against Jimmy Burke and then mention, almost casually, his knowledge of a felony.

The murder of Eaton was not a federal crime, so McDonald had no use for Hill's testimony on that score. But the prosecutor knew two men who did. One was Detective Robert Kohler. The other was Detective Sergeant Joseph Coffey, one of the police department's most famous investigators, noted for his success in breaking Mafia cases. Coffey headed a unit that investigated organized crime murders.

It was not until late 1983 that Coffey and Kohler got to debrief Hill on the Eaton case, for McDonald deliberately sat on the information for some time. During that period, he did not commit a single word of Hill's revelation to paper; while the basketball-fix legal process was under way, he would have been required to turn any such writing over to the Burke's defense attorney under the constitutional stipulation that a defendant had a right to see *all* of the material against him. Therefore, Burke would have been alerted prematurely that Hill had revealed the murder of Eaton.

Coffey was unimpressed by Hill, whom he instinctively distrusted. But as he listened to Hill discuss the Eaton-Burke connection, he noticed Kohler becoming increasingly agitated. And from Kohler's questions, he knew that the Brooklyn detective was finding that Hill's information meshed perfectly with what he had already determined to be the truth. To Coffey's surprise, he realized that Hill was giving them a prosecutable murder case against James Burke.

Hill mentioned a number of other items during the conversation. These Coffey found less compelling, and he summed up their value to Kohler after Hill had finished: "Hill is full of shit. Mostly."

"Mostly," echoed Kohler.

"But he's right about the Eaton thing?" Coffey asked, knowing the answer.

"Yeah, he is," Kohler replied, almost in wonderment. After years of wrestling with a puzzle that lacked one little piece, Kohler now had the corroboration he and Shea had sought for so long.

Kohler rushed with this news to Brooklyn Assistant District Attorney Jon Fairbanks, who welcomed it with something less than total enthusiasm. A young prosecutor who moved and spoke with an almost lubricated smoothness that reminded many people of a psychiatric counselor, Fairbanks had been on the case ever since Eaton's body was found in 1979. Through every step of Kohler and Shea's investigation he had expressed his admiration of their minor classic of criminal investigation. And yet, as much as he liked both detectives and however much he appreciated the job they had done, he had the sad duty as a prosecutor to tell them it was simply not enough; there was no way he could even think of trying the case without that critical corroboration. Now the detectives had brought it, but Fairbanks noted with dismay that the corroboration had come from Henry Hill, a professional criminal whose record for duplicity, untruth, and sheer criminality might cause grave problems of credibility. The case, Fairbanks fretted, was largely circumstantial, hanging by a thread. A witness like Hill, who had performed so badly during the basketball-fix trial in federal court, might be a time bomb just waiting to blow up in their faces.

Fairbanks weighed the matter carefully. What were the prospects that a local jury, watching Hill in action, would return a murder conviction against James Burke? In the end, Fairbanks came to the conclusion that a man like Burke, who had kept the forces of law and order preoccupied (and frustrated) for years with a long list of crimes that remained unpunished, was eminently deserving of prosecution. The case of *The People of the State of New York v. James Burke* would go ahead.

———

As the trial opened in the shopworn old court building in downtown Brooklyn during the early fall of 1984, Fairbanks had more than his share of problems. In addition to his fears about the efficiency of Hill as a witness, there were also questions about the medical evidence. Two medical examiners had come to different conclusions as to cause of Eaton's death. One said it was strangulation; the other listed hypothermia as the cause. It was the kind of difference defense attorneys liked to exploit.

And there was another, more delicate problem, centering on Burke's rumored propensity to buy off cops to beat a case.

Before entering the courtroom, Fairbanks took Kohler aside. "I don't really want to ask you this," the prosecutor began, uncomfortably, "but I have to. Look, uh, Burke got maybe two and a half million dollars from the Lufthansa heist. That's a lot of money and, uh . . ." Fairbanks was trying diplomatically to convey his fear that millionaire Burke might try to buy off the prosecution's chief witnesses.

Kohler was nearly shaking with rage. "No, you didn't hafta ask," he said, in what was nearly a growl. "Look, get this straight: I never took a dime in my life. My badge isn't for sale."

"I'm sorry, Bob," Fairbanks said. "But I had to ask. You know Jimmy has bought a lot of cops in his time—or so we hear."

"Not this one, friend," Kohler said. He stalked away.

If Fairbanks worried what an insulted Kohler might do on the witness stand, he needn't have worried. Kohler had a crisp, no-nonsense style of testifying that usually impressed juries. As Kohler demonstrated during his testimony in the Burke murder trial, he also had a knack for recounting little details that tended to stamp jurors' minds with stark reminders of the crime under discussion. In this case. Kohler had a whole series of them, including one memorable anecdote. He had gone to the morgue, he related, to check Eaton's back for bullet holes or other wounds. The body was frozen stiff, so Kohler stood it upright. It slipped from his grasp and fell to the floor, bouncing "like a piece of marble." The jury, Fairbanks noted with satisfaction, hung on every word and certainly understood what the prosecutor meant when he talked about a murder "in cold blood."

The fulcrum of the trial, however, was Henry Hill. Fearing the worst, Fairbanks led him through the story of Burke's "whacked out" comment, then turned him over to Anthony Lombardino, Burke's defense attorney. A lawyer noted for his flamboyance. Lombardino jumped all over Hill, drawing from him the familiar story of his criminal career. Sensing that his victim was on the ropes, Lombardino pressed ahead.

It was a serious tactical error. As Fairbanks knew, Hill was the type of witness who was initially uncertain, but under repeated body blows, he would gather his strength and start to slug it out toe to toe with a tormenting defense lawyer. The trick was to get to Hill early, cut him up quickly before he had a chance to recover, then stop. But Lombardino went on too long, and Fairbanks, hardly believing his luck, sat back and watched in satisfaction.

He was delighted when Lombardino committed another tactical error: in his summation, he overdid his characterization of Hill. "Courtroom whore," "the devil himself," and "weasel" were some of the milder epithets he used, and too long a string of them had a numbing effect. Moreover, Lombardino tried to appeal to the jury, which consisted of eleven blacks and one white, by alluding to Martin Luther King; this maneuver clearly offended some of them. After a two-week trial, they took only a few hours to return a verdict of guilty on a single charge of second degree murder.

"The bastard died of hypothoimia!" Burke complained to his cell mates, apparently not understanding that the precise method of Eaton's murder—tying someone up, beating him into unconsciousness, and leaving him in sub-freezing temperatures is legally as deadly a method as any—was to a large extent immaterial. That fact of legal life was brought home in December 1984, when Burke was sentenced to twenty-five years to life.

The final fall of James Burke was witnessed by some of his most noted law-enforcement adversaries, among them Edward McDonald. "Hey, Ed, howya doin'?" Burke said, greeting the prosecutor like an old friend. Fairbanks, not quite believing what he was seeing, stared.

During Hill's testimony Burke often glared at another adversary, Special Agent Thomas Sweeney of the FBI. Burke had a general animus for the FBI ("I hate the fucking FBI," he often said), but for reasons that were never entirely clear, he reserved a special dislike for Sweeney. Oddly, he bore no grudge toward Carbone, who had the unsettling experience during the basketball-fix trial of encountering Mrs. Burke in a hallway during a court recess. Mrs. Burke, who seemed to know exactly who Carbone was, spent some time chatting with him about assorted topics of no special consequence. All the while, Carbone felt awkward: here she was, exchanging social pleasantries with the man who had spent a good part of his career trying to put her husband behind bars.

With his conviction for murder—added on to his federal sentence, it meant he was facing life in prison—Jimmy the Gent knew it was all over. In the late winter of 1984, brought back to New York by detectives for one last court hearing on his case, he sat uncharacteristically silent on the flight from federal prison. All during that flight, he stared long and hard out the window as the plane circled Kennedy Airport, waiting for clearance to land.

He gazed down at the huge airport sprawling in every direction. If he had looked hard enough, he would have seen, in the northeast section of the airport, the Lufthansa Air Cargo building. From the air, it looked small and insignificant, with tiny armored cars shuttling in and out.

"And to think," he murmured, "it was mine, all mine."

That was not completely accurate, of course, for other men might have made a broader claim. They were the untouchables, the Mafia dons who had tried to suck the blood out of the airport and who had given their approval to the robbery of Lufthansa Air Cargo.

They had assumed they were beyond jeopardy for that crime. They were not, although justice would come from a direction they never expected.

The rain began just after nightfall on March 18, 1983, a driving, windy storm that made the men gathered inside the cavernous Long Island catering hall grateful they were inside. The attendees at the fourth annual dinner dance of the Private Sanitation Industry Association of Nassau-Suffolk chatted mostly about the storm that was rumbling and rattling outside—a safe topic; they dared not discuss certain more serious topics in that Mafia-infested group.

Especially not with several police detectives lurking about, keeping tabs on what they liked to call "people of interest." Chief among such men of interest was the leading power in the Association: Salvatore Avellino, Jr.

The police were interested in Avellino's movements for

many reasons. For one thing, Avellino was a soldier in the Lucchese family, which harbored several other "people of interest," including Paul Vario, Sr. Additionally, the police were convinced that Avellino was the spearhead of the Lucchese family's takeover of the private carting industry on Long Island.

But, more important, the police were aware that Avellino was the confidant and chauffeur of Antonio Corallo, godfather of the Lucchese organization. That made Avellino privy to a collection of Mafia secrets that any detective would have given his right arm to hear. And considering the fact that Corallo controlled his family's operations at Kennedy Airport, what he and Avellino discussed on that subject could only be imagined.

Of course, Avellino was not about to hold a public seminar on any of those topics. Indeed, both the police and the FBI had been frustrated for years in their efforts to get any hint of the kind of incriminating conversations they imagined transpired between the soldier and his godfather. Avellino had been well schooled in the art of security by Corallo, his partner in crime, who was justifiably proud of his nickname "Tony Ducks"—a tribute to his uncanny ability to frustrate police and FBI surveillance and to his equally legendary reputation for ducking subpoenas.

Like his boss, Avellino avoided conducting or discussing mob business in any location that had even the potential to be bugged. Business transactions were most often discussed in their mobile office: Avellino's new black Jaguar. During the drives, Avellino periodically took steps to shake whatever surveillance the police or FBI might have operating. Further, both men ensured that the car was guarded twenty-four hours a day to forestall any planting of a bug.

On that stormy night on Long Island, while Avellino was sipping his drink and chatting with other garbage industry types, two of his hoods were in the parking lot, watching over his black Jaguar. Although they were under firm instructions never to let the car out of their sight for an instant, their sense of the urgency of the task waned as the rainstorm blew with steadily growing force. They decided there was not much need to watch a car that nobody was about to approach anyway—not in that storm, certainly. They ducked inside the catering hall to get warm and dry, certain that Avellino wouldn't mind if they left the Jaguar unguarded for a while.

Unseen by the hoods, three men were huddled in the dark shadows behind the fence at the far end of the parking lot. This was the moment they had been waiting for. They quickly climbed the fence and, crouching low, dashed toward the Jaguar. In a single deft motion, one man opened the door and simultaneously doused the door light as the two other men rapidly crawled inside. They immediately set to work dismantling the dashboard.

The three men—detectives from the New York State Organized Crime Strike Force—had rehearsed the operation several times on a borrowed Jaguar, but the rehearsal had taken place in dry weather. Now they were trying to plant a bug behind the dashboard of a car that was nearly awash in heavy downpour. Cursing softly, the detectives worked quickly as the wind howled and the rain poured down. The detective holding the door ajar (necessary to allow working room) tried to mop up the rain as fast as it blew into the car. Afraid that a wet interior would tip off the cautious Avellino that his car had been tampered with, the detective wiped frantically with rags, urging the other two men to hurry.

All the while, this same detective had to watch for the return of the guards. If they spotted the three men inside the car, months of preparation, a court order, and a priceless opportunity would be lost, perhaps forever. But as the minutes ticked by, and despite steadily mounting obscenities directed at its manufacturer, the Jaguar dashboard resisted all efforts at haste.

At last, nearly fifty minutes after they had entered the car, they replaced the last screw. Behind the dashboard now lurked unseen a small voice transmitter with homing signal, hooked up into the car's electrical system. It would pick up any conversation in the car and broadcast it nearly a half-mile. One final swipe of a rag, and the team of detectives carefully shut the door and scrambled back over the fence.

Some time later, Avellino left the dinner dance and entered the Jaguar, which a parking lot attendant pulled up to the front entrance. Avellino frowned as he got in; there were wet spots around the front seat. Assuming the parking lot attendant was responsible, Avellino thought no more of it and drove away. As he left the parking lot, Avellino scanned the area for police or FBI surveillance cars. He spotted none and decided that in the pounding storm, even the surveillance teams had taken the night off.

He did not see the van, parked near the road, switch on its lights and slowly pull into traffic far behind the Jaguar. Nor did he see a half-dozen nondescript sedans take up positions in the traffic. And most important, he did not hear the silent homing signal that beeped behind his dashboard.

―――――

The act of a Mafia family soldier driving home followed by police surveillance seemed ordinary enough in the long war between the Mafia and the cops, but in fact that little bug in the Jaguar was a significant move in an all-out frontal assault by the good guys against the Mafia organization in New York, the heart and brain of American organized crime. In a demonstration of what could be achieved when both sides worked together, the FBI and police forces in New York and Long Island had mounted a five-year-long drive against five major Mafia families.

Among the high-priority targets was Corallo's Lucchese family, in large measure because of its grip on Kennedy Airport. And by coincidence, the mob chieftains who had presided over the Lufthansa robbery—and who had ordered the toll of blood and death—confronted a justice from which they had long believed themselves exempt.

―――――

"Those fucking cops would have to be geniuses to follow us today." Corallo laughed as he sat beside Avellino one morning while the Jaguar twisted and turned through a maze of side streets in an attempt to frustrate any surveillance cars.

"Right," Avellino replied, as he wheeled the car through a tire-squealing turn.

The laughter of both men echoed clearly in the headsets of a police team sitting inside a van that was having no trouble following the Jaguar and its electronic signal. In the few days the bug had been operating, a half-dozen cars and the van had followed every zig and zag as the Jaguar drove all over New York. Despite the caution of Avellino and Corallo, the surveillance teams had woven an electronic web around the car: while the van recorded every word the two mobsters said, unmarked police cars leapfrogged back and forth, each one equipped with special electronic repeaters that boosted the bug's signal.

In the weeks that followed, the police, to their delight, found that Avellino, Corallo, and other Mafia passengers in the Jaguar spoke freely of business matters large and small, affording the listeners the most revealing disclosures of Mafia operations ever put on tape. Combined with a series of interlocking investigations, it would result, two years later, in an unprecedented series of indictments against nine major leaders of the New York Mafia families on charges of "operating a criminal enterprise," namely the Mafia itself.

Among those indicted was Corallo, who had in effect indicted himself with his own words spoken so freely as he sat beside Avellino. Those words also led to an indictment of Corallo in suburban Suffolk County on charges that he conspired to control the Long Island garbage collection industry. Avellino was indicted on a similar charge.

The indictments could hardly have enhanced Corallo's failing health. He had suffered a mild heart attack in April 1983 and, while recovering, had assigned Avellino the temporary duty of mediating family disputes. It was a mark of the trust Corallo placed in Avellino's talents (including discretion), a vote of confidence that turned to fury when he discovered that the indictments were based on tapes gathered in Avellino's bugged car. How, Corallo wondered, could Avellino have been so careless as to allow that bug to be installed?

In fact, Avellino, an extremely shrewd hood, had made two small but significant mistakes. The police had watched in dismay at one point while Avellino parked his car in his garage and then flew off to Florida for a vacation. To their frustration, as the car sat in the garage, the bug slowly drained the power from the battery. Since their warrant only covered the car, the police could not legally enter the garage to recharge the bug.

Upon his return to Long Island, Avellino discovered his battery was dead. He called his car dealer to pick up the car and give it a complete checkup, then watched as a tow truck arrived and hauled it away. That was his first mistake: the car was out of his sight. The police were also watching, and just before the car arrived at the dealer's, the tow truck was pulled over by a patrol car. While the puzzled driver of the tow truck tried to answer a senseless battery of questions relating to a "routine vehicle check," two detectives sneaked into the car and disconnected the bug.

With his battery recharged, Avellino drove to a local diner. Deep in conversation with some fellow mobsters, he failed to notice that a van had pulled into the parking lot, blocking his view of the Jaguar. That was the second mistake, for screened by the van, detectives reinstalled the bug.

If Corallo's health suffered from the news of how his own words had been turned against him, the health of Paul Vario, Sr., was even more seriously affected from a related attack, this one from McDonald's Eastern District Strike Force. Already in a hospital suffering from a severe heart ailment, Vario learned in February 1985 that a five-year investigation into Mafia operations at Kennedy Airport had resulted in indictments against eleven persons, including himself, on racketeering, extortion, and conspiracy charges.

McDonald's intent was to break the Mafia's grip on the airport. The indictment of Vario—his first serious legal trouble in the decades of his dominance of the airport—was aimed at the one man who had come to symbolize just what that grip was all about. At the same time, as McDonald did not have to point out, the indictment of Vario represented the final act in the long, often tortuous struggle to get final justice against the "big fish" in the Lufthansa heist.

Still, two of the smaller fish in the Lufthansa robbery remained to be accounted for—two men who had managed to escape the toll of death that had destroyed nearly all the others.

One of them, Frankie Burke, had lived because he was Jimmy Burke's son and because, like his father, the thought of becoming an informant was unthinkable. Burke continued to swagger around Brooklyn and Queens in a tough-guy burlesque meant to suggest that his father's criminal mantle had been passed on to him.

No one took him very seriously. In fact, police detectives watched with some amusement as Frankie tried to convince a skeptical underworld that he was his father's son in every sense of the word. The problem, as Burke's son imperfectly understood, was that he could earn respect only by becoming a moneymaker in the grand style of his father. Frankie, however, was no moneymaker, and while he occupied his time talking tough and waving a gun around, those who knew his father snickered behind his son's back that Frankie would find it hard to boost a candy store.

Some of these snickers may have reached Frankie's ear, because in a forlorn effort to earn the underworld's respect as a tough guy, he became involved in a nasty shooting in Brooklyn. Some nights later, when two detectives stopped Frankie's car after witnesses reported that the car had been at the scene of the shooting, Frankie pointed a gun at the two detectives. It was an especially stupid move, and the police promptly locked him up. No one had to point out that Frankie's father would never have been so stupid as to flaunt a gun at two police detectives.

———

And what of Angelo Sepe, the misbegotten protégé of Jimmy Burke?

Sepe had demonstrated the maximum possible loyalty, shrugging off the best efforts by the FBI and prosecutor Edward McDonald to get him to turn. His reward had been his life, no small matter in the trail of bodies that followed the Lufthansa robbery.

Yet it was a life devoid of much reward. With his mentor and godfather Jimmy Burke in prison, Sepe began to lose his compass. He seemed unable to function, and a criminal career that depended exclusively on Burke's guidance now floundered. At one point he set out to become a major drug dealer—an enterprise that promised the greatest possible rewards for the least possible investment. Sepe failed ignominiously, unable to master even the simplest of the skills required to run a criminal conspiracy. In most of the deals, he was cheated.

The spiral continued ever downward. By the summer of 1984, Sepe, divorced, was living in a one-room basement apartment in a run-down section of Brooklyn. He worked part-time as a security guard for the building in exchange for free rent. For several years, his occasional live-in companion was a young woman who had remained with him, even though Sepe's Lufthansa money was long gone. Despite Burke's patient tutoring, Sepe had never learned that money must make money; he had no grasp of the importance of investing ill-gotten gains in enterprises that would return income.

During that summer, Sepe had finally hit upon a money-making idea—robbing drug dealers. He reasoned that they were not likely to complain to the police, and he knew they walked around with large amounts of cash.

Actually, robbing drug dealers is an extremely dangerous way of earning money, for they have a bad habit of killing people who threaten their livelihood, and stealing a drug dealer's money is the ultimate threat to that livelihood. Like a small boy poking a hornets' nest, Sepe probably had no real awareness of the danger he was in. It is also possible that he did not realize that the police would take a dim view of such activity.

In the summer of 1984, Sepe's robberies of drug dealers came to the attention of police. Picked up for questioning, Sepe groused that he was not being treated with sufficient respect. "Don'tcha know who you're talkin' to?" he demanded.

"Yeah, we know," one detective answered. "Why don't you tell us?"

"I'm the guy who robbed Lufthansa," Sepe said proudly.

This confession was of limited use to Brooklyn detectives, since the statute of limitations on robbery charges in the Lufthansa case had expired the previous December. There was interest, however, in McDonald's office, which retained the hope that federal racketeering charges might be brought, for which the statutes had not expired.

Several men from McDonald's office tried to discuss the Lufthansa matter with Sepe, but the conversations soon disintegrated into a dialogue with the deaf. Having been awarded the desired "respect," Sepe did not want to talk about Lufthansa any further, nor did he want to discuss the robbing of drug dealers.

The experience taught Sepe nothing, for he was soon back to sticking up dope dealers. There was no hope, of course, that any drug dealer would complain to police, but the detectives understood that the drug world has its own system of justice.

Seemingly unaware of any impending doom, Sepe lived his simple life as he had always lived it. When he was not out robbing drug dealers or driving around in his now battered car—the sole tangible sign of his cut of the Lufthansa money—Sepe ministered to his only real companions, save his girl-friend: the small menagerie of animals. By the hour, he cooed to his little birds, to the orphan pigeon whose broken wing he had treated, to the small turtle, to the mangy alley cat who had adopted Sepe as a fellow soul.

In this communion with the creatures whose intelligence most nearly matched his own, Sepe tended to forget the out-side world. He forgot that in the dangerous throw of dice that was now his existence, the time would come when he would rob the wrong dealer, possibly a "connected" dealer, someone who had ties with the mob; someone, perhaps, who was paying protection money to prevent just such an occur-rence. And when the dealer went to the mob to complain, there could be only one possible outcome. Angelo Sepe would be killed, as the macabre mob phrase had it, "for the adver-tising budget." Which meant that Sepe would be gunned down and his body left for all to see as a warning to others that there was no percentage in his line of work.

———

Sometime during the second week of July 1984, Sepe held up a "connected" dealer. The dealer made his complaint, and early in the morning of July 18 two men knocked on Sepe's door. Hearing the familiar voice of a local Mafia hood, Sepe opened the door and confronted two pistols with silencers, both of which were pointed at his head.

Before he could ask the hoods not to harm his girlfriend, they put three bullets into his head. Then they walked into a tiny sleeping alcove. One of the gunman put his gun into the open mouth of the sleeping girl and pulled the trigger.

———

Word of Sepe's murder, the final act in the Lufthansa heist drama, spread rapidly, fueled by newspaper stories that called it the "final link" in the "Lufthansa chain of death."

———

In police precincts around the city, detectives nodded knowingly at the news, surprised only that Sepe had lived for so long.

In the federal penitentiary at Lewisburg, Pennsylvania, James Burke was saddened by the news. Other prisoners saw tears well up in his eyes. He was somewhat depressed anyway, they noticed, often cursing the fate that had brought him to the place. Sepe's death reminded him again of the importance of loyalty in his business, the probable reason why Sepe had continued to live despite what he knew. Burke contrasted Sepe's long record of loyalty and silence with the odious record of Henry Hill.

Hill was to blame, Burke decided. He had not been man enough to withstand the pressure; Hill was responsible for all the trouble. He had put Jimmy Burke in prison. Yet the odd relationship that existed between the two men compelled Burke to understand why Hill became an informant. Burke thought for quite some time on the meaning of it all.

"Henry Hill," Burke said finally, "loved his wife more than he loved me."

———

It was, of course, an inadequate epitaph for the saga of the Lufthansa heist, and served even less as an analysis for Hill's motives. But then, despite his reputation for criminal cunning and intelligence, Burke in the end really had no idea why it all went wrong.

There is some sort of larger meaning in the entire story, and it has little to do with Hill's motivations, Burke's inability to understand, or the thirteen murder victims who lie dead without epitaphs.

It has to do with certain inevitable forces that come into play in a story like this one. They are the powerful forces of greed, loyalty, and betrayal that emerge when human beings decide to tempt the fates.

Oddly enough, the best summation rests today in a small office in Queens, not far from Kennedy Airport. On a wall in the office of the FBI's Stephen Carbone, right behind his desk, there is a small plaque tucked among assorted mementos of his law-enforcement career. Given to him by the agents who once worked in BQ5, it is an engraved tribute to Carbone's direction of the investigation.

About halfway down that plaque is a quotation attributed to someone identified only as "A.S." The initials are Angelo Sepe's, and the quotation, engraved in large block letters, is perhaps the best summation of what this entire story was all about. The quote reads:

YOU GOTTA DO WHATCHA GOTTA DO

Aftermath

With the indictments of the major Mafia figures involved in the Lufthansa robbery, and with the expiration of the statute of limitations, the story of the robbery for all practical purposes came to an end. The heist is no longer being actively investigated by either the FBI or the police, and although the case files remain technically open (there always remains the slim possibility of filing charges someday for murder or racketeering), there is no real hope that any of its lingering mysteries will ever be solved.

There also remains little hope that any of the murders that marked the Lufthansa story will ever be solved. And there is absolutely no possibility that any of the money from the robbery will ever be located. Since the bills were unmarked and unrecorded, authorities have no way to verify that any particular bill is part of the robbery haul. It is conceivable that people are walking around today with fifty or one hundred dollar bills that were stolen that December night in 1978 at the Lufthansa Air Cargo terminal.

As for the people involved in the robbery and the investigation, the Lufthansa heist touched many lives, some of them permanently so. Here is what happened to some of the main characters in that story:

GOOD GUYS

Detective Lieutenant *Thomas Ahearn* is still commander of the 113th Detective Squad.

Richard Broder resigned from the Nassau County district attorney's office. He is now in private law practice.

FBI Supervisor *Stephen Carbone* now heads up the Joint Auto Theft Task Force, an FBI-police operation aimed at breaking up major car theft rings, especially those connected with organized crime. Carbone is highly regarded by police officers assigned to the unit.

Detective *Robert Hernandez* retired from the police department and now handles security investigations for a major insurance company.

Detective *Robert Kohler* retired from the police department.

FBI Assistant Director In Charge *Lee F. Laster* was promoted to head the FBI's New York office, from which he has since retired. He is now in private security work.

Edward A. McDonald in 1982 was appointed chief of the Eastern District Organized Crime Strike Force.

Thomas Puccio resigned as chief of the Strike Force in 1982 to enter private law practice. Subsequently he directed the legal team that successfully defended Claus von Bülow on attempted murder charges.

Detective Sergeant *James Shea* suffered a coronary attack in 1985 and subsequently retired from the police department.

FBI Special Agent *Thomas Sweeney* is now assigned to the Bureau's Organized Crime unit in Queens.

BAD GUYS

James (Jimmy the Gent) Burke is still incarcerated in the federal penitentiary at Lewisburg, Pennsylvania. It it anticipated that he will spend the rest of his life behind bars.

Frank (Frankie) Burke pleaded guilty in 1984 to a reduced charge of illegal weapons possession.

The bodies of *Louis Cafora* and his wife have never been found.

The body of *Thomas DeSimone* has never been found.

Richard Eaton died a pauper.

The family of *Theresa (Terry) Ferrara* still refuses to accept the fact of her death. No one has ever been charged in her murder.

John Gotti, the Mafia *capo* who provided logistical support for the Lufthansa heist, in 1985 made a bid to become godfather of the Gambino organized crime family by arranging for the murder of its reigning head, Paul Castellano.

Peter Gruenwald is now living somewhere in the United States under a new identity.

Henry Hill is now living somewhere in the United States under a new identity. *The Wiseguy*, by Nicholas Pileggi, an account of Hill's criminal career, was published in 1986. Hill continues to testify at various trials and is considered a professional witness.

The body of *Martin Krugman* has never been found. In 1986 he was declared officially dead, and his wife collected $135,000 on his life insurance policy.

The murder of *Paolo LiCastri* remains officially unsolved.

The murders of *Robert (Frenchie) McMahon* and *Joseph Manri* remain officially unsolved.

The murder of *Angelo Sepe* remains officially unsolved.

Paul Vario, Sr., was convicted in 1984 of parole fraud, involving a no-show job he arranged for Henry Hill so that Hill could obtain parole. Sentenced to four years in prison, Vario is now in a prison hospital, suffering from degenerative heart disease. He still faces additional racketeering charges, along with his boss, *Antonio (Tony Ducks) Corallo*.

Louis Werner and *Janet Barbieri* were married following Werner's release from prison. They are now living somewhere in the United States under new identities.

INSTITUTIONAL NOTES

Lufthansa Air Cargo revised its security procedures in the wake of the 1978 robbery. There have been no reported major thefts at its Kennedy Airport terminal since then.

The *FBI* and the *New York City Police Department*, partly as a result of problems that arose during the Lufthansa investigation, have tried to forge a better working partnership between the two agencies. A number of joint task forces have been formed, especially units working on bank robberies, auto theft, organized crime, and terrorism. Both sides rank the task forces highly.

Truck hijackings and cargo theft at *Kennedy Airport* have declined by over 400 percent during the past several years, while the volume of cargo handled at the airport has increased by a similar ratio. Most cargo theft there is now ranked as employee thievery; the days of highly organized rings of hijackers are over. Most authorities credit the turnaround to effective work by the FBI, police, and the Eastern District Strike Force, along with a program by the *Port Authority of New York and New Jersey*, which instituted strict new security rules, holding individual cargo companies responsible for security of shipments. Those companies failing to take adequate security precautions can have their operating leases revoked.

Robert's Lounge has undergone several transformations of ownership and name. In its most recent guise, it was a disco. However, people in Queens continue to refer to the place as Robert's Lounge, adding, "where the big Lufthansa robbery was planned."